The Irish in Baseball

The Irish in Baseball

An Early History

DAVID L. FLEITZ

McFarland & Company, Inc., Publishers
Jefferson, North Carolina, and London

LIBRARY OF CONGRESS CATALOGUING-IN-PUBLICATION DATA

Fleitz, David L., 1955–
The Irish in baseball : an early history / David L. Fleitz.
p.   cm.
Includes bibliographical references and index.

ISBN 978-0-7864-3419-0
softcover : 50# alkaline paper ∞

1. Baseball — United States — History —19th century.
2. Irish American baseball players — History —19th century.
3. Irish Americans — History —19th century.
4. Ireland — Emigration and immigration — History —19th century.
5. United States — Emigration and immigration — History —19th century.
I. Title.
GV863.A1F63   2009   796.357' 640973 — dc22   2009001305

British Library cataloguing data are available

On the cover: (left to right) Willie Keeler, Hughey Jennings,
groundskeeper Joe Murphy, Joe Kelley and John McGraw of the Baltimore Orioles
(Sports Legends Museum, Baltimore, Maryland)

Manufactured in the United States of America

*McFarland & Company, Inc., Publishers
Box 611, Jefferson, North Carolina 28640
www.mcfarlandpub.com*

Acknowledgments

I would like to thank a few people and organizations that helped make this book possible.

The Internet has changed the nature of research, on baseball and all other topics, and I used the computer to perform much of my investigation into early baseball. One helpful web site is called Paper of Record, a historical newspaper search engine that features images of *The Sporting News* beginning with its inaugural issue in 1886. The Brooklyn Public Library has digitized the *Brooklyn Eagle* from the years 1841 to 1902, and the LA84 Foundation, endowed with funds left over from the 1984 Olympic Games in Los Angeles, maintains a digital archive of *Sporting Life* and *Baseball Magazine* for the 1897 to 1920 period. These archives are free, and extremely useful to any sports researcher.

The Eugene C. Murdock collection of baseball books and materials at the Cleveland Public Library was, as always, invaluable, as were Tim Wiles, Gabriel Schechter, and the other knowledgeable staff members at the National Baseball Hall of Fame Library in Cooperstown, New York. I also made use of the SABR (Society for American Baseball Research) Lending Library, a valuable service that is, of itself, a good enough reason to purchase a membership in SABR.

I would also like to thank my wife Deborah, as always, for her editing skills and moral support.

Table of Contents

Prologue

Ireland is a nation with a troubled history. It had been a center of art and scholarship during the early Middle Ages, but the rise of its island neighbor, England, brought an end to Irish independence. After a series of invasions, rebellions, and civil wars, the English conquered Ireland and imported Scottish and English Protestants to colonize the Catholic country. The Protestants failed to subjugate the Catholics, but gained control of the counties of northern Ireland, setting the stage for centuries of religious conflict. After several unsuccessful rebellions against British rule, Ireland officially became part of the United Kingdom (which comprised England, Scotland, and Wales) in 1801. Catholics were still second-class citizens, banned from participating in politics or sitting in the British Parliament, but the Catholic Emancipation Act of 1829 brought hope to the Irish. Unfortunately, these hopes were dashed two decades later, when famine, disease, and emigration decimated the country. By 1911, the population of Ireland had fallen to not much more than half of what it had been in 1845.

The depopulation of Ireland was the result of perhaps the greatest human tragedy of the 19th century. The "Great Famine," which the Irish called *An Gorta Mór,* struck the country with full force in 1845. It was caused by a fungus, introduced to Ireland from continental Europe, which destroyed that year's potato crop, leaving most of the rural counties without food for the harsh winter that followed. The city of Dublin and the Protestant counties of the north were less affected, but the blight laid waste to the largely Catholic areas of the south and west. The potato crop did not recover in 1846, and the following year, remembered in Irish history as "Black 47," saw the worst suffering of all. The conservative government of Great Britain, which ruled the island country, was ineffective or (some say) not interested in providing humanitarian aid to the Irish, and reliable statistics indicate that between 1845 and 1851, more than a million and a half Irish died of starvation, while nearly as many fled the country.[1]

The failure of the potato crop was not a new phenomenon. Earlier versions of the fungus had struck the country several times during the previous 100 years, and as recently as 1830 the counties of Mayo, Donegal, and Galway had suffered widespread starvation. Localized crop failures followed during the next decade and a half, but the Irish were unable to diversify their agriculture. The population of the nation had exploded, from 2.8 million in 1785 to more than 8 million 80 years later, and Ireland had become a country of poor peasant farmers, growing barely enough to feed their families on tiny plots of land. The potato was the only crop that could be grown in enough quantity to feed the Irish people, and the

1

disaster of *An Gorta Mór* was, in retrospect, probably inevitable. In the words of British writer and historian H. G. Wells, "the weary potato gave way under its ever-growing burthen,"[2] with famine and death as the result.

The famine, and the Diaspora which followed, turned Ireland into what Wells described as "a land of old People and empty nests."[3] Ireland was slowly dying, but the United States of America was vibrant and growing. Though the country had existed as an independent nation for fewer than 80 years, it was expanding westward, increasing in population, and building itself into an industrial giant that would one day rival Great Britain as the wealthiest and most powerful nation of the world. It had room for a seemingly limitless number of immigrants, and the desperate Irish, tired of hunger, religious persecution, and British oppression, fled their homeland in droves to build new lives across the ocean. In the nine years immediately following the onset of the famine, some 2,164,000 Irish men, women, and children made the passage to the New World, and the total number of Irish who emigrated by the end of the 19th century topped three and a half million.

Some of these immigrants spoke only Gaelic, the ancient language of the rural counties, but about three fourths of them spoke English, giving those an advantage over arrivals from Germany, Italy, and other European nations. Still, Irish immigrants faced many difficulties in their new land. Most had been peasant farmers and brought no usable talents with them to America. As a result, the only jobs open to them involved unskilled manual labor with long hours and meager pay. Few of the Irish could afford to travel far from their point of entry, so they settled a short distance from where they landed, overwhelming the ability of New York, Boston, and other eastern port cities to absorb them. Irish slums grew quickly in these cities, and the waves of new arrivals made the tenements more crowded and the competition for jobs more fierce. Poverty, chronic unemployment, and crime were the inevitable result, and not until 1855, when the worst of the famine had abated, did the flood of humanity arriving from Ireland begin to slow.

Once settled in their new land, the Irish made incredible strides. Women found jobs as domestic servants (which their upper class employers called "bridgets" or "biddies") while the men gravitated to factory jobs, dock work, and construction projects. They began to build a place for themselves in their new country, and while their work was hard and the hours long, the Irish were determined to succeed. They were proud of their heritage, holding parades on St. Patrick's Day and banding together to fight discrimination, but they were Americans now, with their focus on the future. Immigrants and children of immigrants won political office in the large cities, fought with distinction (in the famous "Irish Brigades") in the Civil War, and integrated themselves into the fabric of their communities and their nation. Perhaps it was inevitable that the Irish would take to the sport which would soon be called the "national pastime" of their adopted country.

Baseball was not yet a professional game during the 1850s and early 1860s. It was a leisure activity, contested on an amateur basis, for young businessmen of the middle and upper classes in New York, Philadelphia, and other eastern cities. It was also primarily a game for native-born Protestants of English ancestry, as members of few other ethnic groups possessed either the time or social standing required to play for one of those amateur teams. Though James Fowler Wenman, a shortstop for the New York Knickerbockers during the 1850s, came from a prominent family of Irish descent, his ancestry was an anomaly in the highest levels of the sport at the time. Many amateur baseball clubs played the English game of cricket as well as baseball, and during the 1850s it was still an open question as to which sport would become more popular in America.

There were two main forms of baseball, the "New York" game and the "Massachusetts" game. The New York version, using rules laid down by the Knickerbocker club, allowed for batters to be retired when a ball was caught on the fly or on one bounce. The Massachusetts form used the older "soaking" rule, in which a fielder put out a batter by hitting him with a thrown ball. Eventually, the New York game grew in popularity and became the dominant style of play, though the Massachusetts version continued in New England for decades afterward. By the early 1860s, the New York game began to evolve into the sport that we know today. It was spread across the country during the Civil War by soldiers from the northeastern states who introduced the game to Midwesterners and Southerners. At war's end, soldiers took the game back to their home states, and a nationwide boom in participation immediately ensued.

As baseball grew in popularity, the influx of hundreds of thousands of young men from Ireland during this era created a potential new source of participants for the rapidly growing sport. Though baseball was unknown in Ireland during the exodus of the 1840s and 1850s, the game claimed an important place in the lives of thousands of immigrants and sons of immigrants during the next several decades. Baseball was an activity that the second-generation Irishman could engage in to become part of his new American community. While the older generation, the folks who were born into hard circumstances back in Ireland, could not always understand this strange new pastime and its appeal, their young men took to it quickly. Through it, they could fit in and excel at something distinctly American. Before long, Irish names began popping up on rosters of amateur teams, especially in Brooklyn, Philadelphia, and northern New Jersey. Irish-American laborers and mill workers formed their own clubs, and their children played the game in vacant lots and pastures.

Sports and games had been an important part of Irish civilization long before the upheaval of the famine. Hurling, a stick and ball game that resembles lacrosse, had been played in some form in Ireland for more than 2,000 years. This ancient sport enjoyed great popularity during the 17th and 18th centuries, while Gaelic football, a cross between soccer and rugby, is said to have descended from a game called *caid*, which was played in medieval times. The Irish came to America, said historian Steven A. Riess, "with a manly athletic tradition and quickly became avid sports fans and athletes in their new country."[4]

From the earliest days of the professional game, many writers have attempted to explain the apparent affinity of the Irish, especially the second-generation Irish, for baseball. Some made the assumption that because a baseball bat bears a resemblance to the traditional Irish wooden cudgel, the "shillelagh," bat-and-ball games had a particular appeal to immigrants from the Emerald Isle. Other observers drew comparisons between baseball and the ancient sport of hurling, while still others spoke of the Irish involvement in baseball in terms of social mobility and assimilation into a new culture. Whatever the reasons, the first- and second-generation Irishmen who filled the large cities of the eastern United States played the new American sport with enthusiasm.

Professional baseball took root in America during the late 1860s, just as the sons of the first wave of famine refugees began to reach adulthood. As amateur ball became more popular during the years immediately after the Civil War, rivalries between cities and towns became more intense, and a leisure activity evolved into a sport with winning as an increasingly important objective. Teams began to pay their star players, covertly at first, and less so afterward. The transformation of baseball into a profession made it even more attractive to the ambitious immigrant, and it did not take long for the Irish to gain a foothold in the rapidly growing sport.

1

Beginnings — The Irish in Boston

When the potato crop in Ireland failed with tragic consequences during the late 1840s, more than a million Irish men, women, and children made their way to America to start life anew. The two main ports of entry for these mostly poor immigrants were New York and Boston, and while many merely landed in those two cities and moved elsewhere, thousands settled close to where they had first stepped off the ship. Boston, a less populous town than New York, was suddenly overwhelmed with immigrants. Its total population in 1840, according to the United States census, was 85,475, but in the year 1847 alone, more than 37,000 struggling Irish settled in the city. By 1855, the Irish made up more than one third of Boston's population, and their presence in what writer Bronson Alcott had proudly called "the city that is set on high" with a morality "more pure than that of any other city in America"[1] changed Boston forever.

For the immigrant, living conditions in Boston were an improvement over those in famine-stricken Ireland, but not by much. The city lacked adequate housing, employment, and sanitation for so large a number of new arrivals, and most of the Boston Irish spent their early years there in squalor and poverty. In addition, Boston's ruling elite, the proud Protestant "Brahmins" of which Bronson Alcott was one, resented the sudden influx of poor, unskilled Catholics. They hired Irish women and girls as servants, but put "No Irish Need Apply," or "NINA," signs in the windows of their businesses. Irish men were willing to perform unskilled manual labor, but the native-born workers resented them for accepting lower wages. The teeming Irish tenements, mostly located near the waterfront, were a breeding ground for crime and disease. Smallpox, which had disappeared in Boston, made a comeback in the overcrowded Irish slums, and a cholera epidemic killed hundreds, mainly immigrants, in 1849.

Still, the Irish continued to pour into Boston, and slowly their communities began to stabilize. They improved their neighborhoods, educated their children, and entered politics, making a place for themselves in a city that would not fully accept them for decades. It was only a matter of time before the immigrants and children of immigrants developed an interest in the leisure pursuits of their adopted country. The English sport of cricket was popular with the Brahmins of the city, but the Boston Irish wanted nothing to do with the game that reminded them of their former British overlords. Instead, they embraced the new American game of baseball.

Though Bostonians, during the 1850s, mostly played the "Massachusetts game" in which a fielder put a batter out by hitting him with the ball, the less dangerous "New York" style of baseball eventually supplanted the local version, growing in popularity during and after the Civil War. Amateur clubs such as the Tri-Mountains and the Lowells gained prominence, and a visit by one of the country's top teams, the Excelsior of Brooklyn, in July of 1862 made an indelible impression upon Boston's sporting scene. The Irish of Boston were eager to involve themselves in this growing sport, so they formed teams of their own and slowly found places on established local clubs. Irish children played the game anywhere they could find the space to swing a bat and throw a ball — on vacant lots and street corners. The Brahmins, still attached to the English game of cricket, mostly ignored this new sport, so the immigrants claimed baseball as their own.

Boston's first Irish-born baseball star, and indeed the first Irishman to succeed in the professional game, came to the Hub by way of Cincinnati. Andrew Jackson Leonard was born in 1846 in County Cavan, when starvation caused by the previous year's ruined potato harvest was beginning to reach its peak. As Cavan, a landlocked county in north-central Ireland, was especially hard hit by the potato blight and the subsequent famine and misery, Leonard's family escaped to America and settled in Newark, New Jersey. The Leonards may already have been looking to the New World for salvation, having named their son after an American icon of Irish parentage. Andrew Jackson, the seventh president of the United States and the first of Irish lineage, was a particular hero of the Irish people during the mid–1800s.

Andy Leonard apprenticed as a hatter but grew into a fine athlete, excelling on the baseball field as a hitter and third baseman. In 1866, when he was 20, Leonard joined one of the leading amateur teams in New Jersey, the Irvington Club, whose members played both baseball and cricket. In 1868 he and teammate Charlie Sweasy, a second baseman, moved to Ohio to play for the Cincinnati Buckeyes, where they impressed Red Stockings manager Harry Wright with their skill. Wright offered contracts to both Leonard and Sweasy for the 1869 campaign, and both men joined the Red Stockings. Sweasy and Leonard each earned a salary of $800 that season.

Because the infield positions were already filled, manager Wright moved Leonard to the outfield, where he continued to excel. The *New York Clipper* marveled at his throwing arm, stating that "as regards accuracy of throwing, Leonard at left field has no superior. He has so repeatedly thrown the ball from that position to the home plate with such unerring precision that the runner on third base has not dared attempt to reach home."[2] Leonard was also one of the club's strongest hitters, with fragmentary statistics crediting him with 211 hits in only 54 games. His outstanding play was a major reason that the Red Stockings defeated all comers in 1869, winning all 57 of its games and claiming the undisputed national championship. More importantly, the Red Stockings proved that the future of baseball lay in the professional, not the amateur, game.

Shortstop George Wright, Harry's younger brother, was the star of the team, but Andy Leonard earned recognition as the best left fielder in the nation. He walloped three homers, one a grand slam, in a 66–4 victory over the Pacific Base Ball Club of San Francisco on September 26, and on July 22 belted a single, triple, and homer in the same inning during a 71–15 bombing of his old team, the Buckeyes. The competition was spotty at best, with the Red Stockings regularly winning games by 40 runs or more, but the team's statistics were impressive nonetheless. They bashed an unheard-of 169 homers during the season, 23 of them by Leonard, and scored 2,396 runs while giving up only 574.

Leonard and the Red Stockings set out to defend their title in 1870, but after 26 more wins they faced the Atlantics of Brooklyn, who defeated them by a score of 8 to 7 in one of the greatest games ever played up to that time. No longer invincible, the Cincinnati club lost four more games that season and fell from the championship picture. The fans, once so thrilled with their winning team, stayed away, and at season's end the club directors decided to disband the Red Stockings and return to the amateur ranks.

The Cincinnati Red Stockings were defunct, but the first professional league, the National Association, came into being after the 1870 season with clubs representing most of the major Eastern cities of the country. The Wright brothers traveled to Boston to form a new team (also called the Red Stockings), while Leonard and four other Cincinnati stars signed with the Washington Olympics for the 1871 campaign. The Olympics finished a distant fourth in the eight-team league, after which Leonard left the nation's capital and rejoined Harry Wright in Boston in 1872. Leonard established himself in left field, though he also saw action at third, second, and short, and batted over .300 each season as this new edition of the Red Stockings dominated the National Association. Wright's Boston team, with Leonard in left field, won four pennants in a row from 1872 to 1875.

When the Association began play in 1871, Andy Leonard was one of only four Irish-born players in the league. Another

Andy Leonard (seated far left) and Jim O'Rourke (seated next to Leonard), Boston's Irish stars of the early 1870s. Cal McVey stands between them.

was Fergus (Fergy) Malone, a well-known player of the day, whose origins have been obscured by the passage of time. Malone was born in Ireland in 1842, most likely in County Tyrone, and grew up in Philadelphia. In 1862 he joined the Philadelphia Athletic Club, which sponsored a team that played both cricket and baseball and emerged as the famous Philadelphia Athletics. Malone was a left-handed catcher, in an era where such was not unusual, and some credit him with being the first catcher, amateur or professional, to wear thin gloves on his hands behind the plate. Malone, already a nine-year veteran of top-level play when the Philadelphia team joined the National Association for its inaugural season, batted .343 as the Athletics won the first professional pennant.[3]

Irishmen were still a rarity in professional ball during the early 1870s, though a new generation of immigrant children was learning the game in the cities. Some of the prejudices attached to the Irish and their culture remained to be overcome. Jim O'Rourke, a talented young outfielder who starred for the short-lived Middletown Mansfields in 1872, was offered a contract to play in Boston for the 1873 campaign on the condition that he change his name. Anti-Irish prejudice was palpable in Boston at the time, and Harry Wright, so the story goes, requested that O'Rourke drop the "O" from his last name to hide his rather obvious Irishness. O'Rourke, a proud son of immigrants who lost his father at an early age, refused. "Mr. Wright," he said, "I would rather die than give up any part of my father's name. A million would not tempt me."[4] Wright, no doubt impressed with the young man's character, signed O'Rourke anyway. With Leonard in left and O'Rourke splitting time between right field and first base, the Red Stockings won the next three pennants by increasing margins.

Harry Wright was born in England and always dreamed of bringing the sport of baseball to his homeland. In 1874 he sent his star pitcher, Al Spalding, to London to arrange a tour of the British Isles for the two-time defending league champion Boston Red Stockings and the Philadelphia Athletics, the 1871 champs. Spalding, a talented organizer, made the necessary connections and arrangements, so in July of 1874 the Boston and Philadelphia teams took an unprecedented three-week break in the National Association schedule and set sail for Europe. At Harry Wright's suggestion, Spalding had padded the itinerary with a trip to the Irish capital. "We must take Dublin in," wrote Wright to the Philadelphia team president, "for with all our Mc's and O'R's, a game there would surely prove attractive and pay handsomely."[5] Indeed, the Athletics featured three Mc's in pitcher-manager Dick McBride, utility man Mike McGeary, and outfielder John McMullen, while the Red Stockings employed outfielders Cal McVey and Jim O'Rourke, along with the Irish-born Andy Leonard. Philadelphia's reserve outfielder Tim Murnane, a second-generation Irishman from Connecticut who spoke in a distinctive brogue, also made the trip overseas. The Irish influence in baseball was growing, and the trans–Atlantic journey served to underscore the maturation of Irish-American baseball talent.

The British showed little interest in baseball, and the highlight of the trip proved to be a cricket match played between a team of 18 Americans and the 11-man Marylebone club, one of the strongest in England. Harry and George Wright were experienced cricketers, but most of the Americans knew next to nothing about the game, so the Wrights conducted a crash course for their countrymen in rules and strategy. However, Al Spalding and several of the Red Stockings, including Andy Leonard, decided to ignore the customary defensive way of playing the game, preferring instead to wallop the ball as far as they could hit it. Harry Wright was appalled, but Spalding tallied 23 runs and Leonard 12 as the Americans defeated the British, 107–105, in a one-inning match.

Although the tour was a money-loser, the players wholly enjoyed themselves. Men of English descent such as Adrian Anson, Al Spalding, and the Wrights explored the sights and sounds of London, Liverpool, and Manchester, while the Irishmen were most impressed with a visit to Dublin and its environs. The teams spent only two days in Ireland, splitting two baseball games in Dublin while besting an "all–Ireland" eleven in cricket by a score of 165 to 79. Despite the presence of Irish ballplayers on the two teams, only about 1,500 spectators watched the two contests in the capital.

Andy Leonard recorded some of his experiences on the trip in a diary:

> [Sunday 23] ... went around the city [of Dublin] in a jaunting car. Visited Phoenix Park, Nelson's Monument on Sackville street, Trinity College, St. Patrick's Cathedral, Royal Barricks Exhibition Buildings, xc xc.
>   Monday, 24. Beat the Athletics. Shelbourne Hotel, Dublin.
>   Tuesday 25. Stopped at the Farnham Arms Hotel, Cavan. Made 26 runs in cricket against the Irish Eleven. Beaten By the Athletics.

However, though Leonard's diary entries were brief, the player's family believes that the Irish-born outfielder made a triumphal entry into his native country. Charles McCarthy, the ballplayer's grandson, has stated, "The notations for Tuesday the 25th are of great interest to us descendents. Oral family history has him returning triumphantly to his hometown, Cavan, as both an American 'champion' ballist and as a native-born Irishman, survivor of the Great Hunger (or Famine) who had battered the English cricket champions silly at their own game. His notes are not particularly helpful in resolving the ambiguities."[6]

Tim Murnane also kept a diary of the trip, in which the Philadelphia infielder (and future *Boston Globe* sportswriter) recorded his observations of the British fans. "Our first game was played at 'Edge Hill' cricket ground on the 30th of July," wrote Murnane, "and won by the Athletics after a ten inning game there was about four hundred spectators present and what a sick looking crowd of ballplayers there was playing before an audience of hundreds where at home we could easily attract thousands. It was rather amusing to listen to the comments one would blurt out — 'Ah, it's the old game of rounders,' then another would say 'Ah, and I think they will beat our cricketers they field so wonderfully well.' If a man hit a long foul ball they were sure to applaud thinking it was a fine hit."[7]

The Red Stockings and Athletics returned to the United States and resumed the pennant chase in early September, but the race was over quickly. Harry Wright's ballclub won 22 of its final 32 games, sweeping to its third pennant in a row. In 1875 Boston's superiority was even more pronounced, as the Red Stockings posted a 71–8 record and won all 37 games played on its home grounds. With solid contributions from its two Irish-American stars, outfielders Andy Leonard and Jim O'Rourke, the Red Stockings won the flag by 15 games over the Athletics. As pitcher Al Spalding admitted many years later, "We rather overdid the thing."[8]

The dominance of the Boston club was a source of pride for the Hub, but did not bode well for the National Association. None of that circuit's final four pennant races were competitive, and weaker teams ran out of money and collapsed in mid-season with dismaying regularity. Players bounced from team to team, club owners sometimes refused to finish their schedules, and the twin ills of gambling and game-fixing filled the headlines of the nation's sporting press. The Association's many inherent weaknesses threatened the very existence of professional baseball. In response, Chicago White Stockings owner William Hulbert created a new organization, the National League of Professional Base Ball Clubs, with strict rules to correct the failures of the Association. Hulbert convinced the Boston Red Stockings and the other important Eastern clubs to join the new circuit, and the National League was born.

However, Boston would not dominate this new organization so easily. In mid–1875, Hulbert had entered negotiations with four of Harry Wright's star players, including pitcher Al Spalding, signing them to contracts for the following season. Spalding, Cal McVey, Ross Barnes, and Jim (Deacon) White, dubbed the "Big Four" by the local newspapers, headed to Chicago at season's end, as did Adrian Anson, the slugging utility man of the Philadelphia Athletics. Hulbert's raid on the Red Stockings made Chicago the powerhouse of the new National League, while Boston, the four-time champion, was faced with a major rebuilding effort.

"No Irish Need Apply" signs still hung in Boston shop windows, but the local baseball club proved more tolerant of immigrants and sons of immigrants. Harry Wright, the English-born manager of the Red Stockings, had apparently accepted the presence of Irishmen on his team after the success of Andy Leonard and Jim O'Rourke earlier in the decade. Leonard and O'Rourke were still with the club in 1876, but when the "Big Four" decamped to Chicago, the defending champions suddenly needed to fill some holes. Wright scoured New England for talented ballplayers and came up with two second-generation Irishmen named John Morrill and Tim Murnane. Morrill was new to the highest level of professional ball, while Murnane had performed for the Philadelphia Athletics and had played against the Red Stockings on the tour of the British Isles two years earlier. Morrill and Murnane would both become important and long-lasting players on the New England baseball scene.

John Morrill, whose parents fled Ireland during the famine and settled in Boston, was born in that city in 1855. By the time he was 20 years old, Morrill had become a star on the Boston sandlots with highly regarded teams called the Our Boys and the Beacons, playing all positions on the field. "We used to play after school and on Saturdays, and we had some fine old times on the Common," said Morrill years later.[9] He was one of the best amateur players in the city. In April of 1876, the Red Stockings played an exhibition game against a team of local all-stars on Fast Day (an old Puritan religious holiday that was later superseded by Patriot Day). John Morrill caught for the "picked nine," as such teams were called then, and performed so well that at game's end Harry Wright offered him a contract to play for the Red Stockings. So began a career that would find Morrill in a Boston uniform for the next 14 seasons.

Morrill, whose most prominent physical feature was an impressive brown mustache, was five feet and eight inches tall and weighed about 155 pounds. He shared second base with Andy Leonard and catching chores with Lew Brown in 1876, the first season of National League baseball. Sober and serious, Morrill, even as a young man, was called "Honest John" by the sportswriters, who appreciated his openness and sincerity. One day, an official scorer gave him an error on a bad-hop grounder, and someone asked Morrill why he did not complain about the ruling, as most players no doubt would have. "Yes, it was an error," explained Morrill. "It hit a pebble, but what of it? I'm supposed to stop those drives. When I don't, you should give me an error."[10] Respected by teammates and fans alike, Morrill succeeded George Wright, Harry's younger brother, as the Boston captain in 1879.

Tim Murnane was another son of Irish immigrants, and the brogue that he inherited from his father remained with him all his life. Born in Waterbury, Connecticut, in 1850, Murnane (whose last name then appeared in the box scores without the final e) had played with his fellow Irish Red Stocking, Jim O'Rourke, on a club in Stratford, Connecticut, in 1870, and again two years later for the short-lived Middletown Mansfields of the National Association. Murnane then spent three years in Philadelphia before making the move to Boston, perhaps because Harry Wright had been impressed with him as a player and as a person during the overseas tour in 1874. Well-spoken and intelligent, Murnane had spent some time at the College of the Holy Cross, making him perhaps the only college-educated member of the ballclub. Wright installed Murnane at first base for the Red Stockings, and with Leonard, Morrill, and O'Rourke also claiming starting positions, the Boston club featured four Irishmen in its lineup.

The new talent took some time to jell, and the Chicago White Stockings, fortified by the

Tim Murnane, an Irishman from Connecticut who turned from playing to sportswriting (Library of Congress).

arrival of the Big Four, claimed the first National League pennant. The Red Stockings finished in fourth position, fifteen games out, mostly due to poor pitching. Starter Joe Borden, signed to a three-year contract by Wright before the season began, pitched so poorly that the club dropped him from the roster in mid–July after a 15–0 defeat at the hands of the White Stockings. Wright, still obligated to pay the unsuccessful pitcher, then put Borden to work as a groundskeeper. Wright realized that better mound work would put his team back in contention, so after the 1876 season he signed the best young pitcher in the game. Tommy Bond, a 21-year-old Irish-born right-hander, soon led the Red Stockings back to the top of the league.

Born in Granard in County Longford in 1856, Tommy Bond and his family left Ireland and settled in Boston, where the youngster played the new American game and decided to make his living at it. He was only 18 when he pitched for the Brooklyn Atlantics of the National Association in 1874, compiling 22 wins and 31 losses, then spent the next two years with the Hartford Dark Blues. Though he weighed a mere 160 pounds, Bond threw perhaps the best fastball in the Association, and in 1875 posted 19 wins for Hartford while playing the outfield on his days off from pitching. He shared the pitching chores in Hartford with Candy Cummings, who taught him the secret of the curveball, which only Cummings and a handful of other hurlers had then mastered. By the time the 1876 campaign was half over, Tommy had learned to throw a better curveball than Cummings, his teacher. He surpassed Cummings as the ace of the Dark Blues, completing all 45 of his starts and winning 31 of them that season.

Tommy Bond was on the brink of stardom, but not in Hartford. His manager with the Dark Blues, and with the Atlantics before that, was Bob Ferguson, one of the game's most respected veterans at the time, but a man with a sharp tongue and a fearsome temper. Ferguson was notorious for driving his men hard, once declaring loudly his intention to "drive my fist down [Jack] Burdock's throat!" after an error by the Hartford second baseman. Ferguson's abusive nature wore on Bond, who had enough of his manager's attitude by August of 1876. Bond, perhaps in a ploy to get off the team, publicly accused his manager of throwing games, a charge that made headlines in the national press. The team's board of directors investigated, cleared Ferguson, and dismissed Bond, freeing the pitcher to sign with his hometown Red Stockings for the 1877 season. Strong and durable, Bond was expected to pitch nearly every game for the Red Stockings, and did so for the next several seasons.

Bond was an excellent pitcher even before he learned how to throw the curve. On October 20, 1874, he nearly became the first professional hurler to throw a no-hitter, blanking the New York Mutuals through eight and two-thirds innings at the Union Grounds in Brooklyn. Joe Start's double to left ended Bond's bid for immortality, and though the next batter followed with a single, Bond completed a two-hit shutout. Joe Borden, Tommy's predecessor with the Red Stockings, threw the first no-hitter the following year. Bond was not the first Irish-born pitcher in the game; that distinction belonged to Hugh Campbell, who won only two of the 18 games he pitched for the Elizabeth Resolutes of the National Association in 1873. However, Bond was the first to reach stardom, and might have earned a place in the Hall of Fame had his career lasted longer.

Off the field, the ownership of the Boston club changed hands in 1877. The new team president and largest stockholder was Arthur Soden, a building contractor who had owned shares in the club for several years. Soden, though wealthy, was no Brahmin, having hailed from Framingham, Massachusetts, before moving to Boston to build his own construction business from the ground up. An enthusiastic baseball fan, Soden had accompanied the team on its tour of the British Isles in 1874 and had even played the outfield in London for Harry

Wright's team. After the club entered the National League, Soden began buying up shares until he owned enough to take control. The second largest stakeholder, J. B. Billings, became the treasurer, and the third, William Conant, served as secretary. These three men ruled the team for the next three decades, and the local papers called them the "Triumvirs," with Soden as the Caesar of the group.

Soden came from the working class, but would never be mistaken for a populist. The Red Stockings had lost money during the previous few seasons, and the majority owner was determined to stem the tide of red ink. "Common sense," said Soden, "tells me that baseball is played primarily to make a profit."[11] Accordingly, he stopped the distribution of free and discounted passes for players' wives and relatives. The only complimentary tickets belonged to the Triumvirs, who received two apiece. He tore out the press box to make room for more paid admissions, cut travel costs to the bone, and ordered Harry Wright and his charges to enter the stands and wrestle the fans for foul balls. He put players to work on the turnstiles before games, and when large crowds gathered at the South End Grounds, Soden and his fellow Triumvirs would man the gates and take tickets themselves. Soden's austerity measures worked, and by the early 1880s the club began to show a profit, little of which went to the players. Though Soden loved baseball, he held no emotional attachment to his employees. "I do not believe in labor organizations or unions," he said. "When a player ceases to be useful to me, I will release him."[12]

The 1877 edition of the Red Stockings was bolstered by the return of Deacon White, who tired of Chicago after only one season and opted to return to Boston. John Morrill switched to third base, with White taking over at first and Andy Leonard moving to the outfield, while Tim Murnane served as an all-purpose substitute. However, Tommy Bond was the main reason for the club's success. He pitched in all but three of the team's 61 games, winning 40 and leading the league in strikeouts. Boston, with Bond winning 18 of his last 19 decisions, swept to the pennant by seven games over the Louisville Grays.

JOHN J. BURDOCK,
BOSTON CLUB, SECOND BASE.

JOHN F. MORRILL,
BOSTON CLUB, FIRST BASE.

Second baseman Jack Burdock and first baseman John Morrill played together in Boston for 11 seasons.

Unfortunately, Boston's 1877 pennant was tainted by revelations that four members of the Louisville club had been paid by gamblers to throw games late in the season, perhaps making it possible for the Red Stockings to win the flag. The club was determined to repeat in 1878 to prove that they deserved their championship, and Tommy Bond delivered another remarkable season. He pitched in 59 games, winning 40 and leading the league in virtually every pitching category as the Red Stockings won the 1878 flag by four games over Cincinnati. The club failed to repeat in 1879, mostly because Boston's star shortstop George Wright joined the Providence Grays and led them to the pennant, but Bond compiled his best season, with a 43–19 record and a league-leading 11 shutouts.

Tim Murnane had left the club after the 1877 campaign, and Jim O'Rourke quit the team and signed with Providence in early 1879 after a dispute with the autocratic Arthur Soden. Reportedly, Soden had decided to charge the players $20 for the use of their uniforms, and O'Rourke had had enough. Andy Leonard, too, was finished after the pennant-winning 1878 campaign, and after spending the following season at Rochester and the next with the Cincinnati Reds, he retired from the game and took a position with the water department in Newark, New Jersey. A few years later, he returned to Boston to work for his old teammate, George Wright, who had started his own sporting goods company.

Even without Murnane, Leonard, and O'Rourke, the Red Stockings were still a largely Irish ballclub, especially after Wright hired O'Rourke's older brother John to play center field. John O'Rourke was not as talented as his Hall of Fame sibling, but proved to be a valuable outfielder, hitting .362 in his first National League season. Another new Irish player was second baseman Jack Burdock, who joined the Red Stockings in 1878 after playing with Tommy Bond on the Hartford ballclub two years before. Burdock, like John Morrill, would spend more than a decade in a Boston uniform.

Bond had pitched virtually every inning for the Red Stockings during the 1877 and 1878 campaigns, but when the schedule increased to 84 games in 1879, manager Wright realized that one man could no longer carry the entire pitching burden. Accordingly, he signed a left-handed pitcher named Charles (Curry) Foley, who had been a minor-league sensation as a pitcher and hitter in Lowell, Massachusetts, during the previous several seasons. Foley, like Bond, was born in Ireland in 1856. He came from Milltown in County Kerry, and arrived in America with his parents at the age of seven. He filled in capably as a substitute pitcher and outfielder in 1879, winning nine games and losing the same number while batting .315.

The departures of two Boston stars, one Irish (Jim O'Rourke) and one not (George Wright), rankled the conservative team president Arthur Soden, who cast about for a way to save money on salaries by restricting player movement. In July of 1878, Soden had discussed the matter with team stockholder N. T. Appolonio, who summarized the talk in a letter to Harry Wright. "Mr. Soden's plan," the letter stated, "is now that if we can hold on to [catcher Pop] Snyder, Burdick [*sic*], they with Bond, [third baseman Ezra] Sutton, and Morrill, would form a pretty good nucleus with which we could afford to be in no great hurry to negotiate with the others."[13] Soden proposed that language be added to the standard player contract that allowed each team to reserve the services of five of its players from one year to the next, at the team's discretion. This proposal, which he presented at the league meetings after the 1879 campaign, was called the "reserve clause."

The other National League owners approved, and the reserve clause remained a part of baseball for more than 90 years thereafter. Soden placed Snyder, Bond, Sutton, Burdock, and John O'Rourke on his reserve list for 1880 (though, perhaps surprisingly, not John Morrill).

With those five key players now unable to negotiate with other teams, the Boston salary list stabilized, as did that of the other National League clubs. It is probably no coincidence that the Boston club began turning a profit after the reserve clause went into effect. By 1885, the league had increased the number of reserved players per team to 11, virtually ending player movement by tying each performer to his club for the duration of his career. The reserve clause put a lid on salaries, as Soden had predicted, but elicited hard feelings between players and owners that would flare into open revolt before the end of the decade.

Though Jim O'Rourke had little use for the penny-pinching ways of Arthur Soden, he admired manager Harry Wright and agreed to return to Boston after one season in Providence. His presence gave the 1880 Red Stockings five Irish starters (the O'Rourke brothers, Morrill, Burdock, and Bond), with Curry Foley in reserve. However, Tommy Bond, at the age of 24, was already on his way out of the major leagues. He had pitched more than 500 innings per season during the previous three years, and by 1880 the strain of throwing curveballs had given him a painfully sore arm. Weak catching also played a role in Bond's decline, and he posted his first losing season since 1874, with 26 wins and 29 losses. Foley won 14 and lost 14, and the Beaneaters finished in sixth place, 27 games behind the pennant-winning White Stockings.

The Boston club, with its largely Irish flavor, had won two of the first three National League pennants, but by 1881 the magic had dissipated. The team finished in sixth place once again, while Tommy Bond pitched in only three games, losing them all and drawing his release in May of that year. Except for a brief comeback in the Union Association in 1884, his career was finished at age 25. Harry Wright, the club's founder and the only manager it had yet known, also left the team at season's end, assuming the leadership of the Providence club. The Triumvirs then named John Morrill as Wright's successor for the 1882 season.

Morrill, the Boston club's first Irish-American manager, proved to be a good choice. He reworked the roster and boosted the club, by now called the Beaneaters to distinguish it from the other Red Stockings in Cincinnati, to third place in 1882. For some reason, the Triumvirs decided to give second baseman Jack Burdock, another Irishman, the reins for the 1883 season, but in mid–July, after a five-game losing streak left the club in fourth place, Morrill regained the manager's post. The club then caught fire, winning 33 of its final 44 games to take its first pennant in five years, breaking Chicago's three-year championship streak. Morrill, honest as always, expressed surprise with his team's great finish. "Good pitching and catching, and lucky hitting won for us," he told the local reporters. "When the season started, I thought we would finish fourth or fifth."[14]

The Beaneaters were not only faced with defending their championship in 1884, but also needed to beat back a challenge from a new league. A St. Louis entrepreneur named Henry V. Lucas believed that the nation could support a third major circuit, so he founded the Union Association to compete with the National League and American Association. Lucas established a team in Boston under the direction of George Wright, the former star shortstop, and Tim Murnane, the onetime utility infielder. Wright was the main backer of the venture, while Murnane was the manager, part-owner, captain, first baseman, and chief recruiter. He signed a group of Boston amateurs and semipros, mostly second-generation Irishmen like himself, and set out to challenge the Beaneaters.

Boston, however, was not interested in a second major league team, and despite the presence of past stars like Tommy Bond and future ones in Tommy McCarthy and Ed "Cannonball" Crane in the lineup, the club lost money in its only season of operation. The Union Association folded at season's end, and Tim Murnane found a new occupation. Hired by the *Boston Globe* as a sportswriter, Murnane eventually became the paper's sports editor. Some say that he virtually invented the daily baseball column, with which he entertained the local baseball fans with news, opinions, and gossip for more than 30 years.

John Morrill's personal popularity and the unexpected 1883 pennant carried him through several lean years that followed. Though the Beaneaters won more than 65 percent of their games in 1884, the Providence Grays went on a winning streak late in the season behind pitcher Charley Radbourn and beat out Boston by ten and a half games. Morrill's club then fell down the standings, finishing fifth in 1885 and 1886 as another largely Irish-American club, the Chicago White Stockings, won two pennants. The Beaneaters failed to top the .500 mark in either season, and although the appeal of baseball to the working-class citizens of Boston, especially the Irish ones, was solid, the club was stagnating. Attendance was flat, the South End Grounds (built when the team was formed in 1871) was deteriorating, and the local papers criticized the club and its management with renewed vigor. The team was profitable, thanks to Arthur Soden's tight control of the budget, but the on-field product was disappointing.

Additionally, the Beaneaters were no longer the automatic team of choice for talented young Irish-American semipro and minor league players from New England. In 1884, John Clarkson, a right-handed pitcher from Cambridge who had posted a 34–9 record in the Northwest League, turned down an offer from Boston and signed instead with the Chicago White Stockings. Hugh Duffy, a Rhode Islander who starred in the New England League in 1886, also rejected the Beaneaters and inked a deal with Chicago, as did Charles (Duke) Farrell, a catcher from Marlborough, Massachusetts. All three became stars, and might have helped the Beaneaters reclaim the top rung on the National League ladder, had they not gone elsewhere.

By the spring of 1887 the Triumvirs had grown impatient. As likable as John Morrill was, time was running out for him to repeat his pennant-winning performance of four years earlier. The Boston owners were determined to improve the Beaneater roster, and the sudden availability of several of the game's most popular Irish-American players appeared to provide the opportunity to do so. If they could no longer develop their own stars, reasoned Soden and his fellow Triumvirs, they would use their profits to buy them.

2

The Irish White Stockings of Chicago

The Irish had settled in Chicago long before the potato famine of the 1840s drove millions from their homes to the new land across the ocean. Thousands of Irish, mostly young men, arrived in the United States during the 1820s to work on canal-digging projects such as the Erie and Lackawanna in New York State. When those were finished, these Irish laborers traveled west to the new city of Chicago, incorporated in 1833, to work on the Illinois and Michigan Canal, a twelve-year project that began in 1836. The Irish population grew as the city did, and more Irishmen found employment in the bustling lumber yards, steel mills, and stockyards of the growing metropolis on the shore of Lake Michigan. By 1860, Chicago had the fourth largest Irish population in America.

Not everyone was happy to see waves of immigrants fill the city. A reporter for the *Chicago Post* once wrote, "The Irish fill our prisons, our poor houses.... Scratch a convict or a pauper, and the chances are that you tickle the skin of an Irish Catholic. Putting them on a boat and sending them home would end crime in this country."[1] However, the Irish were there to stay, and gravitated to city government, the police force, and the fire department. By the 1850s Irishmen were elected to public office as aldermen, and their political power increased as the decades passed, eventually resulting in the election of Irish mayors with names like Kennelly, Kelly, and Daley. The Irish also made their mark in the baseball world, and during the last two decades of the 19th century, many of the top ballplayers in Chicago were Irishmen.

The Chicago White Stockings were one of the top amateur clubs in the nation in the period just after the close of the Civil War. After entering the ranks of professional teams (that is, paying their players openly rather than covertly), they claimed a share of the unofficial national championship in 1870. The team joined the first professional league, the National Association, in 1871, but after the Great Chicago Fire destroyed their ballpark, along with much of the city itself, in October of that year, the club went into hibernation. Not until 1874 did the White Stockings rejoin the Association, with an energetic entrepreneur named William Hulbert in charge of the franchise.

Hulbert despaired of the innate weaknesses of the Association, especially in terms of scheduling woes and problems with enforcing player contracts. In 1875 he conceived a plan to create a newer, stronger league, and managed to convince most of the other Association franchises to accept his leadership. The result was the National League, which began play in

1876. At the same time, Hulbert moved to strengthen his Chicago team by paying top dollar to sign star players away from his rivals. He agreed to contract terms with four key players of the four-time champion Boston Red Stockings, including pitching ace Al Spalding, and also convinced Philadelphia Athletics utility man Adrian Anson, one of the best young sluggers in the game, to travel west and join the Chicago club for the 1876 season. With Spalding serving as field manager, business manager, and star pitcher of the team, the rejuvenated White Stockings won the first National League pennant during the nation's centennial year.

Spalding won 47 games on the mound in 1876, but grew tired of pitching and showed no interest in mastering the curveball, a new pitch that was soon to revolutionize the game. The White Stockings then signed George Bradley to handle the mound chores, with Spalding moving to first base. As a result, the White Stockings failed to defend their championship in 1877, finishing a poor fifth in the six-team National League. Spalding then decided to step down as both player and manager, as he could not serve as business manager and operate his growing sporting goods business while continuing his on-field responsibilities. Many expected Spalding's protégé, Adrian Anson, to succeed him, but team owner William Hulbert sprang a surprise on the Chicago fans. He named the veteran Bob Ferguson to manage the team for the 1878 season.

Ferguson, a former star player and experienced umpire who at the time was one of the most respected personalities in the game, proved a poor fit for the White Stockings. He had always displayed an explosive temper, once breaking an opposing catcher's arm with a bat during a heated on-field argument, and as the 1878 season progressed, his anger began to get the best of him. By mid-season, "Old Fergy" had alienated his players. "He had no tact," complained Spalding later. "He knew nothing of the subtle science of handling men by strategy rather than by force."[2] As the season wore on, the White Stockings tired of their manager's theatrical temper tantrums. The players appeared to be more interested in getting the season over with than in playing well, and by August the White Stockings had fallen out of the pennant race.

Some of the players caused problems for Ferguson with their off-field behavior. Hulbert was a temperance crusader, banning alcohol from the Chicago ballpark and refusing to sign known drinking men, but pitcher Terry Larkin's alcohol problems reportedly cost the team some wins in 1878. Another problem child was Jimmy Hallinan, one of the first Irishmen to play for the White Stockings. Hallinan, born in Ireland in 1849, was a veteran infielder and outfielder who batted .281 and .284 in 1877 and 1878, but his career in Chicago was short because "his habits were such that the management could not depend upon him," according to the *Chicago Telegraph*.[3] Released by Ferguson during the 1878 season, Hallinan died of unknown causes a year later at age 30.

The 1878 White Stockings, riven by dissention and discipline problems, wound up in fourth place, and Ferguson was dismissed at season's end. Left fielder and cleanup batter Adrian Anson, henceforth known as "Cap," was named as field leader for the 1879 campaign.

Anson decided to overhaul the Chicago roster. He moved himself to first base on a permanent basis, and searched both the minor leagues and the other National League teams for talent. Anson discovered and signed several future stars, such as Ed Williamson, a strong-armed third baseman, and Frank (Silver) Flint, perhaps the best young catcher in the nation at the time. With Terry Larkin handling the pitching chores and newcomers George Gore and Abner Dalrymple strengthening the outfield, the White Stockings held first place during the early months of the 1879 campaign. Unfortunately, Anson was forced from the lineup in

August due to illness, and the Chicago club faded in the stretch. However, the new manager sensed that he was on the right track. He recovered his health and went to work, scouting fresh talent for the 1880 season.

By this time, second-generation Irish players were beginning to make their presence felt in the National League, and the new men that Anson signed during the winter of 1879–80 brought an Irish flavor to the White Stockings. One such newcomer was Larry Corcoran, a 20-year-old from Brooklyn who was slated to replace the sore-armed Larkin on the mound. Corcoran, who had spent the 1879 season at Springfield and Holyoke in Massachusetts, was praised by the *New York Clipper* for his "wonderful speed for his strength" and as a "good 'headwork' player in the position."[4] Corcoran was a small man at five feet and eight inches in height and about 140 pounds, but packed so much speed on the ball that minor league catchers found it difficult to control his deliveries. Fortunately for Corcoran, the White Stockings had Silver Flint, one of the best in the game, behind the plate.

Corcoran and Flint made up the first Irish battery in the history of the White Stockings, and the two worked well together from the beginning. The Irishmen worked out a signal system in 1880, the first ever between a pitcher and a catcher in the major leagues. Corcoran chewed tobacco while pitching, so he put the chaw in one side of his mouth for a fastball, and on the other side for a curve. Corcoran became an instant star, posting a 43–20 record for Chicago in his first National League campaign.

Silver Flint, so named for his nearly white hair, had been the first Irish player signed by Anson. Flint, who was born in Philadelphia but moved to St. Louis at a young age, was one of the first products of the highly competitive Mound City sandlots to find stardom in the major leagues. He played for the St. Louis Reds of the National Association in 1875 at age 20, then spent three years playing for Indianapolis, making a name for himself as one of the premier catchers in the game. Anson, impressed by the play of both Flint and outfielder George (Orator) Shaffer, signed both men to play for the White Stockings in 1879. Flint became a great catcher, known for his toughness and his ability to play through pain. During his career, he reportedly fractured every bone in his hands at least once, making his fingers increasingly bent and twisted as his career progressed. In those days of rudimentary protective masks, he suffered many broken bones in his face as well.

Flint was a hard-living individual. He and Shaffer had left a trail of debt behind after leaving Indianapolis, and the local sheriff was waiting for them when the White Stockings traveled to the Indiana capital for an exhibition game in June of 1879. Anson successfully shielded Flint and Shaffer from arrest before the game, but at the end of the contest, the two players made a dash for the team's horse-drawn carriages and bolted out of the ballpark ahead of the pursuing policemen. Flint and Shaffer made it to the train station, where they hid in one of the cars until the crisis passed. The only man arrested that day was Anson, who paid a fine for interfering with the officers.

Corcoran and Flint were both outstanding performers, but another new member of the White Stockings soon earned the title "King of Ballplayers." Mike Kelly was a hard-drinking, fun-loving 22-year-old who spoke in an Irish brogue picked up from his immigrant parents. Born in the Irish enclave of Lansingburgh (which later merged with Troy), New York, Kelly moved with his family to Washington, D.C., when his father served in the Union Army during the Civil War. The Kellys then proceeded to Paterson, New Jersey, when young Mike was in his early teens. Mike apprenticed as a silk weaver, but his heart lay with baseball. By age 15, he had established himself as a catcher for the Paterson Stars, a team that included future major league pitchers Ed (The Only) Nolan and Jim McCormick. In 1877 he and

McCormick moved on to the Columbus Buckeyes of the International Association, and after the season, Kelly signed with the Cincinnati Reds of the National League.

A multitalented youngster, Kelly played for the Reds for two seasons, spending time in the outfield, at third base, and at catcher while steadily improving as a hitter. Inexplicably, he had failed to impress the Cincinnati management in 1879 despite his .348 average, and the Reds did not put his name on their reserve list for the 1880 campaign. Anson took his White Stockings to California that winter to play exhibition games against an all-star team selected from the rest of the league's clubs, and Mike Kelly, the catcher for the all-stars, impressed the Chicago captain with his dash and verve. Anson was already aware of the young man's skill, having played against him for two years in the National League, and the Reds' failure to reserve Kelly gave Anson the opportunity to sign one of the league's most promising talents.

Kelly was young, but he knew his value. He wanted $100 more in salary than the White Stockings were willing to pay, so he refused to sign a contract. Anson and Al Spalding, the business manager of the Chicago club, stood firm, but Kelly was a confident young man who knew that other National League teams would be only too

Mike Kelly, Chicago's "King of Ballplayers," later became the idol of Boston's Irish fans (Library of Congress).

happy to meet his price. After a week-long standoff, the club relented, giving Kelly the salary he desired.

Perhaps the most charismatic player in the game during the 1880s, Kelly quickly became a fan favorite. He turned sliding into an art form, discovering new ways to dodge the tag of an infielder while raising huge clouds of dust. A competitive sort who would do almost anything to win, Kelly was skilled at scoring from second base on a single, partly because he knew that the lone umpire could not tell if he touched third base or not. Kelly sometimes failed to come within 20 feet of third on his way home. A multitalented ballplayer, he spent time at catcher, shortstop, and the outfield, and was known to play right field with an extra ball in his uniform shirt. One day, as darkness approached in the late afternoon, Kelly chased a line drive at top speed in the gathering dusk. He made a spectacular headlong dive, waved the ball happily in the air, then ran off the field to the cheers of the crowd. When Anson complimented him on his catch, Kelly merely laughed. "Not at all, at all," he said. "'Twent a mile above my head."[5]

Charming, cocky, and brimming with confidence, Mike Kelly was already a heavy drinker when he arrived in Chicago, and always insisted that whiskey and ale were good for him. He smoked cigarettes on the bench, and when asked by a fan if he drank during games, Kelly cheerfully replied, "It depends on the length of the game." He was a fine fielder, though sometimes an indifferent one; if he dropped a fly ball, he would simply smile at the fuming Anson and chirp, "By Gad, I made it hit me gloves, anyhow."[6] Despite his carefree attitude, he was a great player, and his presence helped lift the White Stockings back into contention.

Another new Chicago ballplayer was an Irishman like Kelly, though his demeanor could hardly have been more different. Tom Burns was a serious, businesslike shortstop from Pennsylvania who had played in Albany, New York, during the 1879 season. Burns, a levelheaded sort who did not smoke or drink, eschewed the flashiness of a Mike Kelly, performing his job with an efficiency that earned the respect of Anson. He teamed with Ed Williamson to form a solid defensive presence on the left side of the infield, one that would stay intact for the rest of the 1880s.

These three Irish newcomers, teaming with existing stars such as Anson, Flint, and Williamson, propelled the White Stockings back to the top of the circuit. The 1880 Chicago club took the league lead with 14 wins in its first 15 games, then won 21 in a row (with one tie) in June and July to sew up the pennant before the season was half over. Anson's biggest problem that year lay in enforcing discipline on his fun-loving crew. He fined Williamson ten dollars for cursing his manager on the field, and docked Kelly half that amount for loafing on the basepaths. However, the White Stockings were so talented that their bad behavior did not matter. Despite a few off-field problems, mostly involving alcohol and curfew-breaking, the team ended the season with a .798 winning percentage, a mark that still stands as the best in baseball history.

The 1880 pennant was the first of three in a row for the White Stockings. Anson made no major changes for the 1881 season, which saw Corcoran post a 31–14 record, Kelly bat .323 and lead the league in doubles, and Anson himself win the batting title with a .399 average. They cruised to the pennant by nine games over the second-place Providence Grays. In 1882 Kelly displayed his versatility, sharing the shortstop position with Tom Burns and the right field slot with Hugh Nicol, while spelling Silver Flint behind the plate every now and then. Some say that Kelly was the first catcher to give signals to the pitcher with his fingers, a practice that all backstops follow to this day. Kelly, Anson, and Gore were the only .300 hitters in the lineup that season, but the White Stockings won the flag in a spirited race with Providence.

The Chicagoans were a talented bunch, but their success came at a price, and Anson quickly found himself up to his neck in disciplinary problems. Kelly, in particular, was a major headache for the club. "Kelly's habits were not conducive to the best interests of the club or his teammates," wrote Al Spalding, who became team president on the death of William Hulbert in 1882, many years later. "He was of a highly convivial nature, extremely fascinating and witty, and his example was demoralizing to discipline. Particularly objectionable was his influence upon the younger members of the nine."[7] "King" Kelly was a born leader, and many of his teammates were only too willing to follow him in his nightly bar-hopping escapades. When Spalding complained about Kelly's behavior, the "King of Ballplayers" waved him off. "What are you running here?" demanded Kelly. "A Sunday school or a baseball club?"[8]

Kelly made a good salary for the era, but spent more than he brought in. A soft touch, he lent money freely to friends and mere acquaintances, sometimes borrowing from one person in order to give to another. He loved playing the part of the larger-than-life baseball hero, and this son of poor Irish immigrants dressed in silk suits with expensive patent leather shoes and an ever-present top hat and cane. As a child, when his soldier father was stationed in Washington during the Civil War, Mike had seen Union general George McClellan in all his gleaming, polished finery, and the sight left a strong impression upon him. In adulthood, Mike Kelly was driven to dazzle people with his dress, his money, and his personality. "Every baseball team must have a star," said Kelly, "just as a dramatic company must have a leading man."[9] He was the matinee idol of the White Stockings, but the more level-headed Anson knew that trouble was looming. "He was a whole-souled, genial fellow, with a host of friends," said Anson in 1900, "and but one enemy, that one being himself."[10]

Silver Flint was another high-spirited White Stocking who often found himself in trouble. In 1883 a Florida man wrote to Spalding, complaining that Flint and Ed Williamson had borrowed money from him and refused to pay it back. Spalding quickly contacted the two players, threatening to bar them both from the National League if they did not make good on their loans. They did so, and the story was kept out of the papers. Flint was usually broke and always asking for advances on his salary, which Spalding granted at a rate of eight percent interest. The catcher spent most of his Chicago career in a financial hole due to his profligate spending and the many fines he incurred for drinking and bad behavior. Anson, who admired the catcher but despaired of his off-field antics and lack of conditioning, once cost Flint a sizable portion of his monthly salary by levying $170 in fines in a single day.

Kelly and Flint were not the only offenders, nor were only Irish players to blame for the decline in team discipline. Pitcher Fred Goldsmith and infielder Ed Williamson were involved in numerous incidents in beer gardens and taverns, while outfielders George Gore and Abner Dalrymple did their share of wild living as well. Anson and Williamson actually traded punches during a dispute over a card game in 1884. Williamson then retaliated on the field by throwing the ball as hard as he could to his captain, who played first base without a glove at the time. Still, the charismatic Kelly was the leader of the group, and his fellow curfew violators and hard drinkers followed his example. Perhaps the only

Catcher Frank (Silver) Flint. He was Chicago's first Irish-American manager, filling in for Cap Anson during the last month of the 1879 season (Library of Congress).

men Anson could count on were Tom Burns, the quiet, businesslike Irish infielder, and Billy Sunday, a speedy reserve outfielder from Iowa who later became the nation's most prominent evangelist.

Team management introduced disciplinary measures, including bed checks, to keep the players on the straight and narrow, but it appeared to be a losing battle. The *Chicago Tribune* claimed that the White Stockings were engaged in a "late-hour contest for supremacy in the matter of beer drinking," while the *Cincinnati Enquirer* stated that team president William Hulbert "has tried every possible plan to make men out of those who belong to his team. He locked them up on the grounds during the whole day, giving them papers and other necessary material to pass away the time, and still the team contains nine of the greatest drunkards in the league."[11] In 1881, when the National League blacklisted several players for general drunkenness and disorderly conduct, a few of the White Stockings may have narrowly avoided lifetime banishment. Boston club owner Arthur Soden reportedly tried to place Mike Kelly's name on the blacklist, but was blocked by Hulbert.

During the mid–1880s, when the late-night exploits of the Chicago players resulted in listless and disinterested performance on the field, Spalding hired a private detective to tail Kelly and his teammates. The detective compiled a report, which Spalding then read aloud to his men. Players such as Anson, Burns, and Sunday got off easy, but Kelly, Flint, and the rest listened quietly as Spalding recounted what he later described as "stories of drunkenness and debauchery" and "scenes of revelry and carousing that were altogether reprehensible and disgusting."[12] Seven team members were implicated by name in the report, and when Spalding finished, a hush filled the room.

Kelly, after a few tense moments, broke the silence. "I have to offer only one amendment," he told Spalding. "In that place where the detective reports me as taking lemonade at 3 A.M., he's off. It was straight whiskey. I never drank a lemonade at that hour in my life."[13] In the end, Kelly and his six fellow defendants agreed to pay fines of $25 each to defray the cost of the private detective, but their behavior failed to improve. The 1883 club, favored by most observers to win their fourth consecutive National League flag, fell apart in September and finished in second place.

The 1884 team dropped all the way to fourth position, due in part to poor team discipline (though Kelly, the biggest problem child of all, won the batting title and led the league in runs scored), but also because Larry Corcoran was beginning to fade. Corcoran was only 25 years old that year, but had thrown nearly 2,300 innings during his five seasons in a Chicago uniform. In 1880 he had started 60 of the team's 86 games, with second-string pitcher Fred Goldsmith handling almost all the rest. Anson might have had an inkling that the small-statured Corcoran might not be able to stand such a workload because, beginning in 1881, Corcoran and Goldsmith shared the innings more equally. Still, after five years of pitching, Corcoran was wearing down. He threw the third no-hitter of his career in 1884, becoming the first major league pitcher to reach that plateau, but faded as the season wore on. By July, his right arm was so sore that he pitched the ball with his left hand every now and then when the pain became too great to endure.

With the White Stockings out of the pennant chase, Anson spent the last half of the season giving tryouts to minor-league hurlers, including Corcoran's brother Mike, who allowed 14 runs and 16 hits in a loss to Detroit and drew his release after only one game. However, Anson found another second-generation Irishman to complete his pitching staff. John Clarkson, the son of a Scottish father and a mother born in Ireland, would soon surpass Larry Corcoran as the greatest pitcher in the history of the White Stockings.

Clarkson, a tall, thin right-hander, was born in 1861 in Cambridge, Massachusetts, which by the late 1870s had become a proving ground for talented Irish-American ballplayers. Cambridge was the home of Harvard University, where the Irish-born star Tommy Bond served as pitching coach and gave advice to Clarkson and fellow Cambridge native Tim Keefe, among others. Several local Irish ballplayers had already made it to the major leagues by the time Clarkson arrived in Chicago, and more would follow, including two of Clarkson's younger brothers and two of his cousins. Three Cambridge natives (Clarkson, Keefe, and Joe Kelley) would eventually enter the Baseball Hall of Fame.

Clarkson had failed in a three-game trial with Worcester of the National League in 1882, but returned to the minor leagues and re-established himself as a prospect. In 1884 he posted a 34–9 record for Saginaw in the Northwest League before that circuit disbanded in August, making the young pitcher a free agent. He sifted through several offers and, though his father urged him to sign with Boston, near his hometown of Cambridge, John inked a deal with Chicago. He impressed team management by winning 10 games during the last two months of the 1884 season while also filling in capably as an outfielder. Clarkson started the 1885 campaign as the second-string hurler behind Larry Corcoran, replacing the departed Fred Goldsmith, but when Corcoran's sore arm drove him from the lineup after only seven games, Clarkson became the ace of the staff. In early June, the White Stockings unceremoniously released Corcoran and replaced him with the veteran Jim McCormick.

McCormick, a stocky right-hander, was born in Scotland, but grew up in the Irish section of Paterson, New Jersey, where he was a childhood friend and teammate of Mike Kelly. McCormick was a workhorse who had pitched more than 500 innings in a season five times and won 45 games, with 72 complete games, for Cleveland in 1879. Though McCormick was a respected leader, having managed the Cleveland team for which he pitched, he was also an enthusiastic drinker and carouser like his pal Kelly. However, his record spoke for itself, and the White Stockings took him on as a veteran presence to provide support for the newcomer Clarkson. Unfortunately for Anson, Clarkson also proved to be a drinking man and formed a fast friendship with both Kelly and McCormick. Anson no doubt hoped that their collective on-field performance would be worth the disciplinary problems that would inevitably arise.

McCormick did his part, with 20 wins in the 24 games he pitched, but Clarkson was nothing short of sensational in 1885. He won 53 games, the second highest single season win total in major league history, as the two new pitchers almost single-handedly kept the White Stockings in the pennant race. Several of the veteran stars slumped that season, as Silver Flint batted only .209 and Ed Williamson hit .238, but Clarkson and McCormick led the Chicago club to the flag, its first in three years, by two games over the New York Giants. Team president Al Spalding was so pleased with his charges that, according to the *Washington Post*, he awarded each player a bonus of $100 "for having abstained from intoxicating drinks and orgies and for winning the pennant."[14]

Perhaps Spalding spoke too soon. The White Stockings met the American Association champs, the St. Louis Browns, in a post-season "World's Series" in October, but the Chicago players failed to take the matchup seriously. Since the National Leaguers looked down upon the Association as the "Beer and Whiskey League," it appears that Anson's men, though not Anson himself, were satisfied with the league championship and regarded the series with the Browns as a mere exhibition.

The Browns looked to the series with the White Stockings as a chance to prove their equality with the older National League, but the St. Louis field leader had a personal agenda

The 1885 White Stockings featured many Irish-American stars. Top: Gore, Flint, Anson, Kennedy, Kelly, Pfeffer. Bottom: Corcoran, Williamson, Dalrymple, Burns, Clarkson, Sunday (National Baseball Library, Cooperstown, New York).

as well. First baseman and manager Charlie Comiskey was the son of an Irish immigrant who settled in Chicago and rose through the ranks to become a respected and influential city alderman. Charlie, like his father, dreamed of power and influence, but found his niche in the baseball world. He was a young man on the move, becoming manager of the Browns in 1883 at the tender age of 24. Comiskey built a winner in St. Louis, but hoped to someday manage the top baseball club in Chicago, a position firmly held by Cap Anson. Comiskey knew that a victory over the White Stockings would embarrass Anson and Spalding, threatening their position on the top rung of the Chicago baseball ladder and, perhaps, hastening the day when he, Charlie Comiskey, would supplant them.

The 1885 series between the White Stockings and Browns ended in a tie, though Anson's champions were embarrassed by the outcome. George Gore, the Chicago center fielder, made several errors in the first game of the series, and rumor had it that Gore was hung over on the field that day. Anson must have believed the same, for he benched Gore for the rest of the series and replaced him with the more dependable Billy Sunday. John Clarkson, called upon to pitch the seventh and final game, showed up at the park five minutes late, so the fuming Anson started Jim McCormick instead. Charges soon circulated that Clarkson was too inebriated to perform, but McCormick was no world-beater either that day. He allowed 13 runs, mainly due to 17 Chicago errors, and the Browns waltzed away with a 13–4 victory. The series ended with each team winning three games and tying one. Anson and Comiskey, now bitter rivals, were determined to meet again at the end of the next campaign.

The mid–1880s marked the high point of the Irish presence in baseball, as statistics compiled by Baseball Hall of Fame historian Lee Allen reveal that fully 41 percent of new players on major league rosters during the 1876 to 1884 period were of Irish stock, comprising the largest ethnic group in the playing ranks.[15] The Chicago club followed the trend, and though Anson (who prided himself on his family's descent from the British naval hero Lord Anson) grumbled every now and then about his team's behavior, the White Stockings continued to discover and sign talented Irish ballplayers. In 1885, the pitching staff was almost totally Irish, even after the release of Larry Corcoran, with Clarkson, McCormick (a Scot who grew up in an Irish neighborhood), and Ted Kennedy, who spelled the two main starters and won seven games that season. There were a few Germans (second baseman Fred Pfeffer and outfielder Billy Sunday) and a smattering of English (Anson, Williamson, and Gore) on the team, but Irishmen comprised the core of the Chicago club.

Perhaps Anson and Spalding realized that some of their stars were aging quickly, for they continued to scour the country for outstanding young talent. One Irish player who drew their attention in 1885 was Jimmy Ryan, a blond 22-year-old from Clinton, Massachusetts, who batted .462 in three games during the last week of the campaign. Ryan joined the team as a shortstop, but with Williamson and Burns firmly established on the left side of the infield, he soon realized that his future lay in the outfield. He was also a valuable substitute pitcher, hurling in 24 games during his Chicago career and posting a 6–1 record. Ryan was hotheaded and emotional, but multitalented, and would spend the next 16 years in a Chicago uniform, outlasting all the other members of the 1885 championship team.

John Clarkson pitched in 70 games in 1885, completing 68 of them, and with the schedule increasing by 12 games the following year, Anson decided to ease Clarkson's load by adding a third starter to the pitching staff. He released Ted Kennedy, replacing him with another Irish lad, John (Jocko) Flynn, a right-hander from Lawrence, Massachusetts, who weighed only 145 pounds but was, to quote one newspaper, "a perfect terror" on the field. He was a terror off the field too, fitting in all too well with Kelly, Flint, and the rest, but Anson recognized his talent and held high hopes for him. To give support to the aging catcher Silver Flint, Anson signed another Irishman from Lawrence, George Moolic, whose father had fled the famine and found work at a textile mill in that industrial town. Moolic, who worked in the mill as a teenager before baseball provided a way out, had caught Flynn's pitches in the minor leagues the year before.

The 1886 team won the pennant again, Chicago's fifth in a seven-year period, but the race was a challenging one. The Detroit Wolverines, who had absorbed the best hitters from the defunct Buffalo club at the end of the 1885 season, suddenly vaulted into contention and wrested the lead from Anson's men in late July. However, Chicago's depth carried the day. Clarkson posted a 36–17 record, with McCormick at 31–11 and Flynn at 23–6, while Mike "King" Kelly, despite his ever-worsening off-field behavior, won his second batting title with a .388 average. The incredibly versatile Kelly played every position on the field in 1886 except left field and pitcher. The Wolverines closed to a one-game deficit in early October, but a Chicago victory on the last day of the season clinched the flag for the White Stockings.

Anson looked forward to another post-season match against Comiskey and the St. Louis Browns, who once again won the American Association pennant, but his players were not as enthusiastic. John Clarkson defeated the Browns in the first and third games, but Jim McCormick was blasted in the second contest, losing by a score of 12–0. Al Spalding complained that McCormick was "so thoroughly soused, he could not have struck out the batboy," and Anson sent the hard-living pitcher back to Chicago. McCormick pitched no more in the series, and with Jocko Flynn unavailable due to a sore arm, the White Stockings were obliged to pin all their hopes on Clarkson. The half–Irish, half–Scottish ace of the team, who was also troubled by arm soreness, lost Game 4 by an 8–5 score.

Once again, Kelly, McCormick, and many of the Chicago players treated the post-season series as a mere exhibition. Anson, still smarting from the tied outcome of the year before, had demanded a winner-take-all disbursement of the gate receipts, but most of the White Stockings and Browns reportedly paired up and agreed to split their winnings, no matter the outcome. The only two who did not were Anson and Comiskey, the rival first basemen and captains. With no monetary incentive for winning, the unconcerned White Stockings were seen drinking, smoking cigars, and telling jokes in a St. Louis hotel lobby following their defeat in the fourth contest.

Anson drove his men as hard as he could, but a dearth of pitching and a lack of meaningful effort doomed the White Stockings. Clarkson had pitched in three of the first four games, and was so worn out that Anson signed minor league star Mark Baldwin, who had won 23 games in the Northern League that summer. Comiskey, however, refused to allow Baldwin to join the Chicago club at that late date, so Anson was forced to send shortstop Ed Williamson to the mound for Game 5. The Browns batted Williamson out of the box, so outfielder Jimmy Ryan pitched the rest of the contest, which the Browns won 10–3.

The sixth and final game, played in St. Louis on October 23, 1886, was one of the most significant in baseball history. Clarkson took a 3–0 lead into the eighth inning, but the Browns rallied to tie the score after Chicago's Abner Dalrymple dropped a fly ball. Neither team scored in the ninth, and the White Stockings failed to tally in their half of the tenth. In the bottom of the inning, the Browns' Curt Welch singled and went to third on an infield hit and a sacrifice. Doc Bushong came to the plate but never got the chance to swing as the exhausted Clarkson heaved a wild pitch far out of catcher Mike Kelly's reach. As Kelly chased the errant ball, Welch slid across the plate with the game-winning and Series-ending run. Charlie Comiskey and his Browns, pennant winners of the supposedly inferior league, had won the championship of the world.

Kelly, who produced only five hits in 24 trips to the plate during the series, accepted the blame for the wild pitch. "I signaled Clarkson for a low ball on one side," explained Kelly after the game, "and when it came it was high upon the other. It struck my hand as I tried to get it and I would say it was a passed ball. You can give it to me if you want to. Clarkson told me that it slipped from his hands."[16] However, the series was probably lost long before the wild pitch left Clarkson's grip. Even if the Chicagoans had managed to win Game 6, the seventh contest would have required Clarkson to take the mound for the fifth time in seven days.

The unavailability of Jocko Flynn and Jim McCormick, paired with the apparent lack of interest on the part of the Chicago players, caused the loss of the series. It also signaled the demise of the White Stocking dynasty of the early 1880s. In his autobiography, Anson remarked that "had some of the players taken as good care of themselves prior to these games as they were in the habit of doing when the league season was in full swim, I am inclined to believe that there might have been a different tale to tell."[17] The Chicago club, after winning five National League pennants in seven years, was finished, and Anson and Spalding decided that a rebuilding job was in order. They resolved to weed out the troublemakers and start anew.

Several of the White Stockings soon learned that the 1886 season was their last in a Chicago uniform. Jocko Flynn's sore arm failed to heal over the winter, and it was evident that his pitching career was over. He played one game in the outfield during the following season and then disappeared from the major leagues for good. Jim McCormick, whose 31–11 season in 1886 was overshadowed by his off-field antics and failure in the post-season, was shuttled off to Pittsburgh for a young pitcher-outfielder named George Van Haltren.

Spalding had publicly threatened to dismiss two of the more unruly White Stockings, McCormick and catcher Silver Flint, if they did not behave in 1887. McCormick protested and was traded, but Flint remained, though Anson resolved to keep the catcher on a short leash. Two non–Irishmen, George Gore and Abner Dalrymple, were also sent packing, leaving a major rebuilding job for Anson and Spalding as the new season approached.

The biggest player transaction of all, one that struck at the Irish heart of the club, occurred in March of 1887. Mike "King" Kelly had won the batting title in 1886, but his behavior was a major headache for Anson, with his attitude growing more defiant with each passing season. Kelly's simmering resentment with the Chicago management reached the papers when he reacted angrily to Spalding's public criticism of his work ethic and behavior. "The officials of the Chicago Club," said Kelly to a reporter, "never fail to take advantage of any opportunity to impose a fine upon a player. McCormick, Gore, Flint, myself, and several other members of the team were fined for no cause whatever. They say that we were guilty of intoxication. As for McCormick and myself, I will say that there is no truth in this charge. It was simply drummed up in order to lessen the salary list of the club.... One thing is certain, I will never play ball again as a member of the Chicago Club, and if Mr. Spalding refuses to give me an honorable release, I will retire from the profession."[18]

However, Kelly was the game's biggest star, and other National League teams had already begun inquiring about his availability. The Chicago management played a waiting game, with the demand for Kelly's services increasing as the start of the new season drew near. In March, the Boston Beaneaters offered a sum of $7,500 for Kelly, but Spalding demurred. A few weeks later, Boston made a bid of $10,000, the largest amount ever offered for a single player up to that time. The White Stockings accepted, and Kelly decamped for Boston with a parting shot at his former captain. "Anson has claimed right along that it was due to his work that Chicago won the championship," said Kelly. "Next season he will have to prove it."[19]

The dismissals of Gore and Dalrymple, the retirement of Flynn, and the trades of Kelly and McCormick were intended to make the White Stockings a better behaved team. The plan worked, and although the White Stockings did not instantly become a bunch of choirboys, the 1887 squad gave Anson and Spalding fewer disciplinary headaches. However, the overhaul of personnel also cost the team a significant amount of talent that could not be easily replaced. Not until 1906, long after both Anson and Spalding had departed the scene, would the Chicago club win its next National League pennant.

3

Shamrocks, Trojans, and Giants

New York City, the most populous municipality in the nation and the entry point for millions of immigrants, Irish and otherwise, during the 19th century, hosted one of the original franchises of National League baseball when the circuit was formed in 1876. However, when the New York Mutuals and the Philadelphia Athletics, citing mounting financial losses, refused to finish their schedules that September, league president William Hulbert reacted with surprising fury. He expelled both teams from the circuit, leaving his National League without representation in the nation's two largest metropolitan areas. The league struggled to survive during the next few years. By 1879 the state of New York boasted two National League clubs, but neither was based in New York City. These two teams represented the less populous towns of Troy and Syracuse. In 1880 Syracuse dropped out and was replaced by Buffalo. New York City remained outside the National League orbit until 1883, when the Troy club disbanded, giving way to the team that eventually became the New York Giants.

Troy, New York, was one of the smaller cities in the National League, but its baseball roots ran deep. The Troy Haymakers were one of the nation's premier amateur teams during the 1860s, and when the National Association began play in 1871, the Haymakers moved into the professional ranks as one of the new organization's charter franchises. The team employed a diverse group of players, including the first Jewish baseball star, Lipman (Lip) Pike, and the first Latin-American player, Esteban Enrique (Steve) Bellan, who came to America from Cuba to attend college and fell in love with the game. Managed by Pike (the first Jewish manager) and Bill Craver, the 1871 Haymakers finished sixth in the Association. After a fifth-place finish in 1872, money woes forced the team to drop out of the league.

Despite the failure of its National Association club, Troy was a hotbed of baseball, especially among the Irish immigrants who settled there to work in its many mills and factories, which ran on power generated by waterwheels along the Hudson River. Troy and its neighbor to the north, Lansingburgh (which was annexed into Troy in 1900), produced many outstanding Irish-American players who later made their mark in professional ball. Due in large part to the enthusiasm of Irish immigrants and their children, amateur and semipro ball remained strong in the Troy area during the 1870s, and in 1879 a new team, the Trojans, received membership in the National League.

The 1879 Troy Trojans, managed by Horace Phillips and Bob Ferguson, won only 19 of the 77 games it played and finished last in the league, 35 and a half games behind the pennant-winning Providence Grays. A 4–31 skid in July and August buried them in the cellar, and Bob Ferguson, appointed as field leader in early August, recognized that his club could not hope to compete with the more established teams in the league. If top-level baseball was to survive in Troy, the club needed an infusion of talent, which Ferguson was determined to provide. He found three such talented ballplayers, all of them Irish-American, in the city of Holyoke, Massachusetts, some 90 miles southeast of Troy.

Holyoke was a sleepy western Massachusetts town until the late 1840s, when a dam and a system of canals were built to stimulate the growth of industry. Paper mills, powered by water running through the canals, sprouted up, and before long some 25 of them dotted the city. Immigrants from Ireland, fleeing the famine, found jobs there, and Holyoke became one of the most Irish cities in the United States. Even today, several decades after the mills closed, Holyoke still boasts the second largest St. Patrick's Day parade in the country, with only the one held in New York City being larger.[1] Since the townspeople were predominantly Irish, the local baseball team, formed during the national baseball craze of the 1870s, was called the Shamrocks. Most of the Holyoke fans, and many of the players on the club, were Irishmen.

One of the most popular Shamrocks was the starting pitcher. He was called "Smiling Mickey" Welch, but his given name was Michael Walsh. Born on the Fourth of July in 1859 to immigrants from County Tipperary, Michael Walsh grew up in the Williamsburg section of Brooklyn, which at the time was a breeding ground for skilled baseball players. Some of Brooklyn's teams, most notably the Star, Atlantic, and Eckford clubs, were among the best in the nation during the 1860s, and the construction of the Union Grounds, the first enclosed baseball field, in 1862 made it possible for teams to charge admission and brought about the advent of the professional game. Another important baseball innovation with Brooklyn roots was the curveball, developed by a Williamsburg teenager named William (Candy) Cummings shortly after the end of the Civil War. Other hurlers may have experimented with it independently, but Cummings made it popular and changed the nature of pitching forever with his tricky new delivery.

During the 1860s and 1870s, it seemed that almost every vacant lot in Brooklyn was filled with Irish kids playing the American game. It was a highly competitive sport for these city boys, and "Smiling Mickey" Walsh dove right in. He was small, at five feet and eight inches tall, but sturdy, and could throw pitches all day long with his easy underhand motion. "I was a little fellow," said Mickey, "and I had to learn to use my head. I studied the hitters and I knew how to pitch to all of them, and I worked hard to perfect my control. I had a pretty good fast ball, but I depended chiefly on a change of pace and an assortment of curve balls."[2] Mickey was not the fastest pitcher in Brooklyn, but his curveball was one of the best in the city and proved to be his ticket to professional success.

Somewhere along the line, the pitcher's last name changed from Walsh to Welch, possibly because a sportswriter miswrote his name in a box score. Mickey did not mind, perhaps because there were dozens of young men named Michael Walsh in Brooklyn at the time, so he used "Mickey Welch" as his baseball name. However, his family name never changed, and he was Michael Walsh off the field for the rest of his life. His friends called him Mike. He began his professional career in Poughkeepsie, New York, in 1877, and two years later had advanced to the strongest minor league in the country, the National Association, as the main starting pitcher for the Holyoke Shamrocks. Statistics, fragmentary as they are, credit Mickey with a 23–14 record for the Shamrocks in 1879.

Another future Hall of Famer, Roger Connor, was one of Holyoke's batting stars. Connor, born in Waterbury, Connecticut, in 1857, was the tall, powerfully-built son of an Irish immigrant laborer. Patrick Connor had 11 children, of which Roger was the oldest, and the elder Connor expected his boys to find jobs in one of Waterbury's brass factories, not play a useless game till all hours. "Lord help the one who disobeyed" his father, said Roger many years later, for "the punishment was quick and severe."[3] Still, Roger often shirked his chores to play ball on a local field. Roger's love of baseball caused friction between him and his father, and at age 14 the youngster left home to find employment in the baseball world. After a while he returned to Waterbury, only to find that his father had passed away in his absence. Roger then took a factory job to support the family, though he played town and semipro ball for the next few years.

By 1876 he was ready once again to turn his attention to professional ball and gained a spot on his hometown team, the Waterbury Monitors, as a left-handed third baseman. Well over six feet tall and about 200 pounds, he was usually the biggest player on the field whenever he appeared, and in 1878 he joined the Holyoke club. Though his fielding needed work, Roger was already a fine hitter, walloping home runs into the Connecticut River, which ran behind the right field fence at the Holyoke ballpark. Handsome and modest, Roger Connor became one of the most well-liked players on the team.

A third Holyoke star, outfielder Pete Gillespie, is largely forgotten today, but was a pop-

Roger Connor, slugging star of the New York Giants (Library of Congress).

ular player during his era. He, too, was the son of Irish immigrants, and was born in 1851 in Carbondale, Pennsylvania, where his father worked in the anthracite coal mines. Pete, given the Irish nickname "Padney" as a young man, was employed in the mines at a young age as a "breaker boy," pounding large pieces of coal into smaller ones. Fortunately, Gillespie was a good baseball player, and his athletic talent helped him escape the mines. At age 28 he was one of the older players on the Holyoke club, but he batted .411 in 1879, forming a hard-hitting one-two punch with Roger Connor. Connor, Welch, and Gillespie, all future major leaguers, powered Holyoke to the National Association pennant and established themselves as potential stars.

Former major league player and manager Bob Ferguson, a ubiquitous presence in early baseball, managed Holyoke's rivals from Springfield that season. Ferguson, who battled for every game, had thrown a fit during a contest between Holyoke and Springfield, claiming that Mickey Welch's curveball delivery was illegal. Rules at the time did not allow a pitcher to bring the ball above his hip during the delivery. The umpire on duty that day found Welch's pitching acceptable, however, and Welch shut out Springfield by a

Pete (Padney) Gillespie, like Hall of Famers Roger Connor and Mickey Welch, played for the Holyoke Shamrocks before going to Troy and then to the New York Giants (Library of Congress).

score of 1–0 as Ferguson bellowed his objections. Despite the dispute, Ferguson was impressed with Holyoke's three Irish stars, and when he returned to the National League as manager of Troy Trojans in August of 1879, he decided to tap some of that Irish talent. In early 1880, Ferguson signed Connor, Welch, and Gillespie, installing them in the Troy starting lineup.

The three former Holyoke players were not the only Irishmen on the Trojan roster. Outfielder John Cassidy, like Welch a product of the Brooklyn sandlots, had played for Troy in 1879, as had John (Kick) Kelly, a catcher from New York City. Kelly failed to hit and soon passed out of the league, but returned later in the decade as one of the best umpires in the game. Bill Holbert, a native of Baltimore who had started his career several years before as an umpire, performed most of the catching duties despite his .189 batting average. Ferguson also discovered a non–Irishman from Cincinnati, William (Buck) Ewing, a catcher who would become one of the game's biggest stars, but the 1880 Trojans were a predominantly Irish ball-club. With Mickey Welch pitching 64 complete games and compiling a 34–30 record, the Trojans, who had finished last in the National League the year before, improved to fourth place in 1880.

While Troy fought its way up the league standings, another Irish baseball enclave coa-lesced in Buffalo, New York, where the Bisons of the International Association became one of the top teams in the nation during the late 1870s. Buffalo's star pitcher, Jim (Pud) Galvin, was a product of the Kerry Patch district of St. Louis, where he was born to Irish parents on Christmas Day in 1856. Galvin was a stocky right-hander, about five feet nine inches tall and 190 pounds, and his durability and the speed of his sidearm delivery earned him the title "The Little Steam Engine." The fans and sportswriters called him "Pud" because, they said, he made pudding out of opposing batters.

Galvin had apprenticed as a steamfitter, but emerged as a baseball star in St. Louis while still a teenager. In 1875, when the Mound City hosted a team called the Red Stockings in the soon-to-be-defunct National Association, the 18-year-old Galvin pitched in eight games, win-ning four and posting a 1.16 earned run average. The Red Stockings played a non-league schedule in 1876, and Galvin made national headlines with a no-hitter against the Philadel-phia Phillies on Centennial Day, July 4, followed by a perfect game against the Cass club of Detroit on August 17. This performance may have been the first perfect game in baseball his-tory, professional or otherwise, while a hitless game that he completed four years later against Worcester was the first major league no-hitter ever pitched on the road. In 1877 Galvin moved to Pittsburgh, where he performed for the Alleghenies of the International Association and threw a shutout, the first ever in organized minor league play, against Columbus on April 30.

He landed in Buffalo in 1878 and pitched the Bisons to the International Association flag while beating many major league clubs in exhibition games, including a 1–0 victory over the champion Boston Red Stockings that featured Galvin's homer as the game's only run. With Galvin on the mound, the Buffalo Bisons were nearly unbeatable and had nothing more to prove in the minors. The club moved as a unit into the National League for the 1879 season and finished a respectable third, with Galvin posting a 37–27 record. Thus began a major league career that eventually made Pud Galvin the sport's first 300-game winner. He accom-plished this without throwing a curveball, as contemporary reports indicate that Galvin used only a fastball and excellent control to win 365 games and complete 646, the second highest total in baseball history.

Galvin was an unusually durable pitcher, even for his era, and newspaper research shows that he may have been the first major league player to use performance-enhancing drugs. In 1889 Galvin, pitching as well as ever in his 14th major league season, was the subject of an article in the *Washington Post* that revealed that the pitcher took injections of "elixir of Brown-Sequard." This substance was an extract made from animals, usually the brains or sexual organs, and some (but not all) doctors at the time believed the stuff to have life-prolonging properties. As the *Post* reported, "If there still be doubting Thomases who concede no virtue of the elixir, they are respectfully referred to Galvin's record in yesterday's Boston-Pittsburgh game. It is the best proof yet furnished of the value of the discovery."[4]

Another Irishman, Bill McGunnigle, shared the pitching load with Galvin in 1879, but faded out the league after the 1880 season. However, several more Irishmen joined the Bisons and helped put the team in contention in 1881. Jim O'Rourke, the longtime Boston star who had refused the change his last name to please Harry Wright eight years earlier, arrived in

1881 as third baseman and manager of the Bisons. Stubborn to a fault, O'Rourke left Boston after the 1878 campaign and signed with Providence; he was reportedly upset that the club had charged its players $20 for the use of their uniforms.[5] After O'Rourke helped Providence (managed by Harry Wright's brother George) win the 1879 pennant, he returned to Boston, where he played next to his older brother John in the outfield for one season. Jim then left Boston again and joined the Bisons, serving as Buffalo's playing manager for the next five years.

O'Rourke took classes at Yale Law School during the off-seasons, preparing for the day that his baseball career would end. He earned his degree in 1887 and eventually built a successful law practice. He was one of the more intelligent men in the game, a fact which he displayed with his large vocabulary. They called him "Orator Jim" for his flowery pronouncements; as one paper put it, "Words of great length and thunderous sound simply flowed out of his mouth." One day a player asked O'Rourke for a raise. Instead of explaining, as would most managers, that the team could not afford to give the player a bump in pay, O'Rourke saw the request as an opportunity to show off his vocabulary. "I'm sorry," said O'Rourke, "but the exigencies of the occasion and the condition of our exchequer will not permit anything of the sort at this period of our existence. Subsequent developments in the field of finance may remove the present gloom and we may emerge into a condition where we may see fit to reply in the affirmative to your exceedingly modest request."[6] A simple "no" would have sufficed, but they did not call him "Orator Jim" for nothing.

Despite this personality quirk, O'Rourke was popular with his fellow players, who admired him for his honesty. In 1884, with the Bisons succeeding on the field but struggling at the gate, the New York club offered Orator Jim a salary of $4,500 per year to abandon Buffalo in mid-season and join the Gothams (the team that later became the Giants). The deal would have made Jim the highest-paid player in the National League at the time. Much as he enjoyed giving complicated, long-winded speeches to the sportswriters, Jim was uncharacteristically brief in his reply. "No," he said, "I have given my word and will remain to the end of the season."[7]

O'Rourke was a fine hitter, but another Irishman provided the power in the Buffalo lineup. Dennis (Dan) Brouthers, a muscular first baseman, was the son of a printer and a housewife who had set sail for America in 1851 and settled in Wappingers Falls, New York. They called Dennis Brouthers "Big Dan" when he was still a teenager, and his hard hitting and strong arm made him a star in the Hudson River valley. He nearly quit the game in 1877 when he slammed into a catcher during a play at the plate; the catcher suffered a head injury and died the next day. Big Dan, grief-stricken, sat out the rest of the season, but decided to resume his career the following spring. In 1879 he performed well for a team in Lansingburgh, New York, which is now part of the city of Troy. Horace Phillips, then the Troy manager, signed Brouthers, and Big Dan hit the only four homers struck by the Trojans that season. However, Bob Ferguson was less impressed with Brouthers and let him go the following spring after only three games. After spending the summer of 1880 playing for independent teams, Dan landed in Buffalo the following year and quickly claimed the first base position. Big, friendly, and powerful, Dan Brouthers became one of the most popular players in the Buffalo lineup.

The Irish trio of Galvin, O'Rourke, and Brouthers brought the Bisons success in the league standings, but not at the box office. Though Buffalo fans (among then Mayor Grover Cleveland, the future president who knew the Bison players on a first-name basis) enjoyed watching one of the league's strongest hitting attacks, with Hardy Richardson, Jack Rowe, and Deacon White assisting Brouthers and O'Rourke, most Buffalonians stayed away. Pud Galvin did most of the pitching, though in 1882 a 34-year-old Irish-born rookie, Hugh (One-Arm) Daily, threw 29 complete games in support of Galvin. Not even the novelty of a one-armed pitcher could help the club at the gate, and the Bisons struggled for survival year after year.

The Troy Trojans also fought to keep their franchise alive despite poor attendance and financial setbacks. Though the team was weak in some areas, especially on defense, it managed to put several outstanding players on the field, men who would have been stars in any era of baseball. Even without Dan Brouthers, who was released early on, the 1880 Trojans employed three future Hall of Fame honorees in Mickey Welch, Buck Ewing, and Roger Connor during the first half of the season. A fourth player destined for Cooperstown, pitcher Tim Keefe, joined the club in August.

Timothy John Keefe, a quiet and studious young man who was born in Cambridge, Massachusetts, in 1857, was the son of an Irish immigrant named Patrick Keefe, one of three brothers who served in the Union Army during the Civil War. Patrick was a prisoner of war for several years, while the other two, Timothy and John, were killed in battle in 1862. At war's end, Patrick Keefe set high goals for his son Tim, the namesake of both of his departed brothers, but Tim preferred to play baseball. Father and son fought endlessly over Tim's love of the game, but by 1876 Tim had become one of the best amateur pitchers in Boston. He took instruction from Tommy Bond, the Irish-born star of the Red Stockings of the National League, who coached at Harvard University in Cambridge.

A successful stint at Albany, New York, in 1879 brought him to Ferguson's attention, and in August of 1880 the manager signed the 23-year-old Keefe to lighten the load on Mickey Welch, who had pitched nearly all of Troy's games that season. Keefe, a right-hander, pitched in 12 games for Troy in August and September, and though he won only six contests, his earned run average of 0.86 still stands as the best in baseball history for any pitcher with 10 or more decisions in a season. Thus began a partnership between the two Irish-American pitchers, Keefe and Welch, which endured for more than a decade.

Keefe and Welch were both right-

TIMOTHY KEEFE.
ALLEN & GINTER'S
RICHMOND. *Cigarettes.* VIRGINIA.

Tim Keefe, a native of Cambridge, Massachusetts, won 19 games in a row for the Giants in 1888 (Library of Congress).

handers, but differed in both pitching style and temperament. Welch, an outgoing, friendly man who married and started a family at a young age, was a curveball specialist, while Keefe was a quiet, almost taciturn youngster who relied on his outstanding fastball. Welch enjoyed drinking beer so much that he even composed short poems to celebrate his favorite beverage, while the more serious Keefe locked himself away in his room at night with textbooks and taught himself accounting and shorthand. Despite their differences, the two became fast friends, a relationship that lasted for the rest of their lives.

Keefe and Welch handled all the pitching for the Trojans in 1881, with Welch winning 21 and losing 18 while Keefe posted an 18–27 record. Another Irish Trojan, Roger Connor, made history on September 9 of that year when, in a game against Worcester played in Albany, he wiped out a three-run deficit and ended the game with a grand-slam homer, the first ever hit in National League play. However, the Troy club dropped a notch to fifth place, and attendance was disappointing. The popularity of baseball was growing nationally, and cities like Troy, New York and Worcester, Massachusetts, were too small to properly support National League teams, especially since the circuit did not, at the time, have a presence in either New York or Philadelphia. The 1882 Trojans, despite the fine play of Keefe, Welch, Connor and others, fell to seventh place and lost so much money that the club disbanded at season's end.

The fall of Troy, so to speak, created an opportunity for a New York baseball promoter named John B. Day. Day was the owner of the New York Metropolitans, one of the nation's leading independent clubs. The "Mets" were good enough to defeat major league teams in exhibition play, and in 1883 Day decided to move his team into the American Association, the rival of the National League. However, with the dissolution of the Troy club and the sudden availability of stars like Keefe, Welch, and Connor, Day hatched an even more ambitious scheme. He would create a second team in New York, called the Gothams, and join the National League at the same time. Day quickly signed Tim Keefe, Mickey Welch, Roger Connor, Pete Gillespie, Bill Holbert, and Buck Ewing, the elite of the Troy team, for his two New York ballclubs.

Day wanted both his teams to be competitive, so he split up the pitching duo of Keefe and Welch, placing Keefe and Holbert on the Metropolitans and the other four men on the Gothams. Keefe, who had spent the previous three seasons as the number two pitcher behind Welch, blossomed in 1883 as the top pitcher for the Mets, with 68 complete games, 41 wins, and a record 361 strikeouts in 619 innings. Welch, pitching in the stronger National League, posted a 25–23 record as the Gothams finished in sixth place. He did, however, enjoy the honor of pitching the Gothams' inaugural game in the National League before a crowd that included former President and Civil War hero Ulysses S. Grant.

Both New York teams displayed a strong Irish influence. The Mets had Keefe, Holbert, and outfielder John O'Rourke, a former Boston Red Stocking and brother of the more famous "Orator Jim." The Mets also featured left fielder Ed Kennedy, who like Pete Gillespie was a product of the mining town of Carbondale, Pennsylvania. The Gothams were anchored by Gillespie, Welch and Connor, who quickly became popular with the New York fans with his .357 batting average. John B. Day also signed the well-traveled veteran Mike Dorgan, a Connecticut-born son of Irish immigrants and one of the more popular players in the league. The handsome Dorgan, an outfielder, was a good hitter and leader who had captained the Worcester club a few years before, though his off-field behavior was often a problem for his teams. The National League had placed Dorgan, along with nine other players, on a blacklist after the 1881 season for "gross acts of intemperance or insubordination." He sat out the 1882 campaign, stayed out of trouble, and was allowed to play again the next year. Ed Caskins, an infielder who joined Dorgan on the blacklist, also played for the Gothams during the 1883 season.

In 1884, another Irish-American player, Danny Richardson, joined the Gothams and started a major league career that lasted for 11 seasons. Richardson hailed from Elmira, New York, where his immigrant father worked in a shoe factory. The fifth of nine children, Danny starred for one of Elmira's leading amateur teams, the Telegrams, and was signed by the Gothams as a utility player, jumping directly into the National League at the age of 21. Used initially as an outfielder and occasional pitcher, Richardson eventually claimed the second base position, which he held for the remainder of the decade. Though his batting average never crossed the .300 mark in any season, Richardson earned a reputation as a good clutch hitter; as *Sporting Life* once put it, he was "a man worth a dozen ordinary players for his ability to send a man home in the critical stages of a game."[8] On June 11, 1887, he became the first player in franchise history to belt six hits in a game.

Though the Metropolitans won the American Association pennant in 1884, the National League was the more prestigious circuit, and John B. Day realized that a good Gothams club would make more money than a flag-winning Mets outfit. Therefore, in 1885 Day transferred the best Mets players to the Gothams, reuniting Keefe and Welch after two years of separation. The result was a strong, contending club, which became known as the Giants because of the height of some of its players, most notably the six-foot, three-inch first baseman Roger Connor. The newly christened Giants battled the Chicago White Stockings for the league lead all year, while the Mets faded to seventh place. The Giants fell short of the pennant, losing by two games at season's end, but the New York club served notice that it would challenge for the flag for years to come. Day had given the National League a contending club in New York, which strengthened the league and raised the circuit's profile around the nation.

While the New York Giants rose to the top of the league, the Buffalo Bisons sank in a sea of red ink, despite a respectable third-place finish in 1884, and by the end of the 1885 season the team owners were ready to cut their losses. They had already sold off two of their high-priced stars, sending Pud Galvin to Pittsburgh and Jim O'Rourke to the Giants, and a seventh-place performance in 1885 spelled the end for the Bisons. In September, the team owners dissolved the club, selling their slugging "Big Four" of Dan Brouthers, Jack Rowe, Deacon White, and Hardy Richardson to Detroit in a straight cash transaction that instantly turned the Wolverines into contenders. The demise of the Bisons left New York City as the only municipality in the state to host a National League team, a state of affairs that continues to this day.

New York was a city of immigrants, especially Irish ones, and the roster of the Giants reflected the city's population. The team featured an all–Irish outfield in 1885 with Mike Dorgan in center, Pete Gillespie in left, and Jim O'Rourke, acquired from Buffalo before the season, in right. Thomas (Pat) Deasley, born in Ireland, was the substitute catcher and outfielder, while the pitching staff was almost totally Irish, with all but two innings played in 1885 pitched by Irishmen. Mickey Welch carried the biggest load and compiled a 44–11 record, while Tim Keefe won 32 games and Danny Richardson, pressed into service on the mound early in the campaign, made eight starts and posted a 7–1 record. Three other games were pitched by Larry Corcoran, the sore-armed former Chicago star, who unsuccessfully attempted to resurrect his career but was released at the end of the season. Buck Ewing, who took the mound for two innings of relief one day, was the only non–Irish Giant pitcher. The most conspicuous Irish Giant of all was Roger Connor, the big first baseman, who wore a bright green shamrock patch stitched to the sleeve of his uniform shirt. The New York fans called him

"Dear Old Roger," and he responded by winning the batting title that year with a .371 average.

The 1885 season was notable for a pennant race that featured a New York team for the first time, but an off-the-field development was even more significant. The National League had tightened its control over its players during the preceding seasons, keeping salaries as low as possible and restricting player movement with the "reserve clause." This piece of contract language was introduced in 1880 and allowed each team to reserve the services of five players for the following year. By 1885 the reserve clause had expanded to cover most of a team's roster, and the players fervently objected to the restrictions on their freedom that it represented, to no avail. As New York Giants team captain John Montgomery Ward described it in a magazine article in 1887, "Instead of an institution for good, [the reserve clause] has become one for evil; instead of a measure of protection, it has been used as a handle for the manipulation of a traffic in players, a sort of speculation in live stock, by which they are bought, sold, and transferred like so many sheep."[9]

In response to this and other ownership practices (such as lucrative player sales between teams) that the players found offensive, several New York Giants met on October 22, 1885, and founded their own trade association, which they called the Brotherhood of Professional Base Ball Players. Headed by Ward (who, like Jim O'Rourke, had studied law in the off-seasons), the Brotherhood was the creation of nine members of the Giants, six of whom were Irish. The constitution, written in longhand by Tim Keefe, was approved and signed by Ward, Keefe, Roger Connor, Jim O'Rourke, Mike Dorgan, Mickey Welch, Danny Richardson, Buck Ewing, and Joe Gearhardt. Keefe was appointed secretary-treasurer of the Brotherhood due to his self-taught facility in bookkeeping and shorthand.

The National League magnates ignored the fledgling organization, which spent the next several years spreading its message and recruiting new members. As the Giants traveled around the circuit during the 1886 season, they founded chapters of the Brotherhood in every league city, with more than 100 National League players eventually joining. Some of the more radical players wished to take action against the magnates immediately in the form of a strike or similar player rebellion, but John Ward counseled patience. He, Keefe, and the other Brotherhood officers worked to build their organization into a position of strength before taking any action to challenge what they saw as increasingly poor treatment of their members by the team owners.

After their fine 1885 season, the Giants regressed during the next two campaigns, finishing third in 1886 and fourth in 1887. With the number of games on the schedule increasing each year (from 112 in 1885 to 138 in 1888), team management realized that two pitchers could no longer shoulder all the mound duties. Welch and Keefe performed as well as ever during this time, but the Giants' failure to provide support for their two pitching stars consigned them to the fringes of the pennant race.

Mike Dorgan left the Giants after the 1887 season, but another son of Irish immigrants was ready to take his place. Mike Tiernan, a 20-year-old outfielder from Trenton, New Jersey, was the son of a mill worker and spent his teenage years working in a pottery. The Giants bought his contract from Jersey City, where he had excelled as a pitcher, but Tiernan refused to report until the Giants agreed to play him in the outfield, his preferred position. The team relented, and Tiernan wound up spending all 13 years of his National League career in a New York uniform. Tiernan was so quiet that his teammates called him "Silent Mike," but he was a fine hitter who led the league in home runs twice and once scored six runs in a game. He got off to a poor start in the field, setting a major league record on May 16, 1887, with five

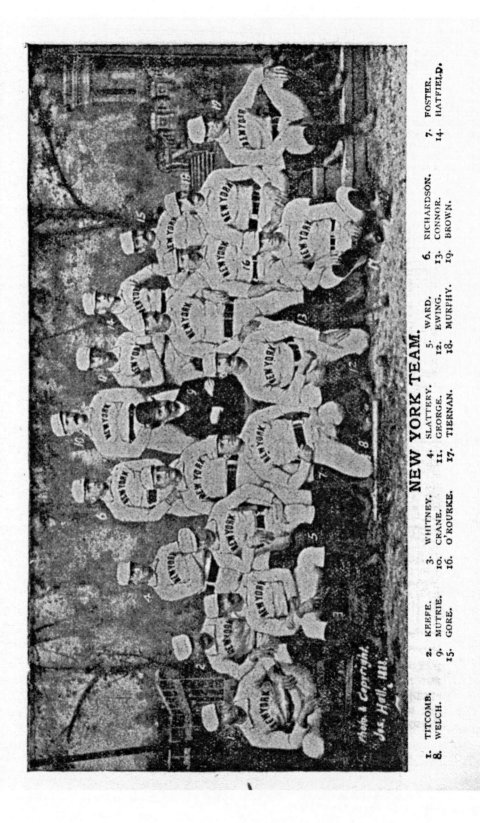

Photo & Copyright.
Jas. Hall, 1111.

NEW YORK TEAM.

1. TITCOMB. 2. KEEFE. 3. WHITNEY. 4. SLATTERY. 5. WARD. 6. RICHARDSON. 7. FOSTER.
8. WELCH. 9. MUTRIE. 10. CRANE. 11. GEORGE. 12. EWING. 13. CONNOR. 14. HATFIELD.
15. GORE. 16. O'ROURKE. 17. TIERNAN. 18. MURPHY. 19. BROWN.

outfield errors in one contest, but he eventually became a good glove man as well. Frequently overlooked because of his reticent nature and disdain for publicity, Mike Tiernan was one of the outstanding players of the 19th century. An article in *The Gael*, an Irish-American literary magazine, stated that Tiernan was "as honest as the sun, a sober gentlemanly professional player ... a credit to his team ... possessed [of] a record of never having been fined for disputing an umpire's decision."[10]

In 1888, the Giants came up with two new pitchers, right-hander Ed (Cannonball) Crane, a second-generation Irishman from Boston, and a left-handed native of Maine named Ledell (Cannonball) Titcomb. Crane made 11 starts, winning five, while Titcomb won 14 games and gave Keefe and Welch more rest between starts. Keefe responded with one of his best seasons, posting a 35–12 record that included a 19-game winning streak in July and August. Though Buck Ewing was the only Giant to bat above .300, Keefe and Welch (26–19) headed the best pitching staff in the league, and led the Giants to their first National League pennant by nine games over the Chicago White Stockings. In the October World Series against another mostly Irish club, the St. Louis Browns, Keefe won four games, and Welch and Crane one each as the Giants defeated the Browns, six games to four.

Titcomb pitched only three games in 1889, but another Irish-American left-hander, Hank O'Day, made 10 starts, winning nine of them as the Giants waged a closely-fought battle against the Boston Beaneaters. Keefe, who held out in a contract dispute for the first few weeks of the season, missed the 30-win circle for the first time in seven years, but the other Irish Giants picked up the slack. Roger Connor batted .317, Jim O'Rourke .321, and Mike Tiernan .335 as the Giants led the league in runs scored and were second overall in pitching. Keefe won 28 games, Welch 27, and Crane 14 as the Giants traded the league lead with Boston through the month of September. On October 5, the last day of the season, Keefe pitched a 5–3 win against Cleveland while Boston's John Clarkson lost a 6–1 decision at Pittsburgh to give the Giants their second consecutive flag.

The 1889 season ended with another World Series win, this time over Brooklyn, but the mood was somber at the team's victory celebration afterward. Relations between the players and owners had deteriorated, especially after the magnates pushed through a salary classification plan. Under this scheme, each player would be assigned a grade from A to E and have his salary fixed accordingly, from $1,500 for an E player to $2,500 for one at the A level. The plan outraged the members of the Brotherhood, especially the usually imperturbable Tim Keefe, whose salary would fall sharply under the plan. "I won't say what the Brotherhood will do, but we will move," he remarked in July of 1889. "There is one thing certain, [that] they won't classify as many men this fall as they think. Why, this talk about [league president] Nick Young classifying men is rot. The clubs send in the salaries, and he puts them in categories to correspond."[11]

The move to which Keefe referred was nothing less than the destruction of the National League, for which Ward and the Brotherhood officers had planned for several years. In November of 1889 Ward announced the formation of what he called the "Players National League," and invited all players, Brotherhood members or not, to quit the established league and join the new one. Almost all of them did so, throwing professional baseball into turmoil and setting off a massive effort by the National League to thwart the new circuit by retaining its existing stars. The effort was only partly successful, and this new baseball war made the winter of 1889–90 perhaps the most conflict-ridden in the game's history.

Opposite: **The pennant-winning Giants of 1888 (1889 Spalding Guide).**

The new Players League had eight franchises, with the Brooklyn entry headed by John Ward and the team in New York under the direction of Buck Ewing. John B. Day, owner of the National League Giants, did his best to prevent as many stars as possible from jumping to the new league, but most of his players turned a deaf ear to his entreaties. Roger Connor, told by Day to "name your price" if he would agree to turn his back on his Brotherhood mates, refused to consider such an offer, while Danny Richardson reportedly "scornfully rejected" a $15,000 salary tender from the established league.[12] Almost all the National League stars, save for Chicago's Cap Anson, Boston's John Clarkson, and a handful of others, bolted for the Players League, leaving Day's Giants and most other National League franchises in a state of near-panic.

The Irishmen on the Giants showed remarkable solidarity in quitting the National League and creating a new circuit, but John B. Day managed to woo two of his veteran performers away from the Players League. One was "Silent Mike" Tiernan, who accepted a three-year contract from Day at a substantial raise in pay. The other, surprisingly, was "Smiling Mickey" Welch, one of the founders of the Brotherhood. Welch considered the matter and concluded that, with nearly 300 wins and more than 450 complete games behind him, his career would most likely not last much longer. Offered a guaranteed three-year contract by Day, Welch quit the Brotherhood and returned to the Giants. "I offered to play with the new club for a salary of $2,000 less than that offered me by Mr. Day," explained Mickey. "The figure suited the leaders of the movement, but the financial men would only guarantee me my salary for 1890. Some time ago Mr. Day made me a big offer, and said that he would sign a three years' contract, he to assume all risks. I am in the business for dollars and cents, and as the offer made by the old League was the better one, I accepted it."[13]

Welch's defection sat poorly with some of his old teammates. "Orator Jim" O'Rourke, one of the most enthusiastic supporters of the new circuit, lambasted the "traitors" in the newspapers. "The poor, miserable wretches who have permitted bribers to label upon their flesh the price of dishonor excited my pity rather than my anger," said O'Rourke, "and I shall allow them to rest in peace if it is possible for them to find it on this green earth."[14] When Day signed shortstop Jack Glasscock and third baseman Jerry Denny away from the Brotherhood, Buck Ewing groused, "Glasscock is a traitor. We are not disappointed, though, for we expected him to desert us."[15] However, Tim Keefe, secretary-treasurer of the Brotherhood (and league president John Ward's brother-in-law), took his longtime pitching partner's decision in stride. "Mike, you are your own boss," said Keefe to Welch, and their friendship continued.

The New York Brotherhood team (which also used the name Giants) built a new park next to the existing Polo Grounds in Manhattan, close enough to allow their fans to see the action in both venues. Ewing's Giants, with most of the familiar New York stars in the lineup, were expected to win the Players League pennant, but faltered and finished in third place despite Roger Connor's league-leading 14 home runs and a .360 average from the 39-year-old Jim O'Rourke. Tim Keefe was held to a 17–11 record after his season ended with a broken finger sustained in practice on August 19, while his new Irish pitching partner, Hank O'Day, led the staff with 22 wins. The Brotherhood team won the box office battle, outdrawing Day's aggregation, but the financial condition of the team, and the new league itself, were shaky at season's end.

Day's Giants, with Tiernan and Welch supported by defectors from the Brotherhood and assorted rookies and castoffs, struggled through the season and nearly collapsed in August, with only an emergency infusion of cash from the National League allowing the club to meet its payroll. Mickey Welch won 17 games, but most of the pitching load fell upon an import from the defunct Indianapolis team, a half–Irish 19-year-old pitcher named Amos Rusie, who excited the fans with his prodigious fastball. Rusie made 63 stars and posted a 29–34 record, while another new Irish-American pitcher, Jesse Burkett, won only 3 of 13 decisions and soon decided to switch to the outfield. Day's Giants finished in sixth place and ended the season in a precarious state, with shares in the club having been sold off to keep it afloat. By the end of 1890, four other National League teams owned stock in the Giants, but at least the club was still alive and ready to battle the Players League again in 1891.

Ward, Keefe, and the rest were willing to continue the fight, but the moneymen behind the new league were ready to surrender. All three major leagues lost money in 1890, but the National League, with its deeper pockets, was able to absorb the blows. In the fall of 1890, several of the financiers behind the New York Players League club, not realizing that the National League Giants team was in nearly as poor a financial condition as they were, raised the white flag. They agreed to merge their two ballclubs and play in the National League in 1891, relieving the Players League of perhaps its strongest team and kicking the supports out from under the new circuit. Within days, the Players League owners in Chicago sold out their interests as well, and when other teams rushed to follow suit, the Players League was dead. In late November, *The Sporting News* declared, "Goodbye Players' League. Your life has been a stormy one. Because of your existence many a man has lost by thousands of dollars. And before long all that will be left of you is a memory — a sad, discouraging memory."[16]

The Players League had been founded largely by Irish-American players, and its demise coincided with the end of Irish domination of the New York baseball scene. One by one, the Irishmen who brought the Giants success during the 1880s left New York, beginning with Tim Keefe, a six-time 30-game winner and, at the time, baseball's career leader in strikeouts. With New York's newest star, Amos Rusie, sharing most of the pitching load for the 1891 Giants with John Ewing, Buck's younger brother, the 34-year-old Keefe found little opportunity to pitch. Perhaps the Giants thought Keefe's best years were behind him, or maybe his status as a Brotherhood officer worked against him, but Tim appeared in only eight games, winning two, before requesting his release at the end of July. He then signed with the Philadelphia Phillies and won 19 games in 1892, but the lengthening of the pitching distance by ten feet in 1893 made his fastball less fearsome. His earned run average nearly doubled in 1893, and in August of that year he pitched his final major league game. After an unsuccessful career as an umpire, Keefe returned to Cambridge, Massachusetts, his hometown, and sold real estate.

Mickey Welch, who quit the Brotherhood and remained with the Giants, also saw his career wind down during this time. He, too, did not pitch much for the 1891 Giants, but his three-year no-cut contract was still in force, and he remained on the bench, pitching only occasionally and compiling a 5–9 record. In 1892, he appeared in only one game and gave up nine runs and eleven hits in five innings. The Giants then demoted him to the minors, sending him to finish the season, and his contract, in Troy, where he had begun his major league career twelve years earlier. Welch, like Keefe, was adversely affected by the new pitching distance, and when he could no longer get minor-league hitters out, "Smiling Mickey" retired to Holyoke, where he and his wife raised their eight children. In 1912, he returned to New York as a night watchman and press box attendant at the Polo Grounds, a job he held for the next two decades.

Roger Connor was dealt to the Phillies after the 1891 season, but returned to New York for the 1893 campaign. He was still a powerful hitter, but in June of 1894 the Giants sold him to the St. Louis Browns and put another Irish-American, "Dirty Jack" Doyle, on first base. Connor played for the Browns for three more years and managed them for a time, with little success. After the 1897 season he left the major leagues and returned to his hometown of Waterbury, Connecticut. He managed and played for the Waterbury entry in the Connecticut State League for the next several seasons, after which he worked as a janitorial supervisor for the local school board. Jim O'Rourke, who hit .304 for the Giants in 1892 at age 42, became president of the Connecticut State League and operated the Bridgeport club, competing on a regular basis with his longtime Giants teammate Roger Connor. He attended to his law practice, but also served as playing manager for his minor league team into the 20th century. O'Rourke, who signed his first professional contract in 1872, finally retired as a player in 1907, when he was 57 years old.

By 1895, all the Irishmen who made up the core of the pennant-winning Giants of 1888 and 1889 were gone, except for "Silent Mike" Tiernan, who patrolled right field until 1899. The Giants finished in second place in 1894 and won the post-season Temple Cup series against the Baltimore Orioles, but fell in the standings after new team owner Andrew Freedman took control in 1895. Freedman, an impatient and impulsive man who changed managers with dismaying frequency, hired Irishmen (Bill Joyce, "Dirty Jack" Doyle) and non–Irishmen (Cap Anson, Buck Ewing) to lead his ballclub, but the team floundered as the formerly dominant Irish became only one of several ethnic groups represented on the New York club. The Giants remained in this sad state until 1902, when new manager John McGraw began to remake the roster, filling it with tough, scrappy Irishmen like himself. McGraw built a ballclub that was even more Irish than the pennant-winning Giants of the late 1880s had been, and his arrival marked the beginning of another successful era of New York baseball.

4

Charlie Comiskey and
the St. Louis Browns

Charles A. Comiskey, founder and sole owner of the Chicago White Sox of the American League, was one of the most respected and successful figures in baseball during the first three decades of the 20th century. Sportswriters dubbed him "The Old Roman," a nickname that probably came from his distinguished Roman nose and profile, and was a shortened version of the more unwieldy moniker, "The Noblest Roman of Them All." His White Sox won the World Series in 1906 and again in 1917, and was the most profitable ballclub in the league during that era. "I started with fifty dollars back in 1877," Comiskey said proudly, "and look where I am now." In 1910 he built a new stadium, which was called Comiskey Park but carried the unofficial title, "Base Ball Palace of the World." He was the king of baseball in Chicago, so popular that he was asked to run for mayor of the city on more than one occasion. His response was always the same: "I'd rather win a pennant than an election!"

Comiskey may have been called "The Old Roman," but his heritage was Irish. He was a second-generation Irishman who made his name in baseball during the 1880s as Charlie Comiskey, a hard-charging, umpire-abusing first baseman and manager of the St. Louis Browns of the American Association. He led the Browns to four league pennants before reaching his 30th birthday, though the methods he employed included fan violence, physical intimidation of umpires and opposing players, and other unsavory tactics. "First place is the only subject of conversation," Comiskey once said. "Everybody chokes up before they get as far as second."[1] Comiskey's transformation from a rule-breaking, win-at-all-cost roughneck to a pillar of civic respectability is one of the more striking narratives of the Irish in the early days of baseball.

Charlie's father was a typical American success story. Born in County Cavan, Ireland, John Comiskey fled the potato famine and arrived in America in 1848. He settled in New Haven, Connecticut, and entered the lumber business. Four years later, despairing of the economic climate of New England, he moved to Chicago, a fast-growing city full of opportunities for hard-working, aggressive individuals like himself. He settled in the city's tenth ward, an area mostly populated by fellow Irish refugees, and involved himself in the political life of the community. John Comiskey married in 1852 and started a family that grew to include eight children. In 1859, the year his third child Charlie was born, John gained election as alderman for his ward, a post he held for the next 11 years. Eloquent, direct, and incorruptible, he was known and admired as "Honest John" Comiskey, whose rise to prominence made him a role model for his fellow Irish immigrants.

John Comiskey was a prosperous brick merchant, bricks being an important commodity in Chicago as the city slowly rebuilt from the devastating fire of 1871. "Honest John" expected his son Charlie to enter the family business that he had worked so hard to build, but Charlie's interests lay elsewhere. The boy was baseball-mad, much to the annoyance of his father, who condemned bat-and-ball games as "frivolous." Years later, Charlie recounted a story of how he set out to deliver a wagonload of bricks one day. He never arrived at his destination, and John, fearing an accident or foul play, set out to find him. He soon came to a vacant lot, where the brick wagon was parked. Charlie, safe and sound, was pitching in a pickup baseball game, having completely forgotten about the brick delivery.

An apprenticeship to a local plumber did not work out for young Charlie, so the elder Comiskey decided that his son needed some time away from Chicago and his baseball-playing pals. He sent Charlie to a Catholic college called St. Mary's in faraway Kansas, no doubt hoping that baseball fever had not yet progressed that far west. His plan might have worked, had

CHARLES COMISKEY.
ALLEN & GINTER'S
Cigarettes.
RICHMOND.   VIRGINIA.

Charlie Comiskey, first baseman and manager of the St. Louis Browns (Library of Congress).

not Charlie happened to meet an Irish-born fellow student named Ted Sullivan, three years ahead of him, who became his baseball mentor.

Ted Sullivan, though largely forgotten today, was one of the most influential promoters and organizers of early baseball. Born in County Clare, Ireland, around 1851, Sullivan arrived in America with his family before he was ten years old, and spent the rest of his childhood in Milwaukee. A sharp, ambitious individual, he attended St. Louis University and, later, St. Mary's College, where he played on the baseball team. It was at St. Mary's that Sullivan made the acquaintance of Charlie Comiskey, a young man every bit as enthusiastic at baseball as he. The Irish-born Sullivan and Comiskey, son of an Irish immigrant, became fast friends as well as teammates.

Charlie was mostly a pitcher at that time, but played other positions on the field as well. When Sullivan pitched he always wanted Comiskey to catch for him. "I picked out Comiskey," related Sullivan years later, "because I considered him the smartest kid on the team. One incident will show how quickly, even in those days, he grasped an opportunity. I noticed that a runner on third was taking a rather big lead. Comiskey signaled for a certain ball. I shook my head. He signaled for another and I repeated. Finally I left the box, all the time upbraiding him because of his bonehead strategy. He never said a word but met me half way, and still bawling him out I slipped him the ball while I returned to the mound. "All set behind the bat and Comiskey whipped the ball to third nailing the runner by ten feet. I did not tell him what to do. I simply wanted to find out if he could think for himself. From that time on I began to have respect for Charles, and he was only a kid at that."[2]

Since Charlie's baseball fever seemed only to increase in Kansas, the elder Comiskey soon transferred his son to Christian Brothers College in Prairie du Chien, Wisconsin. However, Ted Sullivan had left St. Mary's and taken over as manager of a team, called the Alerts, in Milwaukee in 1877. He needed a pitcher, and proposed to hire Charlie Comiskey at a salary of $50 per month. John Comiskey was not happy, but Charlie was a stubborn character, much like his father, and after a series of family discussions John reluctantly gave his blessing to the endeavor. The 18-year-old Charlie was now a professional ballplayer, with his friend and former college teammate Ted Sullivan as his manager.

Sullivan left Milwaukee at season's end to work as a railroad news agent in Dubuque, Iowa, but baseball was never far from his active mind. In 1878 he created an independent team in Dubuque called the Rabbits and convinced his friend Charlie Comiskey to join him. The Rabbits compiled a winning record, but lost money due to the difficulty of scheduling opponents. In early 1879, Sullivan organized the Northwestern League, a four-team circuit that provided his Dubuque Rabbits with dependable opposition. Sullivan fortified his team with a future Hall of Famer, Charley Radbourn, who pitched and occasionally played the outfield. The Rabbits rarely lost a game, and so completely overwhelmed their opponents that the league survived for only three months, folding in July of that season. It was not a lost year for Comiskey, however. He began dating a Dubuque girl named Nan Kelly, a daughter of Irish immigrants, marrying her three years later.

The Dubuque ballclub, which returned to the independent ranks for the next two seasons, employed several players of Irish descent. Besides Sullivan and Comiskey, the team included the Gleason brothers from St. Louis, Bill and Jack, both of whom later played major league ball. Tom Sullivan, another St. Louis boy who played for Worcester the year before and was no apparent relation to Ted, was the catcher. By this time Comiskey had committed to first base on a full-time basis, as his arm had given out and rendered him unable to pitch. He played third base for a while, but his height and quick hands made him ideally suited as a first sacker, and he remained at this position for the next two decades.

The Dubuque nine was one of the best independent clubs in the Midwest, and their star players were coveted by higher-level teams. In 1881, Sullivan's club was invited to St. Louis to play another independent outfit, the Browns, which had signed infielders Bill and Jack Gleason away from the Rabbits earlier in the year. The Rabbits lost by a 9–1 score, but Comiskey's performance impressed the Browns. When the St. Louis club entered the new American Association in 1882, it hired Charlie Comiskey to play first base.

The Browns were the creation of a colorful German immigrant named Chris von der Ahe, a saloon owner whose establishment stood about a block away from Grand Avenue Park, where the St. Louis Reds had played in the National League from 1876 to 1877. Realizing that thirsty baseball fans were good for business, von der Ahe rebuilt the idle park in 1881, then bought a majority of stock in a new baseball club, called the Brown Stockings. In 1882 von der Ahe's club joined the new American Association, giving baseball-mad St. Louis a major league team for the first time in five years. His inaugural aggregation, with ex–Dubuque stars

Comiskey at first, Tom Sullivan at catcher, and the Gleason brothers, Bill and Jack, at short and third respectively, finished a disappointing fifth out of six teams in the Association under manager Ned Cuthbert.

Von der Ahe was an impatient man. He dismissed Cuthbert and, at Comiskey's suggestion, hired Ted Sullivan as manager for the 1883 campaign. Sullivan was an immediate success, winning 53 of the 79 games that he managed, but von der Ahe's constant interference caused friction between Sullivan and his boss. The owner, mostly ignorant of the nuances of the game, expected to win every contest, and fined players for what appeared to him to be bad or sloppy play. Sullivan spent much of his time pleading with von der Ahe not to punish his men arbitrarily, but by late August Sullivan had had enough, and resigned following a final bitter argument with von der Ahe. The owner then appointed the 24-year-old Comiskey as field leader for the rest of the season.

Though Comiskey kept the Browns in the race until the season's final day, losing the flag by only one game to the Philadelphia Athletics, von der Ahe hired a veteran minor leaguer named Jimmy Williams to manage the club in 1884. Ultimately, Williams ran afoul of the difficult owner as had Sullivan, and by early September Comiskey was back in charge. He would remain the manager of the Browns for the remainder of the decade.

Comiskey, having learned much from his mentor Ted Sullivan, emerged as a first-class leader and organizer, though the challenges of dealing with von der Ahe made his job more difficult. The portly owner, who called himself "Der Boss President," wore loud checkered suits and sat in a seat along the third base line, blowing a whistle to get the attention of his players and manager, or to order schooners of beer from his vendors. He liked to boast about his team, his ballpark, and his players to newspaper reporters, though he actually knew little about the game. One day, with manager Comiskey at his side, von der Ahe conducted a tour of his ballpark. "Some plant, eh?" he said proudly. "I have the biggest diamond in the world, and...."

"Chris, all diamonds are the same size," whispered Comiskey in his ear.

"I mean, gentlemen, the Browns are playing on the biggest infield in the world," promptly corrected the owner.[3]

Comiskey, now permanently in charge, put his own stamp on the team by hiring young, aggressive ballplayers, many of them Irish like himself. James (Tip) O'Neill, a Canadian whose grandparents were Irish-born, had failed in a trial as a pitcher with the New York Metropolitans in 1883, but Comiskey signed him and put him in left field. O'Neill, who reportedly earned his nickname due to his ability to foul off pitches until he got one he liked, became the most powerful hitter on the club. In 1887, a year in which walks counted as hits, O'Neill batted .492, a major league record that will most likely never be broken. Removing the walks from his totals gives him a still-incredible .435 average. The biggest and strongest man on the club, O'Neill also served as Comiskey's enforcer in disciplinary matters, sometimes correcting unruly teammates with his fists.

Curt Welch, a hard-drinking center fielder who was reportedly illiterate, was another Irishman brought to the Browns by Comiskey. Welch, from East Liverpool, Ohio, had played for Toledo in 1884, when that city had a club in the Association. He drew notice for his stellar play, though he also angered manager Charles Morton with his antics; among other complaints, Morton claimed that Welch hid a case of beer behind the center field fence before each game and took sips of the brew all afternoon. When Toledo dropped out of the Association in 1885, Welch and teammate Sam Barkley signed on with the Browns. Though a mediocre hitter, Welch was one of the best outfielders of his day, playing a shallow center field and using his speed to run down long flies. He was a fearless headfirst slider and an enthusiastic umpire-baiter who was widely respected for his playing skill, though his behavior often resulted in fines and reprimands.

Bill Gleason, the shortstop, was an Irishman who played aggressively on the field, but was a solid and respectable citizen off it. A St. Louis native, he worked for the fire department during the winter months and managed to save his money and provide well for his family on a baseball salary of $1,800 per year. Comiskey, who admired Gleason's intelligence and passion for the game, roomed with the shortstop on road trips and planned new tactics during long late-night strategy sessions. Comiskey, said Gleason many years later, "never went to sleep at night until he had figured out how he was going to win the game the next day."[4] To opponents, however, Gleason was an enemy, barreling into infielders with spikes high to break up double plays and rattling his adversaries with a constant stream of insults. In 1885, *Sporting Life* magazine offered the opinion that "if [Gleason] should someday break a limb or his neck, not a ball player in the American Association would feel the slightest regret."[5]

CLEASON, S. S. Athletics

A teammate of Charlie Comiskey in Dubuque and with the Browns, Bill Gleason worked for the St. Louis fire department during and after his playing days (Library of Congress).

Verbal abuse of opponents was an important facet of the strategy employed by the Browns. When the Browns were at bat, Comiskey placed two of his most aggressive men, usually Bill Gleason and himself, along the baselines as coaches to direct traffic and upset the fielders with invective. "The chalk lines which enclose the coaching boxes were added to the field diagram after Charles Comiskey had demonstrated their necessity," said Jim Hart, who managed against the Browns during the 1880s. "Comiskey and Bill Gleason used to plant themselves on each side of the visiting catcher and comment on his breeding, personal habits, skill as a receiver, or rather lack of it, until the unlucky backstop was unable to tell whether one or half a dozen balls were coming his way."[6] In 1886 the coaching boxes, clearly marked, became a permanent feature of the infield and remain so to this day.

Umpires, too, were cruelly mistreated by Comiskey and his men. Many arbiters dreaded working games in St. Louis, where the Browns could be counted on to overreact to any decision called against them, and the fans were ready to start a riot on a moment's notice. The Browns, especially Welch, Comiskey, and foghorn-voiced third baseman Arlie Latham, cajoled, harassed, and sometimes physically abused the umpires, and since von der Ahe paid all fines levied by the league, the behavior grew worse with each passing year. The Browns acted in such a manner because it proved to be a winning formula; from 1885 to 1889, they posted an incredible 265–83 record at home for a percentage of .761, while their winning percentage on the road was .597. Intimidating the umpires into calling things their way apparently worked for Comiskey and his rowdy Browns.

Comiskey himself was never much of a hitter, compiling a career batting average of only .259, but his leadership and fielding wizardry at first base made up for his shortcomings at bat. Before the mid–1880s, first basemen never strayed far, if at all, from the bag, remaining anchored to their post to receive throws from the infield, and only leaving it to chase after foul popups near the stands. Comiskey, with his quickness, greatly increased his range (and improved his team's infield defense) by playing several paces away from the bag, knowing that he could get back to the base easily when required. He designed innovative new plays where he fielded bunts and infield grounders and assigned the pitcher to cover first, making the first baseman a much more active participant in infield play. Some say that Ted Sullivan had invented this new way to play first, while others give Comiskey full credit, but by the end of the decade almost all major league first sackers had adopted Comiskey's style. Some historians also claim that Comiskey was the first manager to move his infielders in to the edge of the grass to cut off a run at the plate in a tight situation, something every field leader does today as a matter of course.

The Irish made up the core of Comiskey's club, but other ethnic groups were represented as well. Arlie Latham, a Welshman, played third base and made a name for himself as much for his brawling and umpire-baiting as for his strong throwing and timely hitting. The two starting pitchers, Dave Foutz and Bob Caruthers, were both good hitters and alternated between the mound and right field in an unusual, though successful, arrangement. Joseph (Yank) Robinson, son of a wealthy Tennessee lawyer, was a dependable second baseman, while Albert (Doc) Bushong, of French and Irish extraction, manned the catching position. Bushong had earned a degree in dentistry, and adopted a one-handed catching style to protect his right hand for his future career.

Comiskey had assembled a good team, and although the hitters, aside from Tip O'Neill, were mediocre, the defense and pitching were superb. The club had excellent leadership, thanks to Comiskey, and an aggressive attitude that propelled them to the top of the American Association standings. In 1884 the team had finished in second place, but the following season, Comiskey's first full campaign at the helm, saw the Browns win the first of four consecutive Association pennants. Both Comiskey and O'Neill missed part of the 1885 season due to injuries, but strong defense and the pitching of Foutz (33–14) and Caruthers (40–13) led the Browns to the flag by 16 games over the second place Cincinnati Reds.

In October 1885, the Browns met the National League champions, the Chicago White Stockings, in a "World's Series," but the matchup nearly ended shortly after it began. The teams played to a 5–5 tie in the first game, and in the second contest, a dispute over a foul ball caused Comiskey to pull his team off the field and refuse to continue. As the game was played in St. Louis, the umpire left the park under police protection and later, from the safety of his hotel room, declared the contest a forfeit to the White Stockings. The series may have ended there, but a round of intense negotiations saved it, and the two teams split the next four games. Comiskey and Cap Anson, manager of the White Stockings, agreed to conclude the series with a seventh and final game, which the Browns won by a 13–4 count. However, the embarrassed Chicago club declared the series a tie due to the forfeited second game, not a 3 games to 2 win for the Browns. The disputed outcome was a topic of controversy

The 1884 Toledo team featured former St. Louis star Tony Mullane (standing, fourth from right), and future Brown Curt Welch (third from left). Pitcher and future umpire Hank O'Day is standing, third from right. Catcher Jim (Deacon) McGuire (on the ground at right) would play 26 seasons in the majors (author's collection).

all winter, with the $1,000 winner-take-all prize in abeyance. Finally, the two clubs reportedly split the thousand dollars, though hard feelings between the teams, and the leagues, remained.

The Browns were now the Association's dominant team, and had the opportunity to strengthen themselves further with the return of one of the game's leading Irish-American pitchers in 1886. Tony Mullane, a handsome, solidly-built right-hander with an impressive handlebar mustache, was born in County Cork in 1859 and emigrated to the United States at the age of five. After reaching the major leagues in 1881, he won 35 games for the Browns in 1883, the year Ted Sullivan managed the team. Mullane, nicknamed "The Count" for his regal bearing and supreme self-confidence, was a top-notch hurler who could pitch the ball with either hand, and did so in major league play on at least two occasions. He was one of the first ballplayers to be popular with the female fans. Sportswriter Sam Crane, a former player who competed against the handsome pitcher, wrote that Mullane "was a very fine appearing fellow, and wore a heavy black mustache, as did Tim Keefe, and it was a toss-up between Tony and Tim as to which was the Adonis of the game."[7]

In 1884 Mullane quit the Browns, jumped to the new Union Association, then returned to his former league and signed on with Toledo, where he became fast friends with center fielder and fellow Irishman Curt Welch. Toledo, too, had an Irish presence, with catcher James (Deacon) McGuire playing the first season of a 26-year career, and future umpire Hank O'Day sharing the pitching chores with Mullane. However, Mullane was the star and main drawing card for the Toledo ballclub. He completed 64 of his 65 starts, posted a 36–26 mark, and helped a mediocre club to a surprising fourth-place finish. He compiled this fine record despite his oft-expressed disdain for his catcher, Moses Fleetwood Walker, the first

African-American player in the major leagues. A good hitter, Mullane also played 19 games in the outfield when the second-string hurler, O'Day, pitched.

Mullane was not a smoker, drinker, or carouser, but had trouble honoring contracts. When the Toledo club returned to minor league play in 1885, the pitcher verbally agreed to rejoin the Browns. However, the Cincinnati Reds offered him $5,000 to renege on his agreement, and he fairly leaped at the opportunity. The Browns called foul, and although Mullane was one of the top pitchers in the game at the time, St. Louis owner Chris von der Ahe demanded, successfully, that Mullane be suspended for the entire 1885 campaign. He served his suspension quietly, and when the season ended, von der Ahe persuaded Mullane to let bygones be bygones and return to the Browns. A three-man rotation of Caruthers, Foutz, and Mullane might have made the Browns virtually unbeatable in 1886.

However, the Browns also employed second baseman Sam Barkley, a former Toledo teammate of both Mullane and Welch. Barkley and Mullane had once been close friends, but when the two became enamored of the same Toledo girl, they feuded violently and became mortal enemies. In an exhibition game in New Orleans during the winter months, Mullane nearly hit Barkley in the head with a pitch, and Barkley threatened to belt the pitcher in the head with his bat. It was obvious that the two men could not play on the same team, and in April of 1886 Mullane returned the salary advances that von der Ahe had given him and signed with Cincinnati. Von der Ahe, upset at the loss of Mullane, then released Barkley.

Mullane was unavailable, but with Comiskey and O'Neill staying free from injury and the development of a third starting pitcher in Nat Hudson, St. Louis cruised to the 1886 pennant by 12 games over second-place Pittsburgh. Cap Anson's White Stockings once again won the National League pennant, and the two teams agreed to a rematch in a post-season World Series. This time, the prize money was increased to $15,000, which Anson and Comiskey agreed to contest on a winner-take-all basis. Not only league pride, but also a considerable amount of money, was at stake, and although most of the Browns and White Stockings agreed to split their winnings, Anson and Comiskey stubbornly refused to deal with each other.

The two clubs split the first four games, though injuries and suspensions had left Chicago with only one dependable starting pitcher in John Clarkson, who hurled three of the contests. With Clarkson's arm sore from overuse, Anson had to put shortstop Ed Williamson on the mound for the fifth game, and the Browns bombed the Chicagoans 10–3 to take the lead in the series. The Browns needed only one more win to clinch the championship, and got it in the sixth game when they rallied from a late 3–0 deficit and sent the game to extra innings. In the tenth frame, Curt Welch singled, made his way to third, and scored on a wild pitch, sliding happily across the plate and setting off a wild celebration by players and fans. Charlie Comiskey and his St. Louis Browns were now the champions of the world.

Nat Hudson developed a sore arm and pitched only nine games in 1887, but Comiskey found another young pitching star to take his place. Charles (Silver) King was a 19-year-old right-hander and St. Louis native who had pitched a few games for Kansas City in the National League the year before. King's ancestry was German, not Irish, as his family name was Koenig, but he learned his baseball on the St. Louis sandlots by playing with and against many future stars of Irish-American lineage. A powerfully built man with huge hands, who threw his fastball without a windup, King quickly became the ace of the staff, winning 32 games in his first season with the Browns.

The 1887 team won the pennant again, its third in a row, by 14 games over second-place Cincinnati, but cracks were already beginning to show in the team that Comiskey had so carefully assembled. Owner Chris von der Ahe was becoming disgusted with both on-field and off-field incidents involving his players, especially Curt Welch, who was severely criticized for beating up Philadelphia pitcher Gus Weyhing after a basepath collision in June of that year. Six days later, Welch caused a riot in Baltimore when he plowed into Orioles second baseman Bill Greenwood while attempting to steal second. Welch was arrested by Baltimore police, and von der Ahe was required to pay $200 to bail his outfielder out of jail. Comiskey, too, was losing patience with Welch. A few days after the Greenwood incident, Tip O'Neill, Comiskey's chief enforcer of discipline, let a bat slip out of his hands during practice. The bat struck Welch, standing in the on-deck circle, in the face. O'Neill claimed that the blow was an accident, but the incident put Welch, and the other Browns, on notice.

Von der Ahe was also outraged that September when several of his St. Louis players, Irish and otherwise, refused to play in an exhibition game against the Cuban Giants, a leading African-American team of the era. Comiskey was absent from the club at the time, nursing an injury, and in his absence eight of the Browns drafted a letter in which they declared, "We, the undersigned members of the St. Louis Baseball Club, do not agree to play against negroes tomorrow. We will cheerfully play against white people at any time and think that by refusing to play we are only doing what is right."[8] It was signed by O'Neill, Gleason, Welch, Latham, King, Robinson, Caruthers, and catcher Jack Boyle. Oddly enough, Curt Welch had played on the Toledo team in 1884 with two African-Americans, Moses and Welday Walker, without apparent objection, and the Browns had participated in a match against the Cuban Giants two years earlier without incident. Von der Ahe cancelled the game, though the move cost him a big payday, and never forgot the act of insubordination.

An accumulation of incidents during the 1887 season led to increased public criticism of the Browns and their style of play, and the supremacy of the St. Louis team was becoming harmful to the Association as a whole. Attendance dropped off in several cities, even St. Louis, where the fans were becoming jaded with success. The Browns made a shambles of the pennant race year after year, and their easy dominance threatened the viability of the Association. The New York Metropolitans, who finished 50 games out of the league lead in 1887, dropped out of the circuit and ended the Association's presence in New York, while other clubs, with no realistic chance of winning the pennant, teetered on the edge of solvency. The cry "Break up the Browns!" was heard in many of the league's cities.

The Browns lost a 15-game World Series that fall against the National League champion Detroit Wolverines, and von der Ahe was so critical of his team's sloppy play that he refused to give his players any of the gate receipts. The Browns, understandably, reacted angrily to this news, and the owner responded with a series of player transactions as stunning as they were unexpected. In November 1887 he sold his top two pitchers, Bob Caruthers and Dave Foutz, and catcher Doc Bushong to Brooklyn for a combined $18,250, and sent two members of the Irish core of the club, Bill Gleason and Curt Welch, to Philadelphia for three players and $3,000. With plenty of cash in hand, the owner then sailed to Europe for a vacation, leaving Comiskey to reassemble the team.

Most observers blamed von der Ahe for the destruction of a championship club, but other evidence points to Comiskey as the real guiding force behind the upheaval. *Sporting Life* magazine suggested as much, stating that "very few people know that the sale of Welch, Foutz, and Caruthers was made at Comiskey's request, rather than at von der Ahe's desire. Comiskey wants no man on his team who would not obey him."[9] If so, then perhaps Comiskey had to include his best friend on the team, Bill Gleason, in the trade to Philadelphia in order to be rid of the troublesome Welch. Or, perhaps von der Ahe, still seething over the cancelled game against the Cuban Giants, insisted on Gleason's dismissal. No matter who was responsible for the bust-up, the fact remained that the Browns were shattered, and no one expected the club to contend for the 1888 pennant with so many holes in its lineup.

Comiskey, however, was a keen judge of talent and found a number of fine new players, several of whom were Irishmen. Tommy McCarthy, a five foot, six inch outfielder who had helped Oshkosh win the Northwestern League pennant the year before, joined the team despite von der Ahe's misgivings about his small stature. "Ach! Dat Tommy can't play big ball," the owner spat at Comiskey, but McCarthy remained and claimed the right field position vacated by Caruthers and Foutz. McCarthy had learned to play ball on the streets of Boston, where his parents had settled after fleeing Ireland during the 1850s. He had failed in two previous major league trials, but his intelligence and strategic acumen rivaled Comiskey's. McCarthy brought the trap play, in which he let a fly ball or popup drop on purpose and then forced out the confused base runners, to St. Louis, and soon his innovations in outfield play and baserunning were copied throughout the league. McCarthy quickly became a favorite of the St. Louis fans, especially the Irish ones.

Two Irish lads, Jack Boyle and Jocko Milligan, shared the catching chores in 1888, while infielder James (Chippy) McGarr, who had arrived with Milligan in the trade with Philadelphia, added another Irish name to the roster of the reconstituted Browns. With 20-year-old Silver King leading the league in every major pitching category and Tip O'Neill winning his second consecutive batting title, Comiskey's Browns overcame serious weaknesses at shortstop and center field (the positions vacated by Gleason and Welch) and won the pennant by six and a half games over Brooklyn. It may have been the finest managing job of Comiskey's career.

Unfortunately, von der Ahe's behavior was becoming more unpredictable with each passing year, and when the Browns lost a 10-game World Series that fall to the National League champion New York Giants, the owner publicly blasted umpires John Kelly and John Gaffney. Curt Welch, the former St. Louis outfielder, had drunkenly accosted Kelly at a train station and accused him of betting on the Giants to win, and von der Ahe inflamed the situation when he told reporters that he agreed with Welch. Gaffney and Kelly, unanimously considered the best arbiters in the game (both had earned the nickname "Honest John"), reacted angrily. "I will quit the business before I take any more of that," declared Gaffney, and Kelly concurred, saying, "If Gaffney will not umpire any more games, I won't either."[10] Only a quick, and reluctant, claim by von der Ahe that he had been misquoted (which he had not been) saved the remainder of the series.

The owner wore down his charges with criticism and fines, and by 1889 the players, Comiskey included, were beginning to have their fill of "Der Boss President." The Browns threatened to go on strike after von der Ahe suspended second baseman Yank Robinson in May for insubordination, and though the players soon relented, they dropped three straight contests to the lowly Kansas City club amid rumors that they had done so intentionally. The Browns lost the 1889 pennant by two games, and when the Players League formed in early 1890, Comiskey decided to sever his partnership with von der Ahe. Offered the helm of a new club in his hometown of Chicago, Comiskey left St. Louis for the Windy City and took Tip O'Neill, Silver King, Arlie Latham, and several other St. Louis players with him. The Browns were torn apart again, for the second time in two years, but this time Comiskey would not be around to reassemble the pieces.

Von der Ahe, with a shell of a team under his command, decided to replace Comiskey with another brainy, overachieving Irishman. He appointed Tommy McCarthy as manager of the Browns for the 1890 campaign. However, McCarthy was no disciplinarian, and after a good start in April, the team dropped eight of its first 12 games in early May. During the slump, McCarthy and four of his players broke curfew together in Rochester, New York, drinking at a ball where they "danced the Razzle Dazzle quadrille" at three in the morning, according to an account in *The Sporting News*.[11] The furious von der Ahe fired his manager, though the four men who followed McCarthy in the manager's post that season fared no better. Von der Ahe, by this time, was so flighty and disorganized that he reinstated McCarthy as manager in late August, then relieved him of command again after he won four of five games. The Browns finished in third place, their lowest finish in six years.

Charlie Comiskey would have been happy never to play for von der Ahe again, but when the Players League collapsed after only one season, he reluctantly returned to St. Louis for the 1891 campaign. Tip O'Neill rejoined the Browns, but Arlie Latham, Silver King, and other stars kept their distance. Comiskey was required once again to build a team almost from scratch, and one of the men he hired was one of the most unusual players in baseball history. Willie McGill, a pitcher who stood only five feet and five inches tall, was baseball's first teenage sensation.

McGill, called "Little Willie" or "Wee Willie," was a third-generation Irishman whose paternal grandfather had left Ireland long before the famine and settled in North Carolina. Willie's father was a railroad agent whose work took him to Atlanta, Georgia, where Willie was born in November of 1873. By age 15 Willie was a minor league star, pitching a no-hitter in the Central Interstate League in 1889, and in 1890 he reached the majors as a 16-year-old pitcher with Cleveland of the Players League. "Wee Willie" was the only hurler on his team to post a winning record that year, and his future looked bright. To this day, McGill is the youngest major league pitcher to throw a complete game, pitch a shutout, and join a regular rotation.

Willie won only two of his seven decisions with Mike Kelly's Cincinnati team in early 1891, but Comiskey saw a future star in the teenaged right-hander and brought him to St. Louis that June. At age 17, Willie McGill won 19 games for the Browns, giving him a 21–15 mark for the year and making him the youngest 20-game winner in baseball history. His only problem was self-discipline, and he was absent from the lineup often due to what the papers called "high living." Perhaps his stardom came too easily because he drove managers to distraction with his late-night escapades during his tenure in the major leagues.

Once again, the Browns were a mostly Irish team, with Tommy McCarthy and Tip O'Neill in the outfield, McGill on the mound, Jack Boyle at catcher, and Comiskey on first base, but the magic of the 1880s was gone by 1891. The Browns made a respectable showing, finishing in second position, but the American Association was on its last legs, failing on the field and at the box office. The Association was dying, and the future of major league baseball in St. Louis now rested in the hands of the eccentric, widely disliked Chris von der Ahe.

The Association, as expected, ceased operations at season's end, but von der Ahe managed to keep St. Louis in the ranks of major league cities by moving his franchise into the National League for the 1892 campaign. However, few of his Browns wanted to accompany him to the new league. In October of 1891 Comiskey, McCarthy, O'Neill, and other key players announced that they would refuse to return to St. Louis in 1892, instead making their own deals with other National League teams. Comiskey, McGill, and O'Neill went to Cincinnati, McCarthy signed with Boston, and others scattered, leaving von der Ahe with little talent to work with in the highly competitive National League.

Von der Ahe was a sore loser, as McCarthy soon discovered. The St. Louis owner believed that he deserved compensation from either McCarthy or the Boston club for his outfielder's desertion, but none was forthcoming. Von der Ahe responded by hiring a burglar, who broke into McCarthy's hotel room in St. Louis and stole $19 in cash and a pocket watch. Thus satisfied, von der Ahe considered the matter closed.[12]

The St. Louis Browns never recovered from the loss of Comiskey, or from von der Ahe's mismanagement. The owner hired several Irish-American managers during the next few seasons, including slugger Roger Connor and umpire Tim Hurst, but his impatience increased as the years passed, with the Browns employing as many a five field leaders in a single season. Von der Ahe even took the reins himself for a time, but no one could replace Comiskey, and the team floundered. The Browns spent the rest of the 1890s near the bottom of the standings as the St. Louis fans drifted away, and by 1898 von der Ahe was bankrupt, divorced, and losing control of his team. In early 1899 the Browns were sold at a sheriff's auction to settle the owner's debts, and von der Ahe faded into obscurity. Renamed the Cardinals in 1900, the St. Louis club did not regain its former stature for several decades. The Cardinals did not win their first National League pennant until 1926, long after Chris von der Ahe had departed the baseball scene. When "Der Boss President" died, penniless and forgotten, in 1913, his former manager Charlie Comiskey paid for his funeral.

Several Irish-American members of Comiskey's Browns led successful lives after baseball, while others did not. Curt Welch, the talented but troublesome outfielder, put together a few more good seasons after leaving St. Louis, but during the early 1890s his carefree lifestyle caught up to him. Baltimore manager Ned Hanlon dismissed Welch from the Orioles in 1892 for excessive drinking, after which Comiskey, then leading the Cincinnati Reds, gave him another chance. Comiskey could not reform Welch either, and released him in August of that year. Welch contracted tuberculosis, fell from the major leagues to the low minors, and eventually returned home to East Liverpool, Ohio, where he died in 1896 at the age of 34. A year later, his destitute widow took out an advertisement in *The Sporting News*, offering to sell his jewelry and baseball mementoes to the highest bidder.

Bill Gleason, who never wanted to leave the Browns, quit the game after the 1892 season and joined the St. Louis fire department on a full-time basis. He rose to the rank of captain and spent the next 30 years in the profession, remaining on active duty until his death in 1932 at age 73. Tip O'Neill played for Comiskey in Cincinnati in 1892, then called it a career and returned home to Canada. He never married, spending his life in a large house with his mother and two brothers. He served as an Eastern League umpire for a time before opening a saloon in Montreal, where he died of a heart attack in 1915 at 57.

Willie McGill, the teenaged sensation, might have compiled an enviable record, but a sore arm ended his major league career in 1896 at age 22. His propensity for late hours and poor training habits no doubt contributed to his early flameout. However, he continued to pitch in the minors for many years afterward, and starred in the highly competitive Chicago semipro leagues until he was nearly 40 years old. McGill built a post-playing career as a baseball coach and athletic trainer, and was one of the last surviving members of Comiskey's Browns when he died in Indianapolis in 1944. Tony Mullane, who pitched for Comiskey in Cincinnati and became a police officer in Chicago when his playing career ended, died in that city only three months before McGill's demise. Mullane, with 285 career wins, is one of only four pitchers to win 280 or more games and not gain election to the Baseball Hall of Fame.[13]

Two other Browns enjoyed long careers in the game. Tommy McCarthy went to Boston, his hometown, where he helped the Beaneaters win two pennants and made himself famous as one of the "Heavenly Twins" with his fellow Irish-American outfielder, Hugh Duffy. McCarthy and Duffy ran a saloon and billiard hall together for a while, and after McCarthy retired as a player after the 1896 season he operated his own establishment in South Boston for many years. He was also a respected scout for the local clubs, the Braves and Red Sox, in the years before his death in 1922 at age 59. Tommy McCarthy was elected to the Baseball Hall of Fame in 1946, more for his contributions to strategy than for his statistical record.

Charlie Comiskey, too, wound up in the Hall of Fame, but not for his playing talent. He spent three unsuccessful years as manager of the Cincinnati Reds, then bought the Sioux City, Iowa, franchise in the Western League. He moved the team to St. Paul, Minnesota, and managed it for the next several seasons, donning a glove and making an appearance at first base every now and then. He might have spent the rest of his baseball days with a minor league club, resting on the laurels he had earned with the Browns, but a new century was approaching, and changes were coming to the baseball world. No one knew it yet, but Charlie Comiskey's greatest accomplishments, and most wrenching failures, lay ahead of him.

5

White Stockings, Colts, and Cubs

The Chicago White Stockings of the early 1880s became a National League dynasty, winning five pennants in seven years and boasting some of the game's brightest and most popular stars. The Irish influence in baseball reached its peak during this era, with the White Stockings employing some of the most talented Irish-American players in the game, such as Mike Kelly, John Clarkson, and Silver Flint. However, no great team lasts forever, and a series of post-season embarrassments and off-field incidents led the Chicago management to close this winning chapter of Chicago baseball. After the 1886 campaign, team president Al Spalding and manager Cap Anson decided to dismiss many of their most troublesome players and rebuild their roster.

Mike Kelly, Jim McCormick, and Jocko Flynn were gone when the 1887 season commenced, but the Irish presence on the Chicago club was still represented by John Clarkson, Silver Flint, Tom Burns, and Jimmy Ryan. They were soon joined by new catcher Tom (Tido) Daly, a 22-year-old from Philadelphia, and outfielder Marty Sullivan, a native of Lowell, Massachusetts. Daly was a hard worker, though he liked to play practical jokes, while Sullivan was rumored to have a bit of a wild streak. Taking no chances, Spalding decided to have each player sign a pledge of abstinence for the 1887 season. He declared that he would run the team on the "cold water principle," no doubt hoping to avoid the off-field problems that had caused so much trouble during the championship years.

The White Stockings were a less troublesome bunch in 1887, but they failed to defend their pennant, finishing in third place behind Detroit and Philadelphia. At least Anson and Spalding could take solace in the knowledge that the Boston club, which added the biggest star in the game in Mike Kelly, failed to improve on its fifth-place 1886 finish. Anson's men also ended the career of the onetime Irish pitching star, Larry Corcoran, who was still trying to recover from the arm woes that had forced him out of Chicago. Corcoran, attempting a comeback with Indianapolis, was blasted out of the box by the White Stockings on May 11, losing by a score of 11–6. Five days later, the Giants walloped Corcoran and the Hoosiers 26–6, and the former pitching star drew his release shortly thereafter. Corcoran tried, and failed, to resuscitate his career in the minors for several years before turning to umpiring.

Chicago had featured a nearly all-Irish pitching staff since the early 1880s, but by 1887 John Clarkson was the only son of Erin remaining (except for the versatile Jimmy Ryan, who made three starts and five relief appearances that season). Clarkson, however, was also looking to leave Chicago, as he was upset about the departures of Mike Kelly, Jim McCormick, and other close friends. Clarkson's relationship with Anson soured as the 1887 season wore on, and the pitching ace made noises about quitting the game. He said that he would rather join his father in the jewelry business in his hometown of Cambridge, Massachusetts, than play another season for the White Stockings. Clarkson, who had learned the jewelry trade before entering baseball, wanted to be sent east, where he could live with his family in Cambridge and play with his friend Kelly on the Boston club. "I think it's about time that I should have something to say about where I shall play," said Clarkson to *Sporting Life* magazine. "Chicago won't release me. Very well, then, I shall not play ball at all next season. I will remain in Boston and work at my trade. I mean just what I say. I shall not play in Chicago under any circumstances."[1]

Spalding and Anson were reluctant to lose their ace, but since Clarkson was one of the few players who could quit the game and still be financially secure, they began to listen to offers. Once again, the Boston Beaneaters came calling, and in April 1888, mere days before the start of the new season, the Boston club bought Clarkson outright from Chicago for $10,000, the same price it had paid for Mike Kelly the year before. The Beaneaters now boasted the "$20,000 battery" of Clarkson and Kelly, a new popular attraction to draw the Irish fans of Boston to the ballpark.

Marty Sullivan joined the White Stockings after the departures of Kelly, Gore, Dalrymple, and others after the 1886 season (Library of Congress).

With Clarkson's departure, the White Stockings had no Irish hurlers except for Jimmy Ryan, who pitched only occasionally. Anson had to find a new staff ace, and a powerfully built left-hander named Gus Krock, who had pitched Oshkosh to the Northwest League pennant the year before, filled the bill. However, several more positions on the pitching staff were open as pre-season practice began in the spring of 1888. The Chicago club also sent outfielder Billy Sunday packing to Pittsburgh, putting another roster spot up for grabs and necessitating a search for new blood.

Anson liked to boast of his ability to identify young talent, but he nearly passed up the opportunity to sign one of the best young hitters in the game. Hugh Duffy, a 21-year-old Irish-American shortstop, had led Lowell to the New England League title in 1887. Duffy, a fleet-footed line drive hitter, belted 14 homers that year, including three in one game, and was recognized as the best minor league prospect in New England. The Boston Beaneaters had offered him a contract, but Duffy so admired Cap Anson that he told *Boston Globe* sports editor Tim Murnane that he would play in Chicago for less money. Murnane, a former player and friend of both Anson and Chicago team president Al Spalding, arranged the deal, and Duffy reported to training camp with the White Stockings in the spring of 1888.

Born in Rhode Island in 1866, Duffy, like many second-generation Irish boys in New England, took a job in a textile mill at a young age and developed strong arms and wrists from carrying large rolls of fabric across the factory floor. When he reached his teenage years, he moved to Connecticut, where a job in a mill and a place on a semipro baseball team awaited him. By 1885, at age 19, he was earning a respectable $50 per month as a pitcher and short-stop. Entering pro ball the following year, Duffy's high batting averages and good defense drew attention. His character also impressed Al Spalding, the Chicago team president, who noticed that Duffy never spoke any epithet stronger than "by jingoes." Duffy was not a tee-totaler, but drank only rarely during his lifetime and never smoked or chewed tobacco.

Duffy was a keen competitor, especially when a game was on the line. One day he wheeled around and confronted Washington catcher (and fellow Irishman) Connie Mack, who stood about eight inches taller than he. Mack was skilled at the art of "tipping" bats, reaching out with his gloved hand and interfering with the batter's swing with his large catcher's mitt. The umpire often did not notice it, but Duffy did. "You've been tipping bats," snarled Duffy. "You tip my bat once and I'll break it over your head, you big shadpoke."[2]

Duffy stood only five feet and seven inches tall, and Anson expressed disappointment when he finally met his new recruit. "Duffy," intoned the captain, "you fall about five inches and 25 pounds short of the major league size."[3] Anson ignored Duffy as much as possible, and although the youngster made the team, he rode the bench for more than two months. "Signing with Chicago and playing with Chicago were two different things, I discovered," said Duffy many years later. "This has been found out by many a player since. Anson liked big men. I wasn't big."[4] He finally made his debut with the White Stockings on June 23, after another Chicago rookie from New England, catcher Duke Farrell, suggested that Anson put the young Rhode Islander in the outfield. Duffy played right field and belted two singles in a win over Pittsburgh, but played only sporadically for weeks afterward. He ended the 1888 season, the first of his Hall of Fame career, with an average of .282 in 71 games.

Farrell was another member of a new Irish presence on the White Stockings. His given name was Charles, but he came from Marlborough, Massachusetts, so the nickname "Duke" was most likely inevitable. He worked in a shoe store as a teenager and performed for the Marlborough town team before signing with Salem in the New England League, where he and Hugh Duffy were teammates. At a height of six feet and one inch and weighing 205 pounds, Farrell met Anson's criteria for size in a ballplayer. He batted only .232 in 1888, but his defensive play was superb, and by 1889 he had surpassed two other Irishmen, Tom Daly and the fading Silver Flint, as the number one catcher on Anson's ballclub. Flint, worn out by years of catching and hard living, caught only 15 games for Chicago in 1889 and then called it a career at the age of 34.

John Tener, a pitcher who was born in Ireland, also made his debut for Anson's club in 1888. Tener came from County Tyrone in Ulster, an area which was relatively unscathed by the potato famine, in 1863, long after the first few waves of immigration had carried millions of his countrymen to the Americas. The Tener clan had been relatively prosperous, but after the sudden death of Tener's father, the family decided to start a new life in the United States. John Tener played college ball while attending business school, and by the mid–1880s he had found employment as a bookkeeper while pitching in semipro games on the weekends. A well-educated and dignified young man with a good head for numbers, he impressed Spalding and

Anson, who allowed him to handle some of the business affairs for the club, especially on the road.

Farrell, Duffy, and Tener were all sober, dedicated individuals, three Irishmen whose behavior was considerably less worrisome than that of Mike Kelly and the rest of the fun-loving crew that made Anson's life miserable during the pennant-winning years. The hard-drinking Silver Flint was still on the team, as was the hotheaded Jimmy Ryan, both of whom caused trouble for their manager on a regular basis. Nonetheless, the dependable Tom Burns still held down third base, giving Anson's club another fine Irish role model.

However, Anson was the sort of man who carried grudges. He had been badly treated during the early 1880s by his Irish stars, who made the feat of winning five National League pennants in seven years considerably less enjoyable than it should have been. The Chicago manager still resented the difficulties that Mike Kelly and his friends had caused several years before, and by the late 1880s Anson was no longer inclined to keep his feelings to himself. He began to loudly and publicly disparage the abilities, both physical and mental, of Irish ballplayers, much to the consternation of his teammates.

The Chicago captain already owned a most unpleasant history in dealing with minorities. On August 10, 1883, he had loudly proclaimed his opposition to sharing the field with an African-American player, catcher Moses Walker, during

John Tener, born in County Tyrone, Ireland, served as governor of Pennsylvania and, later, president of the National League (Library of Congress).

an exhibition game in Toledo, Ohio. Faced with the threat of cancellation, and the resultant loss of gate receipts, Anson relented and played against Walker and the Toledo club that day. He angrily resolved never to play against non–Caucasians again, and when the Chicago club returned to Toledo for another non-league game in 1884, Walker remained on the bench. In 1887 the Chicago manager forced the Newark club to remove a black pitcher, George Stovey, from its lineup in another exhibition contest, and a similar confrontation instigated by Anson, once again involving Moses Walker, marred another game in Syracuse, New York, in 1888. The captain was known to disparage blacks in derogatory and demeaning terms, and it appears that his discriminatory attitudes found a target in the Irish as well.

Hugh Duffy was proud of his heritage, as were Ryan, Tener, and the other Irishmen on the club, and Anson's increasingly mean-spirited, bullying condemnations of Irish players sat badly with the young outfielder. Duffy had once so admired Anson from afar that he had turned down a more lucrative offer from the Boston team to sign his first contract with the White Stockings. After one season in Chicago, however, Duffy's view of Anson had changed. He "had no use for the players who had Irish blood in their veins," complained Duffy to the

Chicago Tribune in early 1890, "and never lost an opportunity to insult those men who have played with him in the past."[5] Jimmy Ryan also took offense at Anson's anti–Irish tirades, calling the manager a "big stiff" and nearly coming to blows with his field leader on several occasions. Anson was known to turn surly in the latter stages of an unsuccessful season, but his ill-considered expressions of contempt for the Irish turned many of them against him and damaged the morale on the ballclub.

Ryan, a highly talented but emotional ballplayer, was quickly becoming Anson's biggest disciplinary problem, and the captain's oft-expressed opinions about Ryan's ethnicity did nothing to defuse the situation. Ryan had blossomed into a star by 1888, establishing himself as a consistent .300 hitter, a fine defensive outfielder, and a valuable relief pitcher. His attitude, however, had turned sour, and his relationship with Anson had steadily deteriorated. That winter, during a round-the-world tour of the White Stockings and an all-star team, the Chicago field leader confided to Giants manager John Ward that only "a good thrashing" would set Ryan on the right path. Ward counseled Anson to trade the difficult ballplayer instead.

JAMES RYAN,
CENTRE FIELDER – CHICAGO.

The talented, but mercurial, Jimmy Ryan (Library of Congress).

Anson's relationship with his hotheaded outfielder grew worse as the years passed. At spring training camp in 1891, a group of White Stockings threw a beer keg out a hotel window, nearly beaning Anson, who was standing on the sidewalk outside at the time. "Jim, I think it was you," said the captain to Ryan afterward. "I can't prove it yet, but I'm going to, and when I do, I'm going to give you the worst licking you ever took."[6]

To be sure, Ryan was not an easy man to get along with. At least twice during his Chicago career, he physically assaulted local reporters whose articles displeased him, and in 1896 he scored a one-punch knockout of a train conductor who was trying to quell a disturbance. As Anson, who demanded that his players hustle at all times, said in his autobiography, "[Ryan's] greatest fault was that he would not run out on a base hit, but on the contrary would walk to his base. This I would not stand, and so I fined him repeatedly, but these fines did little good."[7] A Cincinnati paper reported that Anson once told Ryan, "Were it not for my position as captain I would smash you in the face." Ryan responded, "It is a lucky thing for you that you think so well of your position. For if you ever lay hands on me, you big stiff, I will shoot you full of holes."[8]

The 1889 season, in which the White Stockings finished in third place, was played under a cloud. The relationship between major league baseball's players and its owners had been deteriorating for years, due to the expansion of the reserve clause, a proposed cap on player salaries, and other issues. In late 1885, nine New York Giants formed a new association called the Brotherhood of Professional Base Ball Players. This represented the first attempt by major leaguers to start a union, and within two years more than 100 players in both major leagues had joined. However, the American Association and National League owners ignored the Brotherhood, refusing even to meet with its officers before presenting a new salary-limitation plan as a *fait accompli* in early 1889. This was a move that the Brotherhood could not accept, and later that year it announced the formation of a new circuit, called the Players League.

Predictably, many of Anson's Irish stars chose to quit the White Stockings and cast their collective lot with the new league. Jimmy Ryan was one of the first to leave, signing on with a new Chicago club headed by former St. Louis Browns manager (and Chicago native) Charlie Comiskey. Hugh Duffy and Duke Farrell followed, and were soon joined by other old White Stocking standbys such as infielders Ed Williamson and Fred Pfeffer, catcher Dell Darling, and pitcher Mark Baldwin. So successful was Comiskey in raiding Anson's ballclub that the new Players League entry was called the Pirates.

Comiskey, the son of an immigrant from County Cavan, held no prejudice against Irish players; in fact, the Irish presence on his new ballclub rivaled that of Anson's White Stockings of the early 1880s. The Chicago Pirates featured an all–Irish outfield with Duffy in left, Ryan in center, and two-time batting champion Tip O'Neill, whom Comiskey had brought with him from St. Louis, in right. With Comiskey himself on first base and Duke Farrell handling most of the catching, five of the nine Pirates on the field were Irishmen.

Across town, Anson and Spalding found themselves facing a monumental rebuilding task. Veteran third baseman Tom Burns had remained with the White Stockings, as had pitching star Bill Hutchison, but the other key players from the previous season (except for Anson himself, entering his 20th major league campaign) had bolted for the new league. Perhaps men such as Duffy, Ryan, and Farrell would have left the White Stockings in any case, but Anson's dislike of the Irish certainly hastened their departures and left the established club in desperate straits. The proud White Stockings, with almost all their stars gone, now resembled an expansion team.

Anson and Comiskey, bitter rivals in the World Series a few years before, now went to war over the future of baseball in Chicago. "The Brotherhood [Players League] men are all stiffs — just plain stiffs," said Anson to a reporter that spring. "They're all back numbers that have been lost out of the base-ball book. What is needed is young blood, full of life and vigor, and not any stale old stock such as the Brotherhood took off our hands."[9] Comiskey quickly fired back, "It's about time for that big baby to fall on himself ... Anson called us 'stiffs,' does he? Wait until we get him to Chicago and we will assist at his own professional funeral. His club won't draw a corporal's guard at home."[10] The war between the leagues had become intensely personal, especially in Chicago, and it was soon apparent that both circuits could not survive. One would have to drive the other out of business, making the 1890 season perhaps the most divisive and conflict-ridden in the game's long history.

Comiskey's Players League club featured almost all the stars and fan favorites, with men such as Ryan, Williamson, Duffy and others, but Anson assembled a team from minor leaguers and unknowns, supporting holdovers Tom Burns at third, Bill Hutchison on the mound, and Anson himself at first. Some of the new men were second-generation Irish, most notably Jimmy Cooney, a smooth-fielding shortstop from Cranston, Rhode Island (Hugh Duffy's home town), who batted .272 and scored 114 runs for Anson's club in his first major league season. Cooney spent only three years in the National League, but four of his sons played pro ball, and two, Johnny and Jimmy Junior, enjoyed success in the majors. Jimmy Cooney Junior, also a shortstop, manned the same position that his father had played for the same Chicago team, and is best known for turning an unassisted triple play in 1927.

This reconstructed Chicago ballclub, called "Anson's Colts" in the papers, overcame a slow start and nearly won the National League pennant in 1890, finishing second to Brooklyn by six games. It was probably the best managing performance of Anson's long career. Though published attendance figures for both teams during the 1890 season are notoriously inaccurate, with plenty of padding on both sides, it appears that the Colts may have outdrawn the star-studded Players League entry at the box office.

While Anson whipped his young Colts into shape, Comiskey found it difficult to mold the former White Stockings and ex–Browns into a cohesive unit. Hugh Duffy blossomed as a hitter and leader, but Jimmy Ryan, who proved such a headache for Cap Anson, caused problems for Comiskey as well. Ryan could not get along with his fellow Irish outfielder, former St. Louis star Tip O'Neill, who one day rebuked Ryan for failing to slide and received a stream of epithets in return. O'Neill retaliated by standing still in left field, forcing Ryan to cover both center and left. Comiskey took no action against O'Neill, his longtime teammate and friend, and Ryan soon grew disgusted with the Players League in general and Comiskey's Pirates in particular.

Despite Ryan's oft-expressed dislike of Anson, he found Comiskey's leadership inferior. If Comiskey, said Ryan, "would be less afraid of hurting our feelings he would get better work out of the team. I must say I like a captain who will tell you straight out what he wants you to do and insist on your doing it."[11] No doubt the difficult Ryan would have found fault with any field leader, but Comiskey was furious with his best player after Ryan's criticism hit the papers. Had the Players League survived another year, said Comiskey, he would have released the "big-headed" Ryan, despite his .340 batting average. Comiskey's team, talented as it was, stumbled to a disappointing fourth-place finish in the Players League's first, and only, season of competition. The baseball war was over, and all the Players Leaguers were absorbed by the two existing circuits, the American Association (which lasted only one more year) and the National League.

However, several of the defectors refused to return meekly to Anson's embrace. During the summer of 1890, the Chicago manager had kept up a steady stream of pointed criticism of the Players League, viciously disparaging the circuit and its players to reporters in each National League city. "The Brotherhood is making a wonderful bluff," said Anson, a little too gleefully, in July, "but it can't last ... I don't believe [the Pirates] made enough profit to pay half the lumber bills for the grand stand. When the crash comes, you can hear it a mile off."[12] Anson, a stockholder in the Chicago club, could hardly be expected to praise his rivals, but his attitude angered many of his former charges. Players had long memories, and Anson's denunciations of Irish ballplayers, coupled with his enthusiastic heckling of the Players League, turned many of his ex-players against him. The National League won the war between the circuits, but the effort cost Anson the services of several outstanding performers, men who might have brought several pennants to Chicago during the 1890s.

Hugh Duffy, a former White Stocking who led the Players League in hits and runs scored, was one Irishman who had no intention of playing again for Anson and Spalding. "The Chicago club treated not only myself but several other men unfairly [in 1889]," said Duffy to the *Chicago Tribune*, "and I have no earthly use for them."[13] Catcher Duke Farrell, another rising star, and the Irish-born pitcher John Tener also declined Anson's invitation to return to Chicago. Duffy and Farrell opted instead to join the Boston club of the American Association, while Tener quit baseball and returned to the business world. Catcher Dell Darling, a son of German immigrants, wanted no part of Anson either. He followed his Players League manager, Charlie Comiskey, to the St. Louis Browns for the 1891 season.

Jimmy Ryan, however, elected to return to Anson and the team that the papers were now referring to as the Colts. He had grown disillusioned with the Players League adventure, and perhaps a summer with Charlie Comiskey made him more appreciative of Anson's leadership. "Let the men who put up the capital manage the game," said Ryan, "and let the men who do the playing get paid for it and keep still. This is all any ballplayer should ask. There is one thing certain and that is that I will not play again under the same conditions."[14]

Despite the defections of so many stars, Anson's Colts nearly won the National League pennant in 1891. They entered mid–September with a seven-game lead over Boston, a club that had recently received an emotional boost from the return of Mike (King) Kelly, who may have been fading but was still the most popular player in the game. However, the Colts began to sputter, while Boston reeled off 18 wins in a row (with one tie) to take the flag by three and a half games over Chicago. Some of Boston's games, especially against the New York Giants, looked suspicious, and rumors soon abounded that former Players Leaguers in New York (where the Brotherhood was formed six years before) and other cities conspired to throw the flag to Boston to keep it out of the hands of Anson, their sworn enemy. Anson believed as much for the rest of his life, though conclusive evidence of an orchestrated effort is lacking.

Cap Anson managed the Colts for six more seasons, but never again finished higher than fourth place. His teams of the 1890s featured a mix of ethnicities, with Irish and German players in roughly equal portions and a smattering of Englishmen and Welshmen (such as starting pitcher Clark Griffith, beginning a 60-year career in baseball) completing the roster. Anson himself remained in the lineup until he was 45 years old, despite his decreasing production, and innovations in strategy seemed to pass him by. A ninth-place finish in 1897 sealed his fate, and his contract was not renewed for the 1898 season. After 19 seasons as manager and 22 years as a player, Anson's career in Chicago was over.

To take Anson's place, team president Jim Hart (who had succeeded Al Spalding several years before, though Spalding was still the main stockholder in the club) chose Tom Burns, the third baseman of the White Stockings' "Stonewall Infield" of the 1880s. Burns, who had won a pennant at Springfield in the Eastern League three years earlier, had impressed Spalding and Hart as a hard worker who did not drink or smoke. In addition, Spalding no doubt remembered Burns fondly as the only member of Chicago's starting lineup, other than Anson, who did not defect to the Players League in 1890. Burns thus became the second Irish manager in the history of the team, after Silver Flint, who handled the club for a month in 1879 when Anson was sidelined with a serious illness.

Anson did not go quietly. He believed that the Irish players on his team, especially Jimmy Ryan, had conspired to play poorly in 1897 in a bid to get him fired. When Tom Burns, like Ryan a second-generation Irishman, was appointed as manager, Anson made his views public. It may have appeared to be a case of sour grapes on Anson's part, but the veteran manager complained that "underhanded work looking toward my downfall was indulged in by some of the players.... The ringleader in this business was Jimmy Ryan, between whom and the Club's President the most perfect understanding seemed to exist, and for this underhanded work Ryan was rewarded later by being made the team captain, a position that he was too unpopular with the players to hold, though it is generally thought he was allowed to draw the salary as per the agreement."[15]

Burns, a more easygoing individual than Anson, tried his best to manage in a less dictatorial fashion than his predecessor. In March of 1898, during spring training, he arranged an intra-squad game between the Irishmen and the Germans. There had been tension between the two groups the year before, and Burns hoped to defuse it before it got out of hand. However, when Burns named the veteran Jimmy Ryan as team captain, his players rebelled, demanding that star outfielder Bill Lange, a California-born son of German descent, fill the post. The German players threatened to stage a sit-down strike before the season opener at Louisville, and Burns capitulated, naming Lange captain. This incident severely damaged Burns' standing as leader of the club, and although the team finished in fourth place and drew a record attendance in 1898, the new manager was never able to establish discipline in the ranks. An eighth-place finish in 1899 brought Burns' term as manager to a close, and the team foundered until Frank Selee, the former Boston field leader, took over in 1902 and built the team that became a success under his direction. The Chicago club, which the newspapers dubbed the Orphans after Anson's departure, became the Cubs under Selee's leadership, and is known by that name to this day.

Tom Burns did not live to see his old team, managed by Selee and later by Frank Chance, win four pennants and two World Series during the first decade of the 20th century. Burns managed Springfield of the Eastern League in 1900 and Buffalo of the same circuit in 1901, and signed to manage at Jersey City for the 1902 campaign. He might have someday earned another chance to lead a major league team, learning from his mistakes with the Chicago club, but that opportunity never materialized. To the surprise and shock of the baseball world, Burns died of an apparent heart attack in his sleep on March 19, 1902, at the age of 44.

Selee's Chicago club was not nearly as Irish as Anson's had been. The participation of other ethnic groups in the game, especially the Germans, had risen during the previous decade, and by 1900 the number of Germans had surpassed that of the Irish on major league playing rosters. The most notable player of Irish descent on the Cubs of this era was Johnny Evers, an excitable second baseman from Mike (King) Kelly's hometown of Troy, New York. Evers was a third-generation Irishman who teamed with shortstop Joe Tinker and first baseman Frank Chance to form baseball's most famous infield combo. Many of the Chicago stars, such as Tinker, pitcher Ed Ruelbach, outfielder Frank Schulte, and third baseman Harry Steinfeldt, were German, while catcher Johnny Kling was Jewish and several other Cubs were of English and Welsh heritage. Outstanding players of Irish descent would play for the team in the future, but the era of Irish domination of National League baseball in Chicago was finished.

During the early 1890s, four players, three of them Irish, who had helped Anson and the White Stockings rise to the top of the National League ten years before began to pay the price for their profligacy and lack of discipline. Larry Corcoran, the pitcher who won 168 games in only five seasons and threw the first three no-hitters in Chicago franchise history, fell on hard times after his release in 1885. He tried to resurrect his career with the New York Giants and, later, the Indianapolis Hoosiers, but the effort proved unsuccessful, and by the age of 27 his pitching days were over. Corcoran drifted through the minor leagues as a part-time pitcher and umpire for the next few years. After finally leaving the game, he sank into despair and drank heavily until kidney disease, no doubt brought on by alcoholism, destroyed his health. He was only 31 years old when he died of Bright's disease in 1891.

Ed Williamson, the strong-armed third baseman and shortstop, was considered by some to be the greatest player of all time up to that point, but an injury suffered on the world tour virtually ended his career. After an unsuccessful comeback attempt in the Players League in 1890, Williamson tended bar in Chicago, becoming seriously alcoholic. Reduced to poverty, he died in March of 1894 at the age of 36. Two years earlier, the fun-loving Silver Flint met a similar fate. Flint was only 32 years old when his career with the White Stockings ended in 1889, and he failed to catch on with any other team. In January of 1892, he died of liver failure at 34. Cap Anson, usually the most self-controlled of men, wept openly at Flint's funeral.

The most tragic story belonged to Mike Kelly, the "King of Ballplayers." Though spectacularly unsuited to be a manager, Kelly somehow directed the Boston club to the Players League pennant in 1890. Early that season, when Al Spalding offered him $10,000, a princely sum at the time, to abandon the upstart league and return to the National, Kelly thought about it briefly, then turned it down. "I can't go back on the boys," he said, earning the lasting respect of his Players League mates. The new league collapsed after only one season, during which the 32-year-old Kelly batted .326 and played six different positions on the field. It was to be his last successful campaign.

A stint as a player and manager in the American Association in 1891, with the "Kelly's Killers" of Cincinnati, was unsuccessful, and the club disbanded in August. After a four-game stop on Boston's Association team, Kelly wound up back in the National League on Frank Selee's Beaneaters by season's end. His return gave the team an emotional lift, and the Beaneaters won 18 in a row in September to breeze past Chicago for the pennant. However, the Beaneaters were now Selee's team, not Kelly's, and the former star's diminishing skills made him a mere supporting player. He was fading fast, and batted only .189 during 1892, his last season in Boston. He started 1893 with the New York Giants, was released, and ended up in the Pennsylvania State League, barely hanging on to his once-fabulous career.

Kelly slowed down on the field, but not off it. Cap Anson, who bore the brunt of Kelly's wild behavior during their years together in Chicago but carried a grudging admiration for the King, later said of Kelly, "He played good ball for a time, but his bad habits soon caused his downfall ... for baseball and booze will not mix any better than oil and water. The last time that I ever saw him was at an Eastern hotel barroom, and during the brief space of time that we conversed together he threw in enough whiskey to put an ordinary man under the table."[16]

Kelly had earned baseball's top salary during his heyday, but at age 36 he was broke, dissipated, and dispirited. He had thrown stardom and fame away, and he knew it, so he made an effort to warn others of the evils of drink while unable to curb his own addiction to alcohol. By late 1894 he had abandoned baseball for a stage career, reciting "Casey at the Bat" as well as he could remember it for those who still showed interest in him. When he caught a cold in November of that year, he was not strong enough to fight it off, and pneumonia quickly set in. When he was taken to a hospital, the attendants dropped his stretcher and dumped Kelly on the ground. "This is me last slide," he mumbled, and a few days later the "King of Ballplayers" was dead.

John Clarkson, the half–Irish hurler whom most observers, including Cap Anson, called the greatest pitcher in the history of the White Stockings, also came to a sad end. Released by Boston in 1892, he pitched for the Cleveland Spiders for two years before quitting the game in mid–1894. He had always been a highly-strung and emotional individual, traits that seemed to intensify after witnessing a horrific accident in January of 1894. He was on a hunting trip in Kansas with his good friend, Boston catcher Charlie Bennett, when Bennett slipped on some ice on a train station platform and somehow fell under a moving train. Though Bennett survived, the locomotive severed his legs and left the catcher in a wheelchair for the rest of his life. Some say that Clarkson was never the same after the accident.

Clarkson, whose brothers Walter and Arthur also pitched in the major leagues, managed a semipro team and operated a cigar store in Bay City, Michigan, after his National League career ended, but an attempt to expand his cigar business to Chicago ended in failure. His drinking, which he apparently kept under control during his playing days, increased during the early 1900s, and the retired pitcher became increasingly moody, withdrawn, and irritable. Some sources claim that he was suffering from syphilis, which began to compromise his sanity as the years passed. His behavior became so erratic that his wife Ella committed him to a mental institution in 1905, after which his family brought him back to Massachusetts and placed him in a psychiatric hospital in Waverly, not far from his hometown of Cambridge. John Clarkson died there on February 4, 1909, at the age of 47. Dozens of old teammates attended his funeral, and the *Boston Post* said in a headline, "John Clarkson is with Kelly now."

However, for every tragic story of the Irish White Stockings, there was a successful one. Hugh Duffy's career blossomed in Boston, where he starred for the club that won four pennants between 1892 and 1898. In 1894 he batted .438 (revised by later researchers to .440), a National League record that will probably never be broken, while also leading the league in home runs and runs batted in to win baseball's Triple Crown. He was a respected leader, and when the American League began play as a major circuit in 1901 Duffy took the manager's post in Milwaukee, where he proved popular with the largely German-American fans. The American League moved the club to St. Louis in 1902 and installed Jimmy McAleer as manager, but Duffy continued to prosper, eventually serving as field leader of the Phillies, White Sox and Red Sox, as well as several minor league clubs. Elected to the Hall of Fame in 1945, he remained in baseball as a manager, coach, or scout almost until the day of his death in 1954.

Duke Farrell, too, enjoyed a long career in the game. He enjoyed his best season in 1891, when he played for Boston's American Association entry and led the league in home runs with 12 and runs batted in with 110. He bounced around the National League for the next several seasons, and though he battled weight problems every spring, remained a valuable catcher and a solid hitter. While catching for Washington on May 11, 1897, he threw out eight of nine would-be base-stealers, a record that stands to this day. He moved to the American League in 1903, and in May of the following year, when he was 37 years old, he caught Cy Young's perfect game, the first in American League history. He was a steadying influence on the Boston club that won American League pennants in 1903 and 1904 under the direction of another Irish-American star, playing manager Jimmy Collins. Farrell played his last major league game in 1905 and spent another two decades as a coach and scout before his death in 1925.

The Irish-born John Tener experienced the most meteoric rise. After spending the 1890 season with Pittsburgh of the Players League, he left the game to take a position as a bank cashier in Charleroi, Pennsylvania, a town near Pittsburgh, where his wife's family lived. By 1897 the fast-rising Tener was the president of the bank, and during the early 1900s became involved in Republican politics. After serving a term in Congress, Tener won the governorship of Pennsylvania as a Republican in 1910, leaving office four years later only because governors in the Keystone State were then limited to one term. In 1913, the widely respected Tener was named president of the National League, a post he held for five years. Tener refused to accept a salary from the league as long as he also held the governorship, and not until 1915, when he left the governor's mansion in Harrisburg, did he begin to receive compensation from the National League.

At that time, the league presidency was a much more important position than it would become after the commissioner system took effect a few years later, and Tener was called upon to deal with crises and controversies large and small. One of the more troublesome issues of his term concerned the welfare of the aging Cap Anson, Tener's old Chicago White Stockings manager. Anson had fallen upon hard times after his departure from baseball, losing his home to bankruptcy proceedings after failing in both business and politics. The old baseball star was reduced to performing skits and monologues in vaudeville houses, barely earning enough money to keep food on his family's table.

Newspaper columnists across the country had criticized the league for failing to provide for Anson, the first true star of the game, but the fault, such as it was, lay with Anson himself. Two previous league presidents, Harry Pulliam and Thomas Lynch, had offered to supply Anson with a pension, but the ex-manager had turned them down. Though he was bankrupt, Anson's pride and stubbornness prevented him from accepting aid from the league in which he had performed so well for more than two decades. In December 1913, shortly after Governor Tener took office, the topic of helping Anson arose once again at the annual league meetings.

Tener wished to assist his former manager and stop the constant drumbeat of criticism, but knew that the recalcitrant old man could never be persuaded to accept charity. Faced with a difficult situation, Tener addressed the issue with tact and honesty. "Speaking as president of the National League," said Governor Tener to a group of reporters, "I will say that I see no reason why a pension should be voted Captain Anson. The captain is strong, physically and mentally, and is appearing weekly on the vaudeville stage. He is entirely satisfied with the renumeration he is receiving for his talent. In common with his many friends I deplore the continued reference to the National League's failure to provide a pension for the captain's support.

"Mr. Anson is far from being an object of charity and would refuse any pension that any league would vote him. The National League is not unmindful of its heroes and faithful and if there should come a time when Captain Anson should need the organization's support it will quickly and gladly come to his assistance."[17] Tener's measured response cooled the criticism, at least for a while, though the topic of a pension for the aging Anson remained a matter of controversy until the former Chicago manager passed away in 1922.

Tener was a consummate politician, but not even he could solve all the problems dumped into his lap by the quarrelsome and difficult baseball team owners. He stepped down as president in 1918, after an inter-league dispute between the Boston Braves and the Philadelphia Athletics concerning the ownership of a minor league pitcher named Scott Perry. Both teams claimed the pitcher, but when the National Commission awarded Perry to the Braves, Athletics manager Connie Mack went to court and obtained an injunction, keeping Perry in Philadelphia. American League president Ban Johnson sided with Mack, and the furious Tener demanded that the National League cut off all relations with the junior circuit, including canceling the upcoming World Series, until Perry was returned to the Braves. The National League owners refused to support such a bold move, and Tener resigned in August 1918.

The former governor then went into the highway construction business and became a wealthy man. In his later years, the immigrant from County Tyrone was one of Pennsylvania's most respected citizens, though he failed in a bid to regain the governorship. He was prominent in Republican politics, the national Elks Club, and post–World War I relief work. When John Tener died in 1946 at age 83, flags around the state flew at half-staff for 30 days in his honor.

6

Patsy Tebeau and the
Hibernian Spiders

The Irish came to Cleveland in small numbers before the famine of the 1840s, mostly to work on canal-digging projects, but their numbers increased sharply when the potato crop failed in the home country. Several thousand Irish immigrants, the majority of whom came from the hard-hit County Mayo, settled in Cleveland during the late 1840s and 1850s. Though most had been tenant farmers, they found work as laborers, toiling in Cleveland's steel mills and unloading ships on the docks. By 1870, Irish immigrants and their families accounted for about 10 percent of Cleveland's population.

Because the city was so ethnically diverse, the Irish did not build a political machine in Cleveland, though several mayors in the late 1800s and early 1900s claimed Irish descent. However, their cultural influence was well represented by organizations such as the Hibernian Guard, a "band of Irish soldiers" that put on an annual St. Patrick's Day parade and otherwise celebrated their heritage. Many of the young Irishmen of Cleveland also joined military units during the Civil War, drawing praise for their fighting skill.

The "Irishtown" part of Cleveland was a tract that straddled the mouth of the Cuyahoga River, which ran so foul with industrial and other waste that Mayor R. R. Herrick himself called it "an open sewer through the center of the city." Irishtown was a jumble of houses, mills and factories small and large, and churches, all of which were permeated with the smell of industrial discharge. It was a tough place to grow up, but when baseball mania swept the nation after the Civil War, the local Irish boys took up the sport with unbridled enthusiasm. Amateur teams sprang up quickly, and in 1871, when the National Association started play as the first professional baseball league, Cleveland hosted an entry called the Forest City club. It disbanded after one season, but the sport continued to grow there during the 1870s.

Cleveland's first National League ballclub, the Blues of 1879, was perhaps the most Irish team in the game at that time. Jim McCormick, the star pitcher and manager, was born in Scotland but grew up in the Irish enclave of Paterson, New Jersey, as a childhood friend and teammate of Mike (King) Kelly, perhaps the brightest star of the 1880s. Barney Gilligan, a catcher and outfielder, was a product of the Irish baseball scene in Cambridge, Massachusetts, which also spawned the three Clarkson brothers, Hall of Famers Tim Keefe and Joe Kelley, and several other major leaguers. First baseman Bill Phillips, outfielder Bill Riley, catcher Doc Kennedy, and shortstop Tom Carey rounded out the Irish contingent on the club, which boasted six Irishmen in its starting lineup. In 1880 the club added another when Ned Hanlon, son of an immigrant mill worker from Connecticut, made his debut with the Blues, beginning a career that would eventually lead to the Hall of Fame.

Despite their collection of Irish-American talent, the Blues never made a serious run at the pennant and disbanded after a seventh-place finish in 1884. Cleveland spent the next two years outside the orbit of major league baseball until the American Association granted the city a franchise in 1887. This club, also called the Blues, moved into the National League in 1889 and took the name Spiders due to the number of tall, thin players on the club. Though the Spiders, too, would dissolve before the end of the 19th century, the team offered Cleveland fans a decade's worth of highs and lows, mainly produced by players of Irish descent who made up the majority of the ballclub. In an era in which the Irish influence in baseball was at its highest, the Cleveland Spiders of the 1890s were one of the most thoroughly Irish teams in the National League.

The leader of the Spiders was an Irishman by choice, not by birth. Oliver Wendell Tebeau, born in the Goose Hill district of St. Louis in 1864, was the son of a laborer of French ancestry and a woman whose parents came from the German duchy of Baden. Oliver, the fourth of five sons, was sent out to find work when he was about nine years old. He frequented construction sites, running errands for the Irish laborers working there; before long, Oliver could be seen bringing a lunch pail each day and pitching in to help. The construction workers grew to like this young man, eventually awarding him the Irish nickname "Patsy," which he bore proudly for the rest of his life. From then on, Oliver "Patsy" Tebeau was an honorary Irishman. He even spoke with a touch of an Irish brogue that remained with him through adulthood.

The Irish in St. Louis loved their baseball, and the city was dotted with baseball teams, many of them Irish in nature. Patsy Tebeau, who by age 16 was employed as an apprentice to a file maker, and his older brother George, a clerk in a lumber company, became two of the baseball-mad city's star ballplayers during the early 1880s. They learned to play in a take-no-prisoners, no-quarter-given style, as only the strongest and most determined ballplayers could hope to grab the brass ring that professional baseball represented to the sons and grandsons of immigrants. Young men on the St. Louis sandlots played ball as if their lives depended on it, for in many ways, it did.

Patsy Tebeau played first base for one of the Mound City's leading semipro clubs, the Peach Pies, with future major leaguers Jack O'Connor at catcher and Silver King on the mound. From there, he and O'Connor joined a team in Jacksonville, Illinois, where Chicago White Stockings manager Cap Anson saw Patsy and decided to give him a tryout. He batted only .162 in 20 games at the end of the 1887 season and failed to impress Anson, who cared little for Irish (or pseudo–Irish) players anyway. The following campaign found Patsy, now 24 years old, back in the minors, but in 1889 the Cleveland Spiders of the National League gave him a chance and made him their starting first baseman.

When the Players League split from the National in 1890 and took most of the good players with it, Patsy jumped to the new circuit and claimed the first base job with the Cleveland Infants. The Infants were laden with talented youngsters, such as third baseman Ed Delahanty and smooth-fielding center fielder Jimmy McAleer, along with the aging slugger Pete Browning, who batted .373 that season. Still, the Infants were stuck in seventh place in late July when manager Henry Larkin was dismissed. Team management turned to Patsy Tebeau as the new field leader, and his career as a manager was born. The team went 31–40 the rest of the way and failed to rise out of seventh place, but Tebeau lit a fire under his charges and marked himself as a leader to watch in the future.

Oliver (Patsy) Tebeau, despite his nickname, came from French and German ancestry, not Irish (Library of Congress).

The club's best player was Ed Delahanty, a Cleveland native who became one of baseball's most dangerous hitters during the 1890s. Delahanty was a free-swinging slugger whose parents James and Bridget had emigrated from Ireland in 1865 and settled in Cleveland, where Ed was born two years later. Ed was the oldest of five brothers, all of whom played ball in the alleys and vacant lots of Cleveland's Irishtown while their father worked as a laborer and their mother ran a boardinghouse. All five Delahantys—Ed, Tom, Jim, Joe, and Frank—made the major leagues, though Ed was always the star of the family. After a stint on a powerful neighborhood team, the Shamrocks, Ed was signed by the Philadelphia Phillies in 1888. Two years later, he jumped to the Players League to perform for his hometown team.

The Players League collapsed after only one season, with Patsy, McAleer, and most of the other Infants returning to the National League Spiders. Ed Delahanty, however, went back to the Phillies, where he moved to the outfield and made a quick ascent to stardom. He batted over .400 three times, won two batting and two home run titles, and on July 13, 1896, became the second player in major league history to swat four homers in a game. "If Del had a weakness at the bat," remarked Jack O'Connor, "I never could discover it." His presence on the Spiders might have won a pennant or two for Cleveland, as Tebeau's team was always one strong bat short of contending throughout the decade. As it was, the Phillies always drew good crowds when they played in Cleveland because the home fans loved to cheer Ed Delahanty.

Bob Leadley began the 1891 season as manager of the Spiders, but when the club got off to a mediocre start, team owner Frank Robison, a local streetcar magnate, decided that a change was needed. Robison fired Leadley on July 11 and tapped the 27-year-old Patsy Tebeau to take his place. Patsy quickly dismissed some of Leadley's favorites; as teammate Jack Doyle recalled several years later, the new manager "set to housekeeping by weeding out the lobsters who were being toted around the country by his theoretical and cloud-pushing predecessor."[1] Tebeau wanted to build the Spiders in his own image, with fighters and battlers who would turn each contest into a war, as the game was played on the rough sandlots of St. Louis. He already had some of the pieces of a contending team in place, with Cy Young on the mound, Chief Zimmer behind the plate, Jimmy McAleer in center, and himself at first base. Tebeau went to work assembling the rest of the puzzle, and perhaps it should not have surprised anyone when he filled out his roster with his favorite kind of player, the rough-and-tumble Irishman.

Jesse Burkett was one such player who caught Tebeau's eye. Burkett, a small, fleet-footed youngster, grew up in Wheeling, West Virginia, where his immigrant father found work as a laborer and painter in that gritty Ohio River town. Jesse had failed as a pitcher for the New York Giants in 1890, but shifted to the outfield and batted .349 in Lincoln, Nebraska, the following year. In August of 1891, the Spiders bought his contract, and Tebeau put the slap-hitting Burkett in left field. A poor fielder, Burkett worked with his fellow Irishman, McAleer, who taught him to position himself properly, to play the sun field, and to throw to the correct base. Burkett was never a great glove man, but after a few years he became a passable outfielder.

Burkett's greatest value came at the bat. Though he displayed little power, his bat control was second to none, and he could pound the ball out of the reach of the fielders with apparent ease. He was a skilled bunter, perhaps the best in baseball during the 1890s, and before long Burkett was one of the National League's premier batsmen. He won batting titles in 1895 and 1896, clearing the .400 mark in both seasons, and scored more than a run per game for Tebeau's ballclub. Despite his small stature, he was always ready to fight, having learned to use his fists in the Wheeling industrial leagues. "You got to be a battler," he once explained. "If you don't they'll walk all over you. After you lick three or four of them they don't show up any more looking for a fight."[2] Jesse's personality was so prickly that people called him "the Crab," but he was a first-rate leadoff man and a perfect addition to Tebeau's band of fighting Spiders.

Cleveland native Ed McKean, a muscular shortstop, had joined the club in 1887 and had remained with the Spiders during the Players League revolt. McKean, like Burkett a son of Irish immigrants, was a tough character who wrestled and played semipro football in the Cleveland area each year after the baseball season ended. He was Tebeau's enforcer, doling out punishment to unruly opponents and wayward teammates alike. His double play partner was second baseman Clarence Childs, nicknamed "Cupid" for his baby-faced features. Childs, from an old-line Maryland family, had batted .345 at Syracuse in 1890, then became the property of the Boston American Association club when the Syracuse nine disbanded. Tebeau, dissatisfied with the play of the weak-hitting Cub Stricker at second, traded Sticker and another player to Boston for Childs, who became a perennial .300 hitter in Cleveland for the remainder of the decade.

Tebeau also acquired his old teammate from the Peach Pies of St. Louis, Jack O'Connor, who spent time both behind the plate and in the outfield. O'Connor, called "Rowdy Jack," played for the Cincinnati Reds of the American Association in 1887 but was fired by manager Gus Schmelz after a clubhouse brawl. After a stint in Denver, Colorado, with a team in an outlaw league, he moved to Columbus in 1889 only to find Schmelz in place as manager. Still, he lasted for three years in Columbus before being dismissed for excessive drinking during the 1891 season. He returned to Denver for a few months, then joined his childhood friend Tebeau on the Spiders for the 1892 campaign. O'Connor was a versatile man, filling in at catcher and in the outfield and often running the team when Tebeau was absent due to suspension or injury.

Center fielder Jimmy McAleer, whose father had emigrated from Ireland to Canada before finding work as a boilermaker in Youngstown, Ohio, was the youngest of six children and used his baseball skills to avoid a lifetime spent in the boiler works. Jimmy never managed to hit .300 in a high-average era, but was nonetheless one of the most important Spiders. He was the prototypical good-field, no-hit outfielder, but his glove made up for his bat in the eyes of many of his contemporaries. "How he could catch outfield flies!" said an article in *The Sporting News*. "You could write a ream about his great plays."[3] Some say that McAleer was the first outfielder to take his eyes off the ball, run to where it would come down,

JIMMY McALEER
ST. LOUIS.

The smooth-fielding Jimmy McAleer was one of baseball's premier managers and promoters after his playing days ended (author's collection).

and look up again to catch it. He was also a born leader and organizer who would later become a respected manager and promoter.

In 1892, the Spiders boasted an all–Irish outfield with Burkett, McAleer, and O'Connor manning the positions from left to right. They also had half of an Irish infield, with McKean at short and Tebeau, normally a first sacker, at third. Patsy had been severely spiked by Pittsburgh's Jake Beckley in 1891, so he put Jake Virtue at first the following year and planted himself at third to protect his legs from further damage. Patsy shared the position with George Davis, a 21-year-old future Hall of Famer who nonetheless failed to impress his manager. Davis was a quiet youngster, and perhaps Patsy believed that Davis did not fit in with his group of boisterous, fighting Spiders. At year's end, Cleveland traded Davis to New York, where he would soon become one of the league's premier shortstops.

Innovative new strategies had made their way into the game by the 1890s, but Patsy Tebeau showed little interest in the hit and run, left-right matchups, and the like. His preferred style of baseball never changed from the game he learned on the St. Louis sandlots. He believed that games were won by aggressiveness, not brain power, so he filled his team with fighters and scrappers, many of them Irish. "My instructions to my players are to win games, and I want them to be aggressive. A milk and water, goody-goody player can't wear a Cleveland uniform," remarked Tebeau to a reporter.[4] He had spent his early adulthood watching his hometown American Association team, the St. Louis Browns, win pennants by following this same formula under the direction of its Irish-American manager, Charlie Comiskey. Tebeau brought Comiskey's approach to Cleveland in an attempt to bring a flag to a city that had never won a major league pennant.

Tebeau's style of play, which involved a generous helping of umpire intimidation, rule bending, and the occasional brawl on the field, made him one of the least popular men in the National League, but another Irish Spider was even more despised than Tebeau. Jack Doyle was born in Ireland, coming to America from Killorgin in County Kerry before his tenth birthday. Doyle, a catcher and outfielder whose major league career had begun with Columbus of the American Association three years earlier (where he was a teammate of Jack O'Connor), quickly built a reputation for orneriness that earned him the nickname "Dirty Jack." He fought with opponents, manhandled umpires (he beat up arbiters Thomas Lynch and Bob Emslie during separate on-field disputes), and battled his own teammates.

Doyle subscribed to the belief that the basepaths belonged to the runner, and his National League career is littered with incidents in which he trampled, tackled, or spiked opposing infielders. "I was a hard base runner," he admitted in later years. "You had to be in those days.

It wasn't a matter of being rough or dirty. And my base running was just for one purpose — to win."[5] He carried on a long-running feud with a fellow battling Irishman, John McGraw, which came to a climax in 1900 when Doyle spiked his rival severely while sliding into third base. The injury, most likely deliberate, forced McGraw from the lineup for several weeks. Many other infielders found themselves on the business end of Doyle's spikes, and in an era of rough, physical play, Jack Doyle was generally recognized as the most hated player in the National League.

Tebeau liked feisty Irish ballplayers, but Doyle displayed an aggressiveness so extreme that even Patsy could not tolerate it. On June 17, 1892, Tebeau released Doyle; despite his .299 career batting average, "Dirty Jack" would bounce around the league, playing for 10 different teams during his 17-year major league career. Oddly enough, Doyle was known as a friendly, engaging story-teller off the field. He remained in the game, becoming a highly respected scout who signed dozens of star ballplayers in a long post-playing career that lasted until his death in 1958. Despite his wild on-field behavior, Doyle also spent two years as a police commissioner in his adopted hometown of Holyoke, Massachusetts.

Despite Patsy's absence from the lineup for much of the season, the 1892 campaign was one of his most successful as a manager. With the National League operating under a split-season setup, the Spiders ended the first half in fifth place, but won the second part by three games over Boston, the champs of the first half. The Spiders and Beaneaters met in a best-of-nine series for the pennant in October, but after a classic 11-inning scoreless tie between Boston's Jack Stivetts and Cleveland's Cy Young, the Beaneaters swept the next five games to claim the National League flag.

Tebeau had no use for George Davis, so after the 1892 season the Spiders sent the future star to the New York Giants in exchange for the veteran Buck Ewing. Since Ewing's throwing arm was not what it once was, his catching days were behind him, so Tebeau installed him in right field and moved Jack O'Connor into a catching tandem with Chief Zimmer. Tebeau shuttled between the corners of the infield, sharing first base with Jake Virtue and third with another tough Irishman named James (Chippy) McGarr, who fit in so well that in 1894 Tebeau took over first on a full-time basis and gave third base to McGarr, with Virtue relegated to the bench. When O'Connor handled the catching chores, six of the eight Cleveland starters were Irishmen, counting Tebeau himself.

Chippy McGarr earned his nickname for a reason. He grew up in Worcester, Massachusetts, where his Irish-born father worked as a teamster in one of the many local factories. The younger McGarr left school at a young age and followed in his father's footsteps, but was more interested in baseball, and by 1887 he was the regular third sacker for the Philadelphia Athletics of the American Association. Traded to the St. Louis Browns later that year, he fell back to the minors after the 1890 campaign and spent the next three years clawing his way back to the majors. McGarr was only an average hitter, but his toughness more than made up for his bat in Tebeau's eyes. He was a skilled fighter, and made a place for himself with the club that the writers were already calling the "Hibernian Spiders."

McGarr was strong, too. One day he became so flustered with the baserunning antics of Boston's Billy Hamilton that he picked up the much smaller Beaneater, carried him over to the stands, and tossed him into the box seats. Hamilton, like McGarr a product of the Worcester sandlots, was the base-stealing king of the National League at the time and drove a lot of teams to distraction with his aggressive running, but only McGarr took such a direct means of expressing his displeasure. McGarr was nonetheless respected for his baseball knowledge, and coached the sport at the College of the Holy Cross in Worcester during the spring months.

Buck Ewing had been one of the brightest stars in the game during the 1880s, but his Cleveland career was brief. He batted .344 in 1893, but his relationships with his fellow Spiders were strained as a result of the fallout from the failure of the Players League several years earlier. Ewing was a founder of the players' union, the Brotherhood of Professional Base Ball Players, and managed the New York entry in the upstart league in 1890. However, by August of that year he recognized that the new circuit was doomed to failure. He met secretly with Cap Anson, Al Spalding, and other National League officials, perhaps to negotiate a peaceful surrender to the established circuit. Reportedly, the National League offered Ewing a large salary and the managing job in Cincinnati to quit the Players League. Nothing came of the negotiations, and Ewing always denied the charge that he tried to sell out his Brotherhood mates, but the accusation dogged him for the rest of his career. Though Tebeau had approved the trade that brought Ewing to Cleveland, Jack O'Connor, Jimmy McAleer, and other Players League veterans were none too happy to see Ewing arrive.

Another source of tension on the Cleveland club was the presence of the half–Irish John Clarkson, once one of the game's greatest hurlers but now approaching the end of his career. Clarkson was an active member of the Brotherhood and had voted in some of its early meetings. However, he could not resist a three-year contract offer from the Boston Beaneaters of the National League, so he quit the Brotherhood and remained with the established circuit. His fellow union members were angered by his defection, and many friendships with teammates and opponents ended. Released by Boston in mid–1892, Clarkson signed with Cleveland and settled into the pitching rotation behind Cy Young, but some of his teammates were less than enthusiastic about playing behind him. As a result, Clarkson grew irritable and negative as his career waned. He had gotten along well with umpires in past years, but in Cleveland he argued with them on a regular basis, harming his own cause.

The Spiders finished in third place in 1893, but tensions on the club boiled over during the 1894 campaign. Clarkson won seven of his first eight decisions, but then lost three games in a row. The highly-strung and unpopular pitcher believed that one of the Cleveland outfielders was allowing fly balls to drop when he was on the mound, a charge that he made to Patsy Tebeau that June. The offending player, claimed Clarkson, "would throw me down at critical stages of games whenever he had the opportunity. He would dodge flies under the pretext that the sun was in his eyes, and in this way lost many a game, which, of course, was always charged up to me."[6] No one knows which outfielder Clarkson suspected, but it certainly was not Buck Ewing, who played right field. It must have been either left fielder Jesse Burkett, who as a rookie in 1890 was not a member of the Brotherhood but was nonetheless vocal in his opposition to Clarkson and Ewing, or staunch union man Jimmy McAleer in center.

The squabbling grew more intense as the 1894 season wore on, and in early July, after a 2–12 skid, Tebeau decided to act. On July 13 he made two moves, releasing Ewing outright and trading Clarkson to Baltimore for another right-handed veteran, the Irish-born Tony Mullane. Clarkson later claimed that he had quit of his own volition. "I grew disgusted," stated Clarkson, "and one day told Tebeau that I guessed it was no use for me to pitch any longer, and so I packed my baggage and skipped."[7] Neither team benefited from the deal, as Mullane disliked Cleveland and left the team after only two weeks, while Clarkson refused to report to the Orioles and retired from the major leagues at the age of 33. However, the bickering stopped, for the most part, and the Spiders finished in fifth place.

The Baltimore club had won the 1894 pennant using battling, brawling tactics, and Tebeau's Spiders attempted to challenge the Orioles by matching them in the rowdiness department. The Orioles and Spiders, the two National League clubs with the highest percentage of Irishmen, were also the most disorderly, and games between the two clubs often featured fights, beanball wars, and fan violence. Mobs of fans in both cities turned out early to pelt the opponents with garbage, rocks, and bottles as they arrived at the park, and at game's end those same fans would often storm the field and attack the players and umpire. The 1895 season may have been the worst in the game's history for player and fan behavior, with the Orioles and Spiders as the main offenders. Their tactics were successful, however, for the pennant race that year turned into a hotly-contested battle between those two unruly teams.

The umpires found the Cleveland manager a most unpleasant man to deal with, but one of Tebeau's attempts at intimidation failed against Tim Hurst, perhaps the toughest arbiter in the National League during the era. One day, a large crowd at Cleveland's League Park filled all the seats, making it necessary for management to place people behind ropes in the outfield and along the foul lines. The Spiders were facing the hated Orioles that day, and Tebeau, in the pre-game meeting, warned Hurst that if any close calls went against the Spiders, he would cut the ropes and send the crowd charging at the umpire.

Hurst, however, was a tough Irishman who thrived on such challenges. Early in the game, he called Tebeau out at third, then faced the raging manager with his fists ready for action. "Yer out, you (blankety-blank)!" shouted the umpire. "Ye may have beat the throw, but I called yez out! Now go cut them ropes — and if ye as much as turn yer face to that crowd, I'll kill yez dead where ye stand!"[8] Tebeau took Hurst at his word and realized that he was licked. The manager meekly trotted back to the bench, and the crowd accepted the decision without protest.

Tom Lynch, like Hurst a second-generation Irishman, was a more dignified umpire, so Tebeau used trickery instead of intimidation to gain the advantage. One day Cleveland batter Chief Zimmer was nicked by a pitch and trotted down to first. Lynch did not the see the ball strike Zimmer and called him back, but Tebeau put up a fuss from the coaching box. Zimmer stood between first and home as Lynch threatened to fine the player ten dollars if he refused to return to the plate. "If you don't come down here [to first]," roared Tebeau, "I'll fine you $20. Who are you going to listen to, me or Lynch?"

Tebeau then had a flash of inspiration. He pinched Zimmer's upper arm as hard as he could, then said, "Go back to bat and show Lynch where the ball hit you." Zimmer showed the painful bruise to Lynch, who apologized. "Sorry to have doubted you, Chief," said the arbiter. "Take first."[9]

Patsy was never shy about bawling out his own teammates on the field. Cupid Childs, the Spider second baseman, grew up in Maryland, and one day a delegation of fans decided to present a horseshoe of flowers to their favorite son during a game between the Spiders and Orioles in Baltimore. Tebeau hated displays of friendship between players and fans on the road, especially in Baltimore, but as the Spiders were ahead by a 6–0 score when the flowers were presented, the manager merely greeted the scene with a bit of grumbling under his breath. Unfortunately for the Spiders, Baltimore scored eight runs in the next inning and took the lead, partly due to some poor fielding by Childs, the local hero.

Patsy controlled himself for as long as he could, then finally exploded with rage. He raced to the bench, tore the floral display apart with his bare hands, and then hurled the remains into the grandstand. "There's your flowers," he screamed at Childs, "and the next bunch of (blankety-blank) that give flowers to one of me players, I'll fire the player off me club and his damn friends can keep them if they like him so well."[10]

Tebeau's fighting style did not win a pennant for the Spiders during the 1890s, but the team reached the pinnacle of its accomplishment in 1895, when they finished second to Baltimore and met the Orioles in the annual Temple Cup showdown. The Spiders and the Orioles were the main exponents of rowdy play during the decade, and their post-season series was one of the wildest ever seen in the history of the game. Spider fans rang cowbells, blew horns, and threw garbage at the Orioles during the opening game of the series, played at Cleveland, and when the Spiders pushed the winning run across the plate in the bottom of the ninth, the fans carried the Cleveland players off the field. The next two games ended in similar fashion, and the Spiders left town with a lead of three games to none.

This success put the Baltimore fans in an ugly mood, and the fourth game of the series, played in Baltimore, saw a riot that threatened to spiral out of control before a pitch was thrown. Oriole fans, incensed at the treatment their stars had received in Cleveland, attacked the carriages transporting the Spiders to the ballpark with rocks, bottles, and rotten vegetables. It took the police more than five minutes to escort the Cleveland players 15 feet from their carriages to the safety of the tunnel leading to the dugout, and only quick and decisive action kept the dangerously excited crowd under control. Only after the police arrested eleven fans for rioting were the two teams able to take the field, and the game itself, won by the Orioles by a 5–0 score, seemed almost like an afterthought. "One swallow don't make a summer," said Patsy Tebeau as he scurried off the field to safety at game's end. "And we'll get that Cup for they have to face Cy Young again tomorrow."[11] He was right, for Young defeated Baltimore the next day, before a slightly better-behaved crowd, to clinch the Temple Cup for Cleveland.

The Baltimore-Cleveland matchup was an exciting series, but for all the wrong reasons. Rowdiness had taken root in the game, due in large part to the success of the Cleveland and Baltimore teams, and by 1895 the fans had joined in the action to an alarming degree. Though the Temple Cup victory was celebrated in Cleveland, it dealt a blow to the prestige of the game as a whole. A post-game riot at Louisville in 1896, in which Jesse Burkett, Jimmy McAleer, and other Spiders were arrested after they physically assaulted umpire Stump Wiedman, also damaged the standing of National League baseball. Still, the league took little action to curb the bad behavior, and other teams copied the Orioles and Spiders in a bid to emulate their on-field success.

Another dispute, this one featuring Jesse Burkett, marred a doubleheader at Louisville on August 4, 1897. During the first contest, Jesse became embroiled in an argument with umpire Bill Wolf that soon escalated to name-calling. When Wolf thumbed Burkett out of the game, the Crab refused to leave. Tebeau refused to replace him, and Wolf threatened to forfeit the game to the Colonels. "Go ahead," replied Tebeau, whose Spiders had fallen out of the pennant race by this time. "We don't need it." Wolf counted off the required five minutes with his watch, then declared the game a forfeit by the score of 9 to 0. The second game started without incident, but as the innings went by Burkett began to snipe at Wolf again, and by the ninth the arbiter had heard enough. He ejected Burkett, who once again refused to vacate the premises. Wolf then called over two park police officers, who dragged the protesting Crab from the field.[12]

Burkett and third baseman Chippy McGarr lived in Worcester, Massachusetts, and worked together each spring to coach the baseball team at the College of the Holy Cross in that city. During the mid–1890s, Burkett gave batting tips to a phenomenal Native American athlete named Louis Sockalexis, who batted .426 in 1895 and .444 in 1896 for Holy Cross. Sockalexis, from the Penobscot Indian reservation in Maine, was so impressive that both Burkett and McGarr implored Patsy Tebeau to sign him, which the manager did in early 1897.

Sockalexis reported to Cleveland for spring training in March of that year, and the local writers were so taken with the handsome, graceful athlete that they started calling the team "Tebeau's Indians." During the 1897 season, newspapers across the country referred to the Cleveland team as the Indians for the first time.

The 1897 season, Tebeau's seventh as team manager, was the turning point for National League baseball in Cleveland. On May 16, the newly-christened Indians attempted to play a Sunday game at League Park against the Senators, but at the end of the first inning the police invaded the field and arrested all the players on both teams, along with umpire Tim Hurst. A subsequent court case upheld the city's ban on Sunday baseball, which severely restricted the ability of the franchise to operate profitably. The club was aging, as the Irish core of the team had been playing ball in Cleveland for nearly a decade, but the promising newcomer, Sockalexis, flamed out quickly. Most importantly, Tebeau's fighting, brawling style of play had failed to bring a pennant to Cleveland. The rowdier fan element may have liked the on-field product, but most baseball enthusiasts were tired of the thuggish antics of the Cleveland and Baltimore clubs. Attendance in both cities fell in 1897, and would drop further during the remainder of the decade.

The subsequent campaign was the beginning of the end for the team that the Cleveland writers called the "Hibernian Indians." Sockalexis batted only .224 and failed to dislodge Harry Blake from right field, leaving the Cleveland club with the handicap of two light-hitting outfielders in Blake and McAleer. Starting pitcher Nig Cuppy's arm was gone, and while Cy Young and newcomer Jack Powell pitched well, the rest of the staff was weak. Only Jesse Burkett, among the batters, managed to top the .300 mark, and McAleer, while fielding as well as ever, was finished as a hitter. He batted .238 in 1898 with 87 hits, all but three of which were singles.

Even worse, the Cleveland club, deprived of Sunday crowds that would have allowed it to compete financially, was losing money. Most of the Spiders were highly-paid (for the era) veterans, and the crowds at League Park were insufficient to pay their salaries. In desperation, team owner Frank Robison moved most of Cleveland's home games to other cities in the last half of the season. The Spiders played 35 of their final 38 games on the road, and though they ended up in a respectable fifth place, the endless road trip probably doomed their pennant chances. The "Hibernian Indians" were now called the "Wandering Micks" in the nation's newspapers, and the team finished last in the league in home attendance for the second year in a row.

The 1899 campaign proved to be the last for Cleveland in the National League, but Tebeau and his charges — most of them, anyway — would not stick around for the final farewell. In early 1899, the St. Louis Browns, decimated by poor leadership, a bad on-field product, and a stadium fire, were headed to bankruptcy court. Frank Robison, owner of the Spiders, moved quickly to take advantage of the dire circumstances. St. Louis was a great baseball town and, more importantly, allowed Sunday baseball. By March, Robison had gained control of the Browns and moved his best players — Young, Burkett, Tebeau, and all the rest — to St. Louis, leaving only a shell of a team in Cleveland. The only Spiders regular who failed to go west was Jimmy McAleer, who decided to retire rather than choose between playing ball a thousand miles from home and remaining with the gutted Cleveland squad.

The core of the new Mound City team consisted of the Cleveland stars who had made the Spiders/Indians so entertaining for the previous eight years, while a few holdovers from the 1898 Browns rounded out Tebeau's new roster. Among those remaining from the previous St. Louis club were pitcher Willie Sudhoff and outfielder Jake Stenzel. The best player on the previous year's Browns was third baseman Lave Cross, but because every infield position was now occupied by former Clevelanders (Tebeau at first, Childs at second, McKean at short, and Bobby Wallace at third), there was no room for Cross on the new St. Louis team. Robison sent him to Cleveland, where he became manager of the now-hapless Spiders.

Tebeau got off to a fast start as manager of his hometown team, which the newspapers had dubbed the Perfectos in an attempt to leave the memory of the awful Browns behind. The Perfectos won their first seven games and 19 of their first 25 to take the early league lead, and by mid–May Tebeau's men found themselves in a three-team race with Boston, the defending champion, and a Brooklyn team laden with the former stars of the Baltimore Orioles. However, the Perfectos faded in June, and by the end of the month had dropped to sixth place, passed by the resurgent Philadelphia Phillies and the Cap Anson–less Chicago Orphans.

The ex–Browns and the relocated Spiders meshed poorly as the season wore on, and the Perfectos floated along in the middle of the standings. Loyal to a fault, Tebeau kept the fading Ed McKean at shortstop in the early going, though it was clear to all that McKean had reached the end of the line, with his batting average, fielding percentage, and range factor falling below the league average. Not until late July, after the Perfectos had dropped far behind the leaders, did Tebeau bench McKean and move Bobby Wallace to short. He attempted to ship McKean back to Cleveland, but the proud old shortstop retired rather than play for the floundering Spiders.

To replace McKean in the St. Louis infield, Tebeau summoned Lave Cross from the Cleveland club, which had won only 8 of 38 games under his leadership and was well on its way to compiling the worst record in the game's history. The decimated Spiders replaced Cross as manager with the Australian-born second baseman Joe Quinn, a second-generation Irishman who had bounced around the major leagues for a decade and a half. Quinn was a respected veteran leader, but faced the impossible task of competing in the National League with a team of castoffs, semi-pros, and college players. Quinn won only 12 of his 113 games as manager, and the team finished a record 84 and a half games out of first place.

While the Spiders dropped to the bottom of the standings, Tebeau's St. Louis club failed to meet expectations of the local fans. Though Jesse Burkett hit near the .400 mark and both Cy Young and Jack Powell crossed the 20-win barrier, many of Tebeau's old standbys were rapidly aging. Harry Blake's hitting fell off, Cupid Childs was fading at second base, and Tebeau himself batted only .246 in 1899. Still, Patsy believed that the blame for his team's poor performance lay elsewhere. Though his own ancestry was partly German, Tebeau was given to complain publicly about "dumb Dutchmen" who were, in his view, not as mentally quick as Irishmen. His attitude caused friction in the clubhouse and angered the bleacherites, many of whom were German-Americans who had supported baseball in St. Louis since the glory days of the 1880s. In early July of 1899, Tebeau discharged the popular outfielder Jake Stenzel, much to the displeasure of the St. Louis followers. "Why did you release Stenzel?" shouted a fan from the bleachers.

"I released him," replied Tebeau angrily, "because he couldn't think fast enough and was Dutch." The fans exploded in anger, and only a quick intercession by the park police kept the manager from being assaulted by a mob of irate German-Americans. "Tebeau is a great baseball general," said Baltimore's John McGraw to a reporter, "but his temper will get him in a peck of trouble if he doesn't apply a bridle to his untamed wrath."[13]

The Perfectos, who started the season so well, were out of the race by August. Tebeau spent the rest of the campaign juggling his personnel, moving rookie Tim Flood to second base in place of Cupid Childs and sending another Irish lad, Mike Donlin, to center field to replace Harry Blake. The manager also put Ossee Schreckengost at first base and assigned himself more or less permanently to the bench. "I will probably never play again," he told a reporter at season's end. "Schrecken-gost will make a star first baseman and I will manage from the bench hereafter."[14] Patsy, at age 35, recognized that his playing days were over.

Still, Tebeau remained as feisty as ever. In August, a shoving match between Tebeau and a longtime enemy, Baltimore's John McGraw, got out of hand and started a disturbance in which the St. Louis fans pelted the Oriole players with garbage and rotten eggs. A few weeks earlier, Tebeau had berated a spectator in Baltimore so viciously that the fan had Patsy arrested and booked at the local police station. Tebeau emerged from that particular incident unscathed, but in September an argument between the St. Louis manager

John McGraw, who spent one uncomfortable season under Tebeau's leadership with the St. Louis Cardinals in 1900 (1912 Spalding Guide).

and umpire Arlie Latham turned into a near riot, with Tebeau pushing and manhandling the arbiter. Patsy somehow avoided punishment for the incident, probably because the season was nearly over anyway. The Perfectos finished in fifth place, 18 and a half games behind the champion Brooklyn team.

McGraw's Baltimore squad had surprised the league by passing the Perfectos to finish in fourth position, but the Oriole fans had no reason to celebrate. The National League was determined to drop its four weakest and least profitable teams, so the Orioles were disbanded, along with the Washington, Cleveland, and Louisville clubs. The best players from these teams were absorbed by the eight remaining franchises, but McGraw, assigned to St. Louis for the 1900 campaign, was not enthusiastic about playing for Tebeau. He involved himself in plans to revive the old American Association with Baltimore as one of its franchises; when that effort failed, he looked into buying an Eastern League club. Nothing came of that venture either, and in March of 1900 McGraw and his assistant manager, catcher Wilbert Robinson, reluctantly joined the St. Louis team.

Most observers doubted that McGraw, widely recognized as the best young manager in the game, could coexist with his old enemy Tebeau, but the two men made every effort to get along. Unfortunately, Jesse Burkett and some of the other ex–Spiders were none too pleased to see McGraw arrive. Burkett complained loudly when Tebeau named McGraw as team captain, believing that the honor, and the $600 salary bump that went with it, should have gone to Tebeau's old Cleveland running mate Jack O'Connor. Friction between McGraw and several of his new teammates promised to make the 1900 campaign a tough one for Tebeau.

Because the Perfectos had proved themselves to be less than perfect in 1899, a name change was in order for the ballclub. St. Louis teams had traditionally adopted nicknames based on their uniform colors (such as the Reds of the old National Association, the Maroons of the Unions in 1884, and the more recent Whites and Browns), so the club looked to its cardinal red stockings and lettering for inspiration. The result was the nickname Cardinals, which remains to this day.

Though the Cardinals would become one of the National League's premier teams, winning more pennants and World Series than any club during the 20th century save for the Yankees, the first edition of the ballclub never managed to jell. The club posted winning records in April and May, though just barely, but a 5–15 mark in June dropped St. Louis from the race in the newly constituted eight-team league. Despite the presence of stars such as Cy Young, Jesse Burkett, and John McGraw, the team dropped to the second division and wallowed in bickering and in-fighting. McGraw did his best to fit in, praising St. Louis as a fine baseball town and publicly pledging his loyalty to Tebeau, telling his manager to "go ahead and do what you think best."[15] However, Burkett and the other ex–Spiders were incensed that management, to ease the transition of the captaincy to McGraw, sold the popular Jack O'Connor to Pittsburgh on May 22. A 2–15 skid followed shortly thereafter, and the Cardinals were out of the race by mid–June.

Patsy Tebeau grew tired of the turmoil surrounding his hometown team, the endless bickering between factions, and his own demise as a player. He put himself in the lineup only once during the 1900 season, going hitless and making three errors on June 12 in what would be his final appearance as a major league player. Managing from the bench suited Patsy poorly; he drew energy and inspiration from being in the thick of the action, and he appeared listless and uninterested. McGraw, absent from the lineup for weeks at a time with various injuries, and Wilbert Robinson spent many of their afternoons at a nearby racetrack instead of the ballpark. The team floundered with little direction and inconsistent leadership.

Tebeau was too proud a man to continue this way. His talent-laden team was nestled in seventh place, eight games under the .500 mark, when he suddenly resigned after a loss to Cincinnati on August 18. Frank Robison offered McGraw the job, but the former Oriole turned it down, probably because he was already negotiating with the American League for the leadership of a new team in Baltimore for 1901. However, McGraw agreed to name the starting pitchers and direct the team on the field, as a manager without portfolio, for the remainder of the 1900 season. Louis Heilbronner, business manager of the Cardinals, was awarded the title of manager, though he wisely deferred to McGraw on questions of strategy and team leadership. The Cardinals managed to post a winning record for the Heilbronner-McGraw tandem, improving to fifth place by year's end.

John McGraw would rise to greater heights, managing the New York Giants to ten pennants and three World Series titles during the next three decades, but Patsy Tebeau, only 36 at the time of his resignation as Cardinals manager, was finished. He had soured on baseball, and not even the formation of the American League, which doubled the number of major league teams to 16 beginning in 1901, could bring him back to the game. Some of his St. Louis friends, believing that his leadership skills would serve him well as a club owner, offered to back him financially, but Tebeau was not interested. "I'm not one of those fancy guys," he said. "I've been a player, that's all, and they'll never put me on one of those swinging chairs."[16]

Instead, Patsy bought a bar in the Goose Hill section of St. Louis from which he came and managed the establishment for the next 18 years. He gave interviews to newspapers every now and then, but baseball was finished with him, and he with it. As the new century passed, the memory of Patsy Tebeau, one of the most colorful field leaders of the 1890s, slowly faded into the background.

Without baseball to serve as an outlet for his restless energy, Patsy was probably not an easy man to live with after his career ended. In 1890 he married a daughter of Irish immigrants, whom he met while playing for the Spiders, but the union turned sour after a while, and in early 1918 Kate Tebeau and their two children moved to Cleveland, where her family lived. This was a blow from which the old ballplayer could not recover, and in May of that year, Patsy Tebeau put a gun to his head and ended his own life at the age of 54. His wife brought Patsy's body back to Cleveland, the scene of so many of his baseball triumphs and failures, for burial.

The Cleveland Spiders disbanded after the 1899 season, but several of Tebeau's former charges remained in the game for many years thereafter. Jimmy McAleer was a manager, promoter, and team owner, briefly serving as president of the Red Sox before he, too, became disgruntled with the game and left it as had his old boss Tebeau. Jesse Burkett played in the majors until 1905 and then spent ten more seasons in the minors as a player, manager, and team owner in Worcester, Massachusetts. He lived there until his death in 1953, seven years after his election to the Hall of Fame. Another "Hibernian Spider," Ed McKean, managed in the minors before he died at age 55 in 1919, while non–Irish Cleveland stars Cy Young, Bobby Wallace, and Chief Zimmer all lived past their 80th birthdays.

Perhaps the spirit of the Spiders was best exemplified by Tebeau's childhood friend and teammate, Jack O'Connor, whose departure from the sport was one of the most spectacular in history. O'Connor had contributed mightily to the development of the new American League, serving as president Ban Johnson's point man in enticing National League stars to desert the established circuit and join the new organization. O'Connor became manager of the St. Louis Browns in 1910, succeeding his old teammate Jimmy McAleer, and led the club to a seventh place finish. Detroit's Ty Cobb and the more popular Cleveland hitter Nap Lajoie were locked in a race for the batting title, and on the season's last day O'Connor's Browns played Cleveland in a doubleheader. O'Connor, in an effort to help the well-liked Lajoie against the generally despised Cobb, ordered his third baseman to play almost into the outfield grass whenever Lajoie came to bat. Rowdy Jack also put himself in at catcher, though he had not played in a major league game in three years. The Cleveland slugger took advantage, beating out seven bunt singles and adding a triple as he went eight for nine in his quest to catch Cobb for the batting crown.

The league eventually declared Cobb the winner of the title, but O'Connor's machinations were too much for Ban Johnson to stomach. Despite Rowdy Jack's record of service to the league, Johnson drove O'Connor from the game. The St. Louis team fired him, though he later filed a successful suit to recover a portion of his 1911 salary, and O'Connor never returned to the majors. A stint in the Federal League in 1913 ended when Rowdy Jack slugged an umpire, breaking the arbiter's jaw. No one would hire him in any league, major or minor, after that. He spent his remaining years as a boxing promoter in St. Louis, and never got over his bitterness at being expelled from the league he had helped create. In 1937, O'Connor died of natural causes in his hometown of St. Louis. In an interview published in *The Sporting News* four years before his death, he called baseball "a game for sissies."[17]

7

Ned Hanlon and the Orioles

By the early 1890s, more than half of the field managers and captains of National League teams claimed Irish descent, men with names like McGraw, Mack, Duffy, and Comiskey. The game was changing, and though some of the old guard (such as Cap Anson, still leading the Chicago nine after more than a decade at the helm) still clung stubbornly to power, the younger leaders of the 1890s were introducing new strategies and tactics. The hit and run, the trap play (which led to the introduction of the infield fly rule in 1894), and the double steal made their appearance in the game, mainly developed and refined by the younger generation of managers of Irish descent. The proud old Anson, who eschewed such innovative thinking and was so conservative that he continued to play first base without a glove until late in his career, was quickly becoming an anachronism.

One of the new wave of managers was only five years younger than Cap Anson, but built the team that ruled the National League for much of the last decade of the 19th century. Edward (Ned) Hanlon, born in Connecticut in 1857, was the son of a cotton mill worker and a housewife who had fled Ireland a decade before. Ned, the sixth of seven children, worked with his father and older brothers in the mill, but his baseball skill saved him from a life in a factory. Ned first performed in the National League with Cleveland in 1880, then joined the new Detroit Wolverines as a center fielder in 1881. Hanlon was not much of a hitter, but his fielding and baserunning skills made him one of the most valuable Wolverines. In 1882, at age 24, he was named captain of the club, directing the team on the field.

The talent-poor Wolverines were one of the league's worst teams until 1885, when new owner Frederick K. Stearnes bought the failing Buffalo club and put the Bison "Big Four" of Dan Brouthers, Jack Rowe, Deacon White, and Hardie Richardson into the Detroit lineup. The Wolverines immediately jumped into contention, finishing second in 1886 and winning the pennant, Detroit's only National League championship, in 1887. Bill Watkins was the manager, but captain Ned Hanlon earned a great deal of praise for the team's success.

Hanlon was a wizard at strategy, but the Detroit club needed little of it. The Wolverines, with the "Big Four" ably supported by the National League's RBI champ, outfielder Sam Thompson, were the best hitting team in the game, and simply slugged their way to the pennant. They led the league in virtually every offensive category, and with a strong one-two pitching duo in Charles (Lady) Baldwin and Charlie Getzien, the Detroit club easily outpaced the resurgent Philadelphia Phillies and Anson's rebuilding Chicago team. They then faced the St. Louis Browns in a 15-game World Series, winning 10 games to clinch the world championship.

The Wolverines' success was short-lived, with injuries dropping the club to fifth place in 1888. At the time, Detroit was the smallest city in the National League, and the club, barely profitable when it was winning, became a money-loser. It disbanded at season's end, and Hanlon was sold to Pittsburgh, where he became the playing manager of the Alleghenies (later called the Pirates) in 1889. He helped develop several star players there, most notably a tall, gangly Irish catcher named Cornelius McGillicuddy (who went by the shortened moniker Connie Mack). Hanlon managed the Pittsburgh entry in the Players League in 1890, then returned to the same city as a National Leaguer in 1891. Unfortunately, his Alleghenies were a hard-drinking lot, and Hanlon already recognized that poor discipline was fatal to a club's pennant chances. He fined, suspended, and released popular players for violating his rules, and by mid-season the Alleghenies were ready to revolt. Hanlon was fired as manager in late June, though he remained in center field and stayed on as captain.

Hanlon expected to play for Pittsburgh in 1892, but a severely broken leg suffered in spring training brought his playing career to a sudden halt. He was not out of work for long because the Baltimore Orioles were looking for a new manager after starting the new season with only three wins in their first 19 games. Like Pittsburgh, Baltimore was an unruly team in dire need of discipline, and Hanlon had proven his willingness to establish and enforce rules without regard to his personal popularity. In May of 1892, the Orioles tapped Hanlon as their manager and gave him the job of building the team into a contender. Hanlon, seeking to consolidate his position, bought 25 percent of the stock in the club and had himself appointed team president. He demanded, and received, full control of all facets of club management, including player transactions, and before long the majority owner, a German immigrant beer baron named Harry von der Horst, found himself with little to do. When the sportswriters came to von der Horst for information, he would simply point to a button on his coat that said, "Ask Hanlon."

The talent-poor Orioles finished in last place in 1892, Hanlon's first season in charge, but he was already setting the stage for future success. His predecessor, star outfielder George Van Haltren, had remained with the club but grumbled about the new manager's tactics and strategies. Hanlon traded him to Pittsburgh for a young, unproven outfielder named Joe Kelley and $2,500. "I had my eye on [Kelley] for a long time," explained Hanlon to the *Baltimore Sun*. "I think it is better to have a good, steady ballplayer than to have a great player who, for some reason, does not play as well as he should."[1] Kelley, a native of Cambridge, Massachusetts, had failed in previous trials in Boston and Pittsburgh, but Hanlon saw potential in the 21-year-old outfielder.

Kelley, like Hanlon, was an Irishman, but the manager did not keep players around because they shared his ethnic heritage. An Irish catcher and first baseman named Jocko Halligan was one of the most popular players in Baltimore, but when Halligan broke teammate Cub Stricker's jaw in a clubhouse fight in August, Hanlon released him the next day. Curt Welch, a star outfielder with the St. Louis Browns during the previous decade, was a charismatic Irish-American star who brought fans to the ballpark, but his out-of-control drinking forced Hanlon to dismiss Welch from the team in mid–July. Hanlon discarded the drinkers, complainers, and carousers, and filled the Baltimore roster with talented youngsters and a few serious-minded veterans.

A keen judge of talent, Hanlon knew which players to keep and which ones to send away. John McGraw was a teenaged third baseman who had not yet enjoyed success with the Orioles, but Hanlon recognized that McGraw was an intelligent, competitive youngster with a nearly fanatical will to win. Born in Truxton, New York, in 1873, John McGraw was the son of an Irish immigrant farmer, also named John McGraw (or McGrath, as the family spelled it back in Ireland) from County Tipperary. The younger John had lost his mother and four siblings during a diphtheria epidemic, then left home at age 12 to escape the wrath of his embittered father. He took up residence at a nearby boarding house, hustling magazines and candy for a living while playing ball on the Truxton town team in his spare time. From there, he clawed his way quickly up the minor league ladder, arriving in Baltimore in 1891 at the age of 18.

McGraw appeared to have little natural athletic talent, but made it to the major leagues on sheer will and perseverance. He was also determined to stay there. On his first day as an Oriole, a veteran player shoved him off the end of the bench. McGraw immediately jumped on the older and much larger man and pummeled him until several of his new teammates intervened. They left him alone after that. He hit well enough to earn a place on the team, but his erratic fielding and throwing made him a mere substitute during his first season in Baltimore. His first manager, Billy Barnie, left him home on road trips, and put him to work taking tickets, in full uniform, before home games during the 1891 season. Ned Hanlon continued to use McGraw as a substitute infielder in 1892, but the teenager was hungry for stardom, and worked harder than any other Oriole.

McGraw, who reportedly weighed only 121 pounds when he joined the club, had little power at the plate but recognized that getting on base was crucial to a team's success. Consequently, he taught himself to choke up on the bat and punch hits to all fields. An accomplished bunter, he was also a master at drawing walks, fouling off pitches in the days when foul balls were not counted as strikes. He would slap away ball after ball until he walked or got a good pitch to hit. McGraw also prevailed upon the Baltimore groundskeeper, an Irishman named Tom Murphy, to pack hard clay directly in front of the plate. The rock-hard ground made it profitable for McGraw to hit the ball straight down, a maneuver called the "Baltimore chop." The ball bounced high over the infielders' heads, enabling McGraw to reach first before it came down. John McGraw was Hanlon's kind of player, and in 1893 the manager made the 20-year-old McGraw the starting third baseman of the Orioles.

McGraw was barely tolerated by the Oriole veterans when he arrived in 1891, but he formed a fast friendship with a portly catcher named Wilbert Robinson, nine years his senior. Robinson, whose parents and grandparents had been born in America, always gave his ancestry as English, though he grew up in an Irish neighborhood, played ball with Irish teammates, and married into an Irish immigrant family. The Robinsons were Episcopalians, but in adulthood, after he married an Irish-born Baltimore woman named Mary O'Rourke, Wilbert converted to Catholicism. He fit in so well with the other Irish Orioles that most people assumed that he, too, was an Irishman.

A friendly man with a large handlebar mustache, Robinson was the son of a butcher and fish dealer from Bolton, Massachusetts, and had spent five years as a catcher with the Philadelphia Athletics before arriving in Baltimore for the 1891 season. "Robinson was a great catcher from the first day we placed him behind the bat, but to my mind his greatest quality was, and is, his personality," said William Prince, Robinson's first minor league manager. "His good nature was a sure remedy to drive away all the blues. No cliques could last while Robbie was around. He taught us to look at all such things as a joke, and drew us together as a sociable, harmonious club."[2] His easygoing nature hid a fierce will to win and a sharp baseball mind, and he and McGraw bonded instantly. Hanlon, too, appreciated Robinson's qualities and named him captain of the Orioles.

Hanlon kept McGraw, Robinson, and pitcher John (Sadie) McMahon, but turned over almost all the rest of the roster within two years. Some of his moves puzzled the Baltimore fans, especially one in which he sent veteran outfielder Tim O'Rourke to Louisville for a red-headed rookie shortstop named Hugh Jennings, who hailed from the coal mining country of eastern Pennsylvania. Jennings, a fine fielder, had hit poorly for Louisville, but Hanlon saw the makings of a future star who, like McGraw, had a driving need to win. The 1893 Orioles, with the steadily improving McGraw, Jennings, and Kelley leading the way, rose four notches in the standings to eighth place.

Wilbert Robinson preceded both Hanlon and McGraw to Baltimore. His ancestry was English, but his wife was Irish-born, and most of his teammates were Irishmen (author's collection).

Hanlon executed his most important player transaction in January of 1894, when he made another of his apparently inexplicable deals. He sent two solid contributors, infielder Billy Shindle and outfielder George Treadway, to Brooklyn for a little-used young outfielder named "Wee Willie" Keeler and a 36-year-old fading star, first baseman Dan Brouthers. The fans were surprised at this turn of events, though Shindle, whom Hanlon had often criticized for a lack of hustle and effort, forced the trade by threatening to quit the game rather than return to Baltimore for another season. Shindle was a popular player, but Hanlon regarded the 33-year-old infielder, whose skills were on the decline, as a disruptive influence. Besides, Hanlon saw Keeler as a potential star, even if the Brooklyn club did not, while Brouthers was a proven veteran performer who might have one more good season left in him.

The 1894 Orioles were a mostly Irish ballclub, and it may have appeared that Hanlon was purposely trying to fill his roster with as many Irishmen as possible. Five of the starting eight (McGraw at third, Brouthers at first, Jennings at short, and outfielders Kelley and Keeler) were second-generation Irish like Hanlon himself, as were starting pitchers Sadie McMahon and Kid Gleason. Another starter, the veteran Tony Mullane, was born in Ireland, having left County Cork as a young man and settled in the coal mining region of western Pennsylvania. Second baseman Heinie Reitz claimed German descent, while right fielder Walter (Steve) Brodie was a Scotsman, but the rest of the team spoke with Irish accents. In an era when the influence of the Irish was at its highest, the Baltimore club was the most thoroughly Irish of all.

Wee Willie Keeler, despite his German-sounding name, was every bit as Irish as McGraw, Jennings, and the rest. Born in Brooklyn in 1872, his birth name was O'Kelleher, though his family adopted the name Keeler at some unknown point. Standing only about five feet and four inches tall, Keeler generated almost no power at the plate, as more than 80 percent of his career hits were singles. However, his bat control was outstanding, and only Cleveland's Jesse Burkett rated with him as a bunter. Wee Willie produced prodigious batting averages, topping out at .432 in 1897, and regularly averaged more than a run per game. "Hit 'em where they ain't," he said, and his skill as a leadoff batter keyed the Oriole offensive attack.

Another Irish Oriole who underwent a name change was Joe Kelley, who was a Kelly at his birth in 1871. According to legend, an admiring newspaper writer added an extra "e" to Joe's last name because "Kelley" was supposed to be a classier handle than the more common "Kelly." Joe, perhaps tired of being confused with the more popular Mike (King) Kelly, kept the extra letter for the rest of his life. Raw and unproven upon his arrival in Baltimore in 1893, Kelley learned the fine points of playing center field from the former outfielder Hanlon, who sometimes required Kelley to show up for practice as early as eight o'clock in the morning. Kelley, already a good hitter, was perhaps the most talented man on the team, speedy enough to bat at the top of the order and powerful enough to hit in the middle of the lineup if needed. He was also the most handsome Oriole, and the left field bleachers in Baltimore were filled with female fans who wanted to see Kelley up close. That section of the ballpark was known as "Kelleyville" for as long as Joe played for the club.

Dan Brouthers, who came to Baltimore with Willie Keeler in the trade with Brooklyn, bore almost no resemblance to Keeler despite their shared Irish ancestry. "Big Dan," a muscular slugger more than six feet tall and well over 200 pounds, had played top-level baseball since breaking into the National League with Troy in 1879. A friendly and good-natured man, Dan had been a vice-president of the Brotherhood and was one of the major figures behind the Players League rebellion of 1890. He was also famous for being tight with his money. Rumor had it that he took his salary each year in silver dollars, which he put in a sack and buried on his farm in his hometown of Wappingers Falls, New York. His friend and teammate Mike Kelly was so surprised when Dan bought a round of drinks one day that he took the dollar bill from the bartender and had it framed.

Dan had been one of baseball's great power hitters for more than a decade, leading his leagues in slugging percentage seven times and in home runs twice. He was also one of the most well-traveled men to play major league ball, having performed for seven teams in three leagues before arriving in Baltimore. He won the National League batting title, his fifth, in 1892, but slumped dreadfully the following season, and was considered by most to be washed up at age 36. Ned Hanlon, who had been Dan's teammate on the Detroit Wolverines several years before, did not share this view. He had men with high on-base percentages, Keeler and McGraw, at the top of his lineup, and he needed some power behind them. If anyone could provide it, reasoned Hanlon, Dan Brouthers was the man.

Shortstop Hugh Jennings, too, was the son of immigrants, his parents having settled in the coal-mining town of Pittston, Pennsylvania, in 1851. Like most of the town's residents, Jennings's father James worked 12 hours a day at the Pennsylvania Coal Company mine to feed his growing family. Unlike many, James Jennings took a temperance pledge and stayed away from the many bars and taverns that ringed the mining district and soaked up much of the miners' wages. James imparted his strong work ethic to his children, of whom Hugh was the ninth, and by the time Hugh was 12 years old he, too, went to work at the mine as a mule driver. He lied about his age to get the job, claiming to be two years older than he really was, and the discrepancy in his birth date followed him into baseball.

Jennings' mother was Scottish, but his father was a proud Irishman from County Galway. One day late in the 1897 season, James Jennings paid a visit to his son in Baltimore. While watching a practice session, he immediately noticed one of the Orioles wearing a bright red sweater. "Who's that bloke in shortfield, Hughie?" demanded the bewhiskered old miner. "He looks like an Irishman, but he's flashing the wrong color."

"That's Joe Quinn," responded Hughie. "He is Irish, father."

The elder Jennings marched onto the field. "Quinn," he proclaimed, "I don't know you personally, but you're flashing the wrong colors. A red sweater on a Mick makes a turncoat out of him. It's a disgrace to your country." Quinn, no doubt amused by the old gentleman's agitation, exchanged his red sweater for a green one, earning the approval of James Jennings.[3]

With the Irish heart of the team firmly in place, the Orioles surprised the league in 1894 by winning 24 of their first 34 games and sprinting to the top of the standings. The Baltimore pitching was mediocre, as ten different hurlers earned at least one decision and six men threw at least 100 innings, but the Orioles' fielding and hitting more than made up for the lack of a true staff ace. Besides, 1894 was a hitters' year, the most extreme offensive explosion in the game's history, with Baltimore's incredible .343 team batting average only the second best in the league. Hanlon knew that outstanding pitching in such a year was a luxury, but not a necessity. Mediocrity on the mound was sufficient for a team that averaged more than nine runs per game.

Strategy was an important part of baseball during this era, and the Orioles practiced and refined the hit and run, the double steal, and other maneuvers designed to keep their opponents on edge. Hanlon gave his Orioles a great deal of responsibility, making the players, especially John McGraw, accountable for their own successes and failures. Rising to the challenge, McGraw, Kelley, Jennings, and the other young Irish Orioles drove themselves, and each other, to greater heights. "Hanlon didn't have to scold or punish a player for failing to do his part," said McGraw. "We attended to that ourselves.... Woe betide the player who failed us! His life on the bench was not a pleasant one. He never forgot the roasting and never failed to deliver one if somebody else failed."[4]

They called Hanlon "Foxy Ned" for his baseball acumen, but the Orioles were quick learners, and devised strategies of their own. They were close off the field as well. "Jennings, Kelley, Keeler, Wilbert Robinson and myself organized ourselves into a sort of committee," said McGraw many years later. "We were scheming all the time for a new stunt to pull. We talked, lived, and dreamed baseball. We met every night and talked over our successes and failures. If it was a trip to the theater, all of us went and sat together. Every year later on we had a reunion. The players even looked after each other for years afterward. It was like an old college football team."[5]

National League umpires were no fans of the Orioles, for the Baltimore players quickly discovered that intimidating and manhandling the arbiters not only increased their chances of winning games, but also went unpunished for the most part. The decade of the 1890s was the worst in baseball history for the umpiring profession, in no small measure due to the behavior of Hanlon's Orioles. Almost any decision against the Orioles, no matter how mundane, could instigate a wild, unruly protest that sometimes involved the fans as well as the players on the field. When trouble started, as

Edward (Ned) Hanlon, who led the Orioles to three consecutive pennants (author's collection).

it too often did, the lone umpire (the league would not use two officials until later in the decade) often found himself surrounded, pushed, and jostled by a mob of angry Orioles. Such antics, and the league's lack of interest in enforcing discipline on umpire abusers like McGraw and his teammates, forced many arbiters to call things Baltimore's way, much to the disgust of opposing teams and fans.

With the umpires sufficiently cowed, the Orioles directed a steady stream of rough, physical play against their opponents, especially on their home field. Tripping, shoving, and blocking base runners were daily occurrences, and McGraw perfected the art of interrupting an opponent's progress around the bases by grabbing the runner's belt and holding on. On offense, the Baltimore players, urged on by McGraw's command, "Get at 'em!" slammed into and trampled over infielders and catchers, often with spikes flashing dangerously, leading to a large number of on-field brawls. One such tussle, at Boston's South End Grounds in May of 1894, caused a fan riot that resulted in the stadium burning down. Boston sportswriter Tim Murnane, an Irishman and a former player himself, claimed that the Orioles played "the dirtiest ball ever seen in this country," and complained that Hanlon's men were "ready to maim a fellow player for life [in] just retribution for trying to stop them in their temporary flight."[6]

The team slumped in July, falling five games behind the defending Boston champions, but Hanlon shook up the lineup by putting Joe Kelley in the leadoff slot and moving John McGraw to the cleanup position. The Baltimore pitching was inconsistent, and Hanlon tried to strengthen the staff by trading the Irish-born veteran Tony Mullane, nearing the end of his long career, to Cleveland for another fading star, John Clarkson. However, Clarkson refused to report and retired instead, leaving the Orioles in the lurch. Somehow, Hanlon coaxed good performances from a pitching corps devoid of real stars. John (Sadie) McMahon, a portly right-hander who grew up in Wilmington, Delaware, and ran with an Irish street gang in his youth, was the best of the lot, winning 25 games as part of the "Dumpling Battery" with the equally hefty catcher Wilbert Robinson. The pitching stabilized late in the season, and the Orioles went 28–3, with 18 straight wins, in September to win the flag by three games over the resurgent New York Giants.

The National League was the only major circuit remaining after the collapse of the American Association in 1891, but the club owners recognized that post-season championship play was popular and profitable. To this end, they accepted a plan authored by Pittsburgh businessman William Temple, who proposed that the first- and second-place teams meet in October of each year to vie for possession of a large silver trophy known as the Temple Cup. The inaugural Temple Cup match was played after the conclusion of the 1894 season, between the pennant-winning Orioles and the runner-up New York Giants.

Apparently, neither Temple nor the league magnates had considered that the players might be less than excited about playing in a post-season series after concluding a grueling pennant race. Temple had proposed that the winning and losing teams divide the gate receipts in a 65–35 split, but the Orioles protested, demanding a 50–50 division of the proceeds. This idea was rejected, as it would have removed any incentive for either club to give its best effort. The 65–35 arrangement stood, but the canny Orioles found a way around it. Each Oriole simply paired up with a member of the Giants and agreed to split their winnings evenly, regardless of the outcome.

The Orioles were highly favored to win the series, but McGraw, Keeler, and their teammates appeared satisfied with the National League pennant and attached no significance to the Temple Cup. The Giants swept the series in four games, with pitchers Amos Rusie and Jouett Meekin winning two games apiece from the listless Orioles. "They could not have beaten Towsontown or Hoboken in those games," a Baltimore newspaperman griped afterward. "They were not in condition to beat anybody."[7] To add insult to injury, all but one of the Giants reneged on their commitments to split their winnings. Amos Rusie gave Baltimore's Joe Kelley $204, the difference between the winning and losing shares, after the final game, but the other New Yorkers went back on their promises and kept all of their money.

The Orioles found tougher going in the National League during the early days of the 1895 season. Dan Brouthers, after his fine performance the preceding year (he drove in 128 runs and batted .347), was finally, irreversibly finished at the age of 37. Never a great glove man, Big Dan was, at this point, almost immobile at first base and Hanlon decided to replace him with George (Scoops) Carey, a weak hitter but a much better fielder. On May 8, Brouthers' 37th birthday, Hanlon sold the big first baseman to Louisville for $500 in cash. Carey batted only .261 in 1895, but his contributions on defense made up for his weak bat, as Hanlon had no doubt expected.

The 1894 Orioles were remarkably healthy all year long, but John McGraw played in only 96 games in 1895 due to illness (later diagnosed as malaria), while second baseman Heinie Reitz spent much of the season on the sidelines nursing various injuries. Hanlon, as usual, identified a replacement and put him in the lineup. The player's name was William (Kid) Gleason, who was, not surprisingly, another second-generation Irishman who, like McGraw, had an almost fanatical will to win and never backed down from a fight.

Kid Gleason, born in Camden, New Jersey, in 1866, had made his name as a pitcher in the rough coal mining towns of eastern Pennsylvania. By 1888 he had attracted the notice of Harry Wright, manager of the Phillies of the National League, who signed Gleason and put him on the mound. In 1890 he was recruited by the Players League, but his loyalty to Wright outweighed the opportunity to make more money. "Harry Wright gave me my chance two years ago when I was just a fresh kid playing coal towns, and I'm not running out on him now," he told a local newspaper reporter.[8] Gleason rewarded Wright with 38 wins in 1890 and 24 more in 1891.

Traded to St. Louis for the 1892 season, Gleason clashed with the Browns' owner, the German-born beer baron Chris von der Ahe. Kid was one of the few good players on an awful Browns team, but lasted only two seasons in St. Louis, possibly because von der Ahe found that the youngster was not an easy man to push around. One day Gleason opened his pay envelope and found his check short by a hundred dollars, due to a fine for some offense the Kid did not even know he had committed. Gleason stormed into the owner's office.

"Hello, Kid, how you vas?" asked von der Ahe in his thick accent.

"Look here, you big fat Dutch slob," shouted the enraged ballplayer. "If you don't open that safe and get me the $100 you fined me, I'll knock your block off."[9] Gleason got his money, but was traded to Baltimore in mid–1894.

Gleason's pitching arm went bad soon after the trade, but Hanlon recognized that Gleason was a talented all-around athlete, serviceable at bat and in the field. Kid was a good hitter, so Hanlon moved him into the everyday lineup, filling in for McGraw at third or Reitz at second. He also cut a swath through the league as a first-class fighter. Gleason, said John McGraw, was "the gamest and most spirited ball player I ever saw. And that doesn't except Ty Cobb.... He could lick his weight in wildcats and would prove it at the drop of a hat."[10] Needless to say, Gleason fit in well with McGraw and the other battling Orioles.

Gleason hit .309 in 1895, while Jennings, Kelley, and Keeler all batted .369 or better, as the Baltimore offense scored more than 1,000 runs for the second consecutive season. Pitcher Bill Hoffer, a German-American rookie discovered by Hanlon on one of his scouting expeditions, posted a 31–6 record and stabilized the pitching staff, while the half-Irish pitcher Arthur (Dad) Clarkson, younger brother of the recently retired John Clarkson, arrived in mid-season and won 12 of his 15 decisions. The 1895 pennant race was a spirited one, but the Orioles claimed the flag again by three games over Cleveland. The only blemish on the campaign came in the Temple Cup series, which the Orioles lost to the Spiders four games to one.

Ned Hanlon never hesitated to make changes in his personnel. Heinie Reitz and John McGraw appeared to have recovered from their maladies well enough to perform well in 1896, so the manager deemed Kid Gleason expendable. Hanlon was unhappy with Scoops Carey's offensive production, so he released Carey and traded Gleason to Washington for first base-man "Dirty Jack" Doyle, a tough Irishman who had already made a name for himself as the least-liked player in the National League. Willie Keeler, for one, still held a grudge against Doyle, who had played for the Giants during the 1894 Temple Cup series and reneged on his promise to split his winnings with Keeler. Doyle solidified the first base position, though his effect on the Orioles would be felt in the next few seasons.

Perhaps Hanlon soon wished that he had not traded Gleason, for in early 1896 McGraw fell ill with typhoid fever. He was unable to return to the lineup until August, and played in only 19 games that season. Hanlon made do, importing another Irish player in mid-season from St. Louis. Joe Quinn was a 31-year-old veteran who began his career in the Union Association during that circuit's only season of play in 1884. Quinn, who assisted his father-in-law in running a funeral home in the winter months, was a part-time player by 1896, but batted .329 while filling in capably at second, third, and the outfield. Quinn is remembered today, if at all, as the first major league player born in Australia, where his Irish parents settled before boarding a ship for America when their son was seven years old. No other Australian-born player followed Quinn into the major leagues until 1986, when infielder Craig Shipley broke in with the Los Angeles Dodgers.

McGraw's extended absence harmed the team, but the talented Orioles weathered their leader's absence, pulling away from the Cleveland Spiders late in the season and winning their third pennant in a row by 10 games. They then decided to bear down and play to win in the post-season Temple Cup series, defeating Cleveland easily to solidify their position at the top of the National League.

The Orioles were now the dominant team in baseball, and other clubs moved to copy their success. Since the Oriole manager, Ned Hanlon, and most of the key players were Irishmen, most observers credited the success of the Baltimore ballclub to its predominantly Celtic roster. New York Giants manager Bill Joyce, an Irishman who grew up playing ball on the highly competitive sandlots of St. Louis, spoke for many when he described the ethnic makeup of a winning ballclub. "Give me a good Irish infield," said Joyce, "and I will show you a good team. I don't mean that it is necessary to have them all Irish, but you want two or three quick-thinking sons of Celt to keep the Germans and others moving.

"Now you take a German," continued Joyce, "you can tell him what to do and he will do it. Take an Irishman and tell him what to do, and he is liable to give you an argument. He has his own ideas. So I have figured it out this way. Get an Irishman to do the scheming. Let him tell the Germans what to do and then you will have a great combination."[11]

The 1896 season proved to be the last pennant-winning campaign for the Orioles in the National League. The 1897 club featured McGraw, Kelley, Keeler, and Jennings at the collective peak of their Hall of Fame careers, but the revamped Boston Beaneaters were gaining ground. The Orioles and Beaneaters quickly broke away from the pack and turned the season into a two-team race for the flag, producing one of the most exciting pennant chases in National League history. Not until September 25, when Boston's Kid Nichols pitched a wild 19–10 victory over the Orioles at Baltimore, did the Beaneaters bring Baltimore's reign at the top of the league to an end.

To be sure, internal tensions among the club's Irish stars helped derail the team's pennant chances. John McGraw's demanding nature wore upon his teammates, and as one player later put it, the Oriole third baseman "had a mean way of nagging a man that worked against the success of the team." Even the usually mild-mannered Willie Keeler took exception one day to an on-field dressing down by McGraw, and a confrontation afterward in the locker room ended with McGraw and Keeler, both naked, grappling on the floor of the shower. Jack Doyle, who always enjoyed a good fight, grabbed a bat and threatened to clobber anyone who intervened. McGraw eventually yielded, but the tension grew among the players all season long. McGraw also grew snappish at Hanlon, reportedly shouting at his manager, "We made you what you are and here you go putting on airs.... You were a stiff until we boosted you!"[12]

Doyle, too, was a disruptive force on and off the field. He had not wanted to leave New York, and balked at taking orders from McGraw. Doyle had not changed the hyper-aggressive style of play that had gotten him released by Cleveland and traded by the Giants, and though he batted .354 with 101 runs batted in that season, he quickly wore out his welcome in Baltimore. In August 1897 Doyle, always willing to settle disputes with his fists, beat up umpire Thomas Lynch during an on-field argument, and he and McGraw reportedly traded punches on several occasions. "I got a bat," said McGraw after one such scrap, "and would have broken [Doyle's] jaw if manager Hanlon had not stopped me."[13] At the conclusion of the 1897 season, Hanlon traded Doyle and second baseman Heinie Reitz to Washington for first baseman Dan McGann and second sacker Gene DeMontreville, a rising star who hit .348 for the Senators the year before. DeMontreville added a dash of speed and youth to the lineup, but the dismissal of Doyle promised to help the team even more.

McGann was an interesting, and mysterious, player. Born in Kentucky in 1871, his given name was Dennis (or the Irish style Denis), but he used an older brother's name during his baseball career. His parents were Irish-born, and his father Joe worked as a stone mason. Not much more is known about McGann's background, which was probably the way he wanted it. There must have been much turmoil, and perhaps mental illness, in his family, for two of the player's siblings ended their lives by suicide, and another brother died in an accidental shooting. McGann, at six feet tall and about 190 pounds, more than held his own in the brawling department, and though he sometimes found trouble off the field, proved an effective replacement for the departed Jack Doyle.

The Irish stars of the club, despite their occasional disputes, were close friends as well as teammates. Shortly after the conclusion of the 1896 Temple Cup series, McGraw, Keeler, Jennings, Kelley, and pitcher Arlie Pond vacationed together for a month in Europe, where they visited London, Paris, Rome, and their ancestral homeland of Ireland. In March of 1897, when McGraw married a Baltimore girl named Minnie Doyle (no apparent relation to Dirty Jack), Jennings served as best man, with Keeler and Kelley as groomsmen. In October of that year, Kelley married Margaret Mahon, daughter of a prominent Baltimore politician, with Keeler as best man. McGraw and Wilbert Robinson co-owned a bowling alley in Baltimore, while McGraw and Jennings coached baseball together during the spring months at St. Bonaventure College in western New York state, receiving free tuition in lieu of pay. The Oriole club, or at least the Irish contingent, was undoubtedly the closest-knit group of players in the game at the time.

This camaraderie was an unwelcome sight to Ned Hanlon in the spring of 1898, when Kelley, Jennings, and Keeler decided to hold out together for more money. Kelley was especially adamant about his salary. He had batted .362 or better during each of the previous four seasons, establishing himself as the best all-around player on the team and one of the finest in the game. He earned the National League maximum salary of $2,400, with an extra $200 for serving as assistant captain, but wanted more now that he was married and planning a family. He refused to report for spring training, and threatened to move back to Cambridge, Massachusetts, and join his brother in a hauling and cartage business rather than play another season without a raise in pay. Kelley cared little that his salary was already at the maximum amount decreed by National League rules, as it was a poorly kept secret that players on other teams received more money under the table.

Keeler and Jennings, who were also at or near the maximum salary, were unhappy as well. Keeler had won the 1897 batting title with a mark of .432 (revised by later researchers to a still-impressive .424) and his 239 hits fell only one short of Jesse Burkett's year-old sin-

KEELER, N. Y. AMER.

Wee Willie Keeler, an Irishman from Brooklyn, won two batting titles while playing for the Orioles (Library of Congress).

gle-season record. Jennings had batted .401 in 1896, still the highest mark ever posted by a shortstop, and led the league in fielding in 1897 for the fourth year in a row. All three men were at the top of their game, and with the Orioles drawing well in 1897, both at home and on the road, the players wanted a bigger slice of the apparent profits.

Hanlon, for his part, was reluctant to raise salaries across the board, for he foresaw that the 1898 season would be a difficult one for the baseball business, both locally and nationally. The Spanish-American War turned the country's attention away from the sports news and sent thousands of young men, many of whom were baseball fans, into the military and away from the ballparks. Additionally, Hanlon and others sensed that the Baltimore fans had become jaded with success. The April home opener drew only 6,500 fans, which proved to be the largest crowd of the campaign. The Oriole team already owned the most expensive payroll in the game, and the falling attendance boded ill for the future of National League baseball in Maryland. With little money available for salary increases, Hanlon, after much effort, convinced his three Irish holdouts to sign in exchange for small raises shortly before the start of the season.

The 1898 campaign was the final one

in Baltimore for Hanlon, Kelley, Keeler, and Jennings. The club won games at a .644 clip, a good enough percentage to win the pennant in most seasons, but the Beaneaters followed up their 1897 championship with 102 wins, outpacing the Orioles by six games. Hugh Jennings batted .328, but was crippled by shoulder problems, and his arm was so sore that he could barely throw the ball to first from his shortstop position. His arm never recovered, and a series of serious beanings (including one by Amos Rusie in 1897 that nearly killed him) made Jennings a part-time player after 1898. However, McGraw, Keeler, and Kelley were still going strong, and the Orioles, with newcomers McGann and DeMontreville performing well at first and second base respectively, hoped to make another pennant charge in 1899.

Unfortunately, the Baltimore club had lost money in 1898, with home attendance dropping to less than half that of the championship seasons, and majority owner Harry von der Horst hit upon a plan to stem the tide of red ink. In February 1899, von der Horst and Ned Hanlon met with Brooklyn Dodgers owners Frederick Abell and Charles Ebbets and agreed to combine their two teams in a scheme that gave each ownership group a 50 percent stake in both clubs. Since Brooklyn was a bigger city and a better baseball market than Baltimore, the new ownership group moved Baltimore stars Willie Keeler, Joe Kelley, Hugh Jennings, Dan McGann, and several others to Brooklyn for the 1899 campaign. Hanlon, who now held a stake in the combined Baltimore-Brooklyn franchise, assumed a dual role as manager of the Dodgers and president of the Orioles.

Willie Keeler, who grew up in Brooklyn, was happy to play for his hometown team, but Joe Kelley was reluctant to follow suit. Only an appointment as captain of the club (renamed the Superbas after a popular vaudeville act), and the salary increase that came with it, persuaded the reluctant Kelley to join Hanlon in Brooklyn. John McGraw and Wilbert Robinson, however, dug in their heels and refused to leave Baltimore. Both men owned homes and had business interests there and furiously resisted efforts to induce them to play for Brooklyn. "I have gotten all the glory I can out of baseball and am not interested in getting more. I'm more interested in getting money.... Baltimore is good enough for me," said McGraw to the *Baltimore Sun*.[14] He and Robinson spent the winter months searching for investors to buy the Orioles from Hanlon and von der Horst. They failed, but remained adamant about playing in Baltimore, or nowhere, in 1899.

McGraw, whose relationship with Hanlon had become strained since the pennant-winning years, was determined to become a manager himself, and his stubborn refusal to follow his teammates to Brooklyn ultimately paid off. In early 1899, Abell and Hanlon appointed the 26-year-old McGraw as new manager of the Orioles, with Wilbert Robinson as his chief assistant. Though Hanlon and von der Horst had transferred all the best players to Brooklyn, leaving the Orioles almost bereft of talent, McGraw immediately got down to business, assembling a collection of no-name players and putting them through a grueling spring training regimen. The new Orioles responded to his leadership, and many National League observers were surprised when McGraw's band of unknowns won two of three practice games from Hanlon's Brooklyn team in Augusta, Georgia.

Like Hanlon, McGraw was an outstanding judge of talent with a penchant for signing Irishmen like himself. One future Hall of Fame player that he discovered was Joe McGinnity, a 28-year-old right-handed pitcher who had played for Peoria in the Western Association in 1898. McGinnity, whose original family name was McGinty, was born in Illinois but moved to the Indian Territory, which later became part of the state of Oklahoma. He had worked for his father-in-law in an iron foundry, which led to his nickname, "Iron Man." His easy sidearm motion put little strain on his arm, and McGraw installed McGinnity as his staff ace.

The Iron Man paid dividends, pitching 366 innings and winning 28 games in his first major league season.

McGinnity, a quick-fisted, no-nonsense Irishman, was McGraw's kind of player. During his minor league career, he had owned a saloon in Springfield, Illinois, and acted as his own bouncer. McGinnity's fights with opposing players were the stuff of legend, and he served several suspensions for on-field incidents during his ten seasons of major league play. His career almost ended in 1901 when he spat in the face of umpire Tommy Connolly, after which the pitcher escaped with a 12-game suspension only when he agreed to apologize publicly to the arbiter. A few years later, McGinnity beat up Pittsburgh's Heinie Peitz and drew a 10-game ban after National League president Harry Pulliam accused the pitcher of "attempting to make the ball park a slaughterhouse."[15]

While McGraw assembled his new Orioles from scratch, Hanlon had an embarrassment of riches to work with in Brooklyn. The club had finished in tenth place the year before, but added Keeler, Kelley, Jennings, and McGann from the Baltimore club. They joined an existing crew of Irishmen that included veterans such as catchers Duke Farrell and Deacon McGuire, second baseman Tom Daly, and pitchers Bill Kennedy and "Wild Bill" Donovan. The Superbas, like the champion Orioles of several years before, were heavily Irish in character and were exactly the kind of team that Ned Hanlon preferred to lead. They spoke Hanlon's language, responded to his leadership, and quickly turned the pennant race into a runaway. The defending champions from Boston tried to keep up with the Superbas, but Brooklyn's 20–2 streak in August and early September ended the race by Labor Day.

Hanlon's star-laden Brooklyn club coasted to the pennant, as expected, but McGraw's no-name Baltimore team surprised the league by running in the first division all season long. McGraw batted .391, played a fine third base, managed with flair and passion, baited and intimidated the umpires, and got the best out his talent. He also pulled off several good trades, getting ex–Oriole Gene DeMontreville from Washington (to which Hanlon had traded him after the 1898 season) to firm up his infield. The 1899 Orioles ended the season in fourth position, and had McGraw not left the lineup in late August after the sudden death of his young wife Minnie from appendicitis, the club might have finished even higher.

The 1899 Orioles were an exciting, hustling ballclub, thanks to McGraw, but attendance remained stagnant, and the team lost money yet again. When the National League decided that winter to eliminate its four least profitable clubs, the Orioles found themselves on the chopping block. McGraw fought to keep the Orioles alive, but the league magnates could not be persuaded to allow the club, which had been a perennial money-loser, to continue operations. In late 1899 the league disbanded the Baltimore franchise, along with those in Cleveland, Louisville, and Washington, and the players of the four defunct teams were distributed around the league. The championship club that Ned Hanlon built, and that John McGraw tried his best to keep afloat, was no more.

McGraw and Wilbert Robinson, still adamantly refusing to play for Brooklyn, were shunted off to St. Louis, where they spent an uncomfortable season playing for their old Cleveland Spiders rival Patsy Tebeau. Joe McGinnity and several other ex–Orioles moved over to Brooklyn, where Hanlon directed the Superbas to another pennant in 1900, but a war between the National League and the new American circuit loomed on the horizon. When it was over, three years later, John McGraw's star was on the rise, while Ned Hanlon, the architect of the brawling, battling Oriole champions of the 1890s, was unable to repeat his success in the new century. McGraw had many pennants and World Series victories ahead of him, but Hanlon, his mentor, never won another title.

Hanlon's final seven seasons as a major league manager were uneventful and disappointing. The Brooklyn club was severely damaged by player defections to the new American League beginning in 1901, and the team's winning percentage fell in each of the next five seasons. In 1905 the club dropped all the way to last place, winning barely 30 percent of its games. Hanlon then took over the managerial reins of the Cincinnati Reds, replacing his old Baltimore outfielder Joe Kelley as field leader, but the undermanned Reds finished in sixth place in both 1906 and 1907. Hanlon's magic was gone, so after the 1907 campaign he resigned his position with the Reds and returned to Baltimore, his adopted home town. Still, baseball insiders never lost respect for his talent. "I always rated Ned Hanlon as the greatest leader baseball ever had," said Hanlon's old catcher, Connie Mack. "I don't believe any man lived who knew as much baseball as he did."[16]

After a brief ownership stint in the Federal League in 1914 and 1915, the man they called "Foxy Ned" left baseball for good and retired, a wealthy man, to his home near Baltimore. He kept in touch with the game and could not help but notice that he had spawned a group of baseball's finest managers, most of them Irish and all of whom learned their strategy and leadership skills from him. Four of his Oriole stars of the 1890s (John McGraw, Wilbert Robinson, Kid Gleason, and Hugh Jennings) managed pennant winners, 16 in all, during the first three decades of the 20th century. Ned Hanlon outlived them all, and when he died in 1937, he was buried in New Cathedral Cemetery in Baltimore, not far from the graves of two of his most famous pupils, McGraw and Robinson.

8

The Heavenly Twins and
the Boston Irish

Boston's National League team, known as the Red Stockings or Red Caps in its early days and the Beaneaters afterward, was one of the most successful franchises in baseball during the first 19 years of its existence. Under founder Harry Wright, the club won four National Association pennants in a row from 1872 to 1875, then joined the National League and won flags in 1877, 1878, and 1883. The success of the club in this city of immigrants helped spread the popularity of the sport throughout New England and attracted fans from the next several generations of Irish-Americans. In a city with a large and ever-growing Irish-American population, the team featured many stars of Irish descent, none more famous or popular than Mike Kelly, the "King of Ballplayers," who arrived in Boston with much fanfare in the spring of 1887.

Mike (King) Kelly was a charismatic, multitalented catcher and outfielder who had led the Chicago White Stockings to five pennants in seven years beginning in 1880. Born to Irish immigrants in Lansingburgh (now part of Troy), New York, Kelly had grown up in Paterson, New Jersey, and played amateur and semipro ball until signed by the Cincinnati Reds in 1878. After two years in the Queen City, he joined Cap Anson's Chicago White Stockings and, with a host of other Irish-American stars, took control of the National League. The White Stockings won three consecutive pennants beginning in 1880, and, after Boston and Providence took the next two flags, Kelly and company recaptured the championship in 1885 and 1886. The handsome, mustachioed Kelly, a two-time batting champion, was not only one of the game's best players, but also the first true matinee idol in baseball. The Irish fans, whose numbers increased with each passing season, saw Mike Kelly as one of their own, and thousands of them, in Chicago and elsewhere, flocked to the ballparks to cheer the "King of Ballplayers."

Kelly reveled in the adoration he received from the fans, and enjoyed bantering with the folks in the bleacher seats. Playing right field in St. Louis on Queen Victoria's birthday in 1886, Kelly turned to the predominantly Irish-American attendees in the bleachers and taunted them. "So yer Kerry Patchers, eh?" he said. "Well, this is the 24th of May! God save the Queen! I'm coming up yer way tonight and start an Orange lodge. I expect all of yez ter join up."[1] He was so popular that he could get away with it, and his apparently carefree attitude toward the game and genuine charisma made the Irish fans admire him all the more.

He was also such a disciplinary problem that Al Spalding, the Chicago team president, was eager to rid himself of the game's biggest star after the 1886 campaign. Kelly had batted .388 and won his second batting title that year, but his off-field behavior had grown so troublesome that Spalding hired detectives to keep tabs on Kelly and the other White Stockings who followed his lead. Spalding and his manager, Cap Anson, were weary not only of Kelly's drinking and nighttime escapades, but also of his effect on his teammates, especially the younger ones. Spalding and Anson decided to break up their championship team after the 1886 season, and the Triumvirs were only too happy to take "King of Ballplayers" off their hands.

J. B. Billings, the Boston club treasurer, worked hard to persuade his fellow Triumvirs (Arthur Soden and William Conant) to pay Chicago the sum of $10,000 for Kelly. His efforts succeeded, and on February 14, 1887, the Beaneaters completed the transfer of Kelly in the largest player transaction in baseball history up to that time. Several years later, Billings recalled the excitement occasioned by the addition of Kelly to the Boston lineup:

> The advent of Kelly in the Boston team, created an enthusiasm among those who have followed its career for years such as would follow the acquisition of no other player in the profession. Everybody knows that the Chicago Club has always been one of the best drawing cards of the League in Boston, and this has been due largely to the presence of Kelly ... the good-natured raillery which has invariably greeted Lieutenant Mike on his appearance at the South End grounds has been caused by his good nature, while using every effort and taking advantage of every point to win. Nowhere has Kelly more friends than in Boston, and they will receive him with enthusiasm which ought to make him play ball even better than he ever did before, if such a thing were possible.[2]

One problem, however, was Kelly's desire to be named captain of the Beaneaters. He had chafed under the strict rule of Anson during his seven-year tenure in Chicago, and the King believed himself ready to be a field leader. John Morrill was both manager and captain of the club, but Kelly's presence dictated a change in leadership that needed to be made carefully. In the end, the Triumvirs decided that Kelly would direct the team on the field, while Morrill would remain in charge at all other times. "No better captain can be found for a winning team than John Morrill," explained Billings, "but he is of so sensitive a nature that during the time of defeat he does not play the game of which he is capable. No man is more respected on the ball field than John Morrill, and he will still manage the nine, having entire charge of the men at all times, except when they are in their uniforms. As captain, Kelly cannot fail to inspire every man in the field to play ball all the time to do his very best to win."[3]

This arrangement was doomed to fail, as Kelly soon clashed with Morrill over every issue imaginable. Morrill, still the starting first baseman for the Beaneaters, appeared to resent taking orders from the newcomer Kelly, while Kelly was disinclined to submit to anyone's authority off the field. His great popularity in Boston made him the most powerful member of the club, and although the local papers often criticized his behavior, the fans were solidly in Kelly's corner. "Trouble was Kelly's shadow," said Boston writer Harold Kaese, "and it was a dark day for Honest John Morrill when that shadow fell on him."[4]

Though the Beaneaters repeated their fifth-place finish in 1887, the Irish fans hardly seemed to mind, so thrilled were they with Kelly's presence on their ballclub. They showered him with gifts, including a horse and carriage to convey him to the ballpark each day, innumerable trophies, floral arrangements, and gold jewelry. Crowds of people followed "King" Kelly from his home to the South End Grounds, and sometimes became so enthusiastic that they unhitched the horses from his carriage and pulled the vehicle themselves. In 1889, his Boston admirers provided Kelly and his wife Agnes with a fully furnished house to show their appreciation. No athlete in any sport had ever been so lionized, and it can be said that hero-worship of professional ballplayers began with Mike Kelly and his mostly Irish fans in the Hub.

The Boston pitching staff was weak, so in April of 1888 the Triumvirs bought John Clarkson, the best pitcher in the game, from the White Stockings for $10,000, the same sum they had paid for Kelly one year earlier. Clarkson, a good friend of Kelly from their Chicago days, completed the "$20,000 battery," providing another attraction for the Irish fans. To appease John Morrill, who still had his supporters despite his declining production, the club restored him to the captaincy, abandoning the two-leader arrangement of the previous season. Still, the Beaneaters finished fourth, even with Clarkson winning 33 games and Kelly batting .318, while tensions between Morrill and Kelly continued unabated.

Another longtime Irish-American favorite, Jack Burdock, saw his career end ignominiously that season. Burdock had joined the club in 1878, its third season in the National League, and had held down the second base position ever since. He had played a major role in the 1883 pennant chase, but injuries had dragged him down since then, as had a serious beaning at the hands of Tim Keefe in August of 1886. By 1887, he was only a shell of the hitter that he once was. He had begun drinking to excess, and rooming with Mike Kelly on the road only exacerbated this problem. In May of 1888, the Triumvirs released Burdock after 11 seasons in Boston, removing one of John Morrill's chief friends and supporters from the club.

At season's end, Kelly wrote a letter to the *Sporting Times*, in which he stated that Morrill "will not in any way be connected with the club [in 1889]. If he is, I will not wear a Boston uniform. Some may think this is idle talk, but nevertheless it goes." Morrill, for his part, complained about Kelly's status. "The trouble with 'Kel' is that he is getting too much money," said the captain to *Boston Globe* writer Tim Murnane.[5]

Morrill's position was weakened by the fact that, after 13 seasons on the team, his usefulness as a player was rapidly dissipating. He batted only .198 in 1888, an incredibly low average for a first baseman in any era, and it appeared that his career was coming to a close at the age of 34. Still, he defiantly played every game that season, though he drove in only 39 runs and sported the lowest slugging percentage of any Boston starter. He also held out for a higher salary before the 1889 campaign, causing the Triumvirs to abandon their loyalty to him. The team was not big enough for both Morrill and Kelly, and the Triumvirs came down firmly on the King's side when they ordered Morrill to head up the reserve team on the annual Fast Day exhibition contest, with Kelly handling the starters. Morrill pointedly refused, and was traded to Washington the next day, ending his long tenure with the club.

"The directors saw yesterday that the patrons of the game are divided between Morrill and Kelly," said team president Arthur Soden in a statement. "It came down to who should go. Morrill has many friends in this city and is a perfect gentleman. Kelly is a ballplayer. So it was for us to choose between the men, and we picked out Kelly as the one who could win the most games."[6] Jim Hart, who had led Milwaukee in 1888, was hired as manager, and Kelly became the captain. As Hart had never played in the major leagues and had produced only middling results in the minors, the Beaneaters became Kelly's team. Hart was content to stay in the background and leave the decision-making to Kelly.

The Beaneaters added another Irish star in the person of Dan Brouthers, recently purchased from the disbanded Detroit club. Brouthers, the leading power hitter in baseball at the time, added a jolt of energy to the Boston lineup, and with John Clarkson compiling one of his finest seasons, the Beaneaters grabbed the early lead in the pennant race under Kelly's direction. They held first place until September, when the defending champion Giants made a charge and passed Boston in the standings. The two teams, both powered mainly by Irishmen, swapped the lead for two weeks before the Giants lost to Pittsburgh on October 1. The Beaneaters defeated Cleveland that day behind Clarkson, and Boston regained the lead by percentage points.

However, October 2 was a black day for the Beaneaters. Mike Kelly had gone on what one newspaper called "a jollification during last night with several theatrical friends,"[7] and was too hung over to play the pivotal game against the Spiders in Cleveland that afternoon. He sat on the bench, shivering under an overcoat, as his teammates carried on without their captain and guiding force. Worst of all, he caused an ugly scene during a dispute with the umpire, a man named McQuaid, and was dragged out of the park by the Cleveland police. Jim Hart quickly bought Kelly a ticket to get back onto the grounds, but the local cops would not allow the King to return. He stood outside helplessly as the Beaneaters lost to Cleveland by a 7–1 score, surrendering the league lead to the Giants once again. Three days later, the Giants clinched the pennant when the overworked John Clarkson failed in a bid for his 50th win of the season, losing a 6–3 decision to Pittsburgh.

It had been a disappointing end to a promising campaign, but the race was soon forgotten as the Beaneaters, and indeed the entire National League, faced a fight for survival. Four years before, the players had formed a trade association, called the Brotherhood of Professional Base Ball Players. The Brotherhood chafed under the autocratic rule of the club owners, and at the conclusion of the 1889 season the Brotherhood formed its own circuit, the Players League. Within weeks, most of the National League clubs were decimated by player defections, with the Boston Beaneaters especially hard hit. The team, which relied so heavily on Irish-American stars such as Kelly, Dan Brouthers, and others, saw almost all of the best players decamp for the new league. Recently hired manager Frank Selee, who had won several pennants in the minor leagues but had never led a team in the majors, was faced with the task of building a new Boston team almost from scratch.

John Clarkson, who had nearly pitched the 1889 Boston team to the pennant with his 49–19 record, was one of the few National League stars who did not jump to the Players League. He had joined the Brotherhood and voted in some of their meetings during the fall of 1889, but when the Triumvirs offered the half–Irish pitcher an unprecedented $25,000, three-year contract, Clarkson decided to remain with the Beaneaters. His former Brotherhood mates cried foul, labeling Clarkson a "traitor," and the incident colored the rest of the pitcher's major league career. Even Mike Kelly, one of Clarkson's best friends, publicly condemned the pitcher for his defection. Catcher Charlie Bennett, a solid and well-respected veteran, also stayed with the established league, giving Frank Selee a first-rate battery around which to build.

Selee, who had spent the previous season at Omaha in the Western League, filled the holes in his club by importing players who had impressed him in the minors. He brought Charles (Kid) Nichols, a 20-year-old pitcher who had won 39 games in 1889, from Omaha, and signed left fielder Bobby Lowe from Milwaukee and shortstop Herman Long from Kansas City. All three claimed German descent, but Irishmen remained in the majority. James (Chippy) McGarr, a former Philadelphia third baseman, and outfielder Marty Sullivan, who had played for Cap Anson in Chicago two years before, were two new Beaneaters of Irish heritage, while another outfielder, 25-year-old rookie Patrick (Patsy) Donovan, was a native of the island, having been born in County Cork. Selee also scored a coup when he signed the batting champion of the American Association, Tommy Tucker, to play first base.

Tucker was one of most colorful and popular players of the 1890s. He was born in 1863 in Holyoke, Massachusetts, a mill town that was a magnet for Irishmen looking for work in the burgeoning local paper industry. Most of the workers were Irish immigrants, as were Tommy's parents, and by the age of 12 Tommy had left school to join his older siblings at work in one of Holyoke's many paper mills. However, Holyoke was baseball-mad, and the local team, the Shamrocks, was a source of pride for the immigrants and sons of immigrants in the town. Holyoke had already sent several young men to the major leagues, and Tommy Tucker was determined to follow their example rather than spend his life in the mills. In 1887, after three seasons in the minors, he landed in the American Association as a first baseman for the Baltimore Orioles.

"Noisy Tom" Tucker was a good hitter, winning the Association batting title in 1889 with a .372 average, but was best known as a foghorn-voiced, aggressive battler. He was a popular first base coach, celebrated for his humorous asides to the fans while rattling opponents and arguing enthusiastically with umpires in "a voice like a steam calliope," said *The New York Times*. Opposing pitchers hated him, causing Tucker to lead the league in being hit by pitches in five different seasons, but the home fans enjoyed his hustle and attitude. After one rain-soaked game in 1893, the *Boston Globe* reported that Tucker "looked like an invited guest to a boiler explosion. His clothes were covered with mud, but he felt good — his fielding bordered on the phenomenal, and the spectators cheered him all through the game for the interest and life he put into the boys."[8] Sam Crane, a former player turned sportswriter, lauded his animated style of play. "Tom Tucker's earnestness is refreshing," wrote Crane. "He grabs at thrown balls as if to say 'Come here, I want to eat you.' And he eats them."[9]

Other National League teams held little love for Tucker, and his aggressive baserunning and defensive play drew comparisons to another Irishman, the hated "Dirty Jack" Doyle. Tucker was a master at blocking runners off the first base bag, using elbows and knees as weapons, often sitting on the bag to prevent the runner from touching it. He refined the art of tripping runners when the umpire wasn't looking to a science, and was never reluctant to trample infielders while running the bases. In May of 1894, Baltimore third baseman John McGraw kicked Tucker in the head as he slid into the base, igniting a brawl between the Beaneaters and the Orioles that continued even as smoke billowed from the stands. A discarded cigar or cigarette probably set some trash ablaze while the fans' attention was riveted on the fight, and Boston's South End Grounds burned down, along with 170 other buildings in the neighborhood. Tucker's relations with the Orioles were especially unpleasant; in 1898, the *St. Louis Star* reported that "[Hugh] Jennings complains that when playing off first Mr. Tucker resents his attempts to return suddenly by putting his knee in his face or else sitting down on him. Mr. Tucker says that Mr. Jennings always returns spikes first and with malicious intent."[10]

While Selee labored to build the Beaneaters, Boston's Players League club, called the Reds, fortified its lineup with several popular Irish-American stars. Slugger Dan Brouthers, the well-traveled veteran first baseman, provided the power, while Joe Quinn, a second-generation Irishman and the first major leaguer born in Australia, manned second base. The catching chores were shared by the little-known Morgan Murphy and the game's most popular player, Mike Kelly, who had been offered the sum of $10,000 to desert the Players League and return to the National. After a short period of reflection, Kelly turned down the offer and threw in his lot with the Brotherhood. One surprising presence on the club was John Morrill, the former Beaneater manager who was driven off the team by Kelly after the 1888 season. Morrill did some scouting work for the Reds and also played in two games.

Kelly owned a long history of off-field incidents, drunken behavior, and curfew-breaking, and it surprised most observers when the new club announced that Kelly would manage the Reds in 1890. There may not have been a less likely candidate for a manager's post in the history of the game, but somehow Kelly was able to get his men to play winning baseball. He led by example with a .326 average while playing six different positions on the field, and kept the players loose with practical jokes and a relaxed approach to discipline. The pennant race was close, with the Reds holding first by only one game on August 20, but a 22–4 streak by Kelly's charges solidified their hold on the lead. The Reds wound up winning the first, and only, Players League pennant by six and a half games over Brooklyn.

The 1890 Beaneaters finished in fifth position for Frank Selee, but more importantly, the Players League failed after only one season. The Reds had drawn well, most likely winning the battle of the box office with the established Beaneaters, but the new league was unable to survive and collapsed in October of 1890. However, the American Association was still standing, though just barely, so almost all of the Reds moved as a unit to the Association for the 1891 season. Most of the new Boston Reds were the same men who had won the Players League flag, with the addition of two more Irish stars in center fielder Hugh Duffy and catcher-third baseman Duke Farrell.

Mike Kelly transferred his services to the Association as well, but not with Boston. He was offered the manager's position with a new team in Pendleton, Ohio, outside of Cincinnati, where he had begun his major league career 13 years before. The team did not even use the name Cincinnati; they were simply known as "Kelly's Killers," and were one of the wildest, most carefree clubs in the game's history. Perhaps Kelly believed that team discipline was unnecessary, as his Players League club had won a pennant without it, but Kelly's Killers did not have the talent to overcome poor behavior both on and off the field. The team was also hampered by the illegality of Sunday baseball in Pendleton, and on several consecutive weekends, the Killers began a Sunday game, only to be arrested and marched down to the local police station. The authorities booked Kelly and his men, after which the players returned to the ballpark and resumed the game as if nothing had happened.

As the season wore on, it appeared that Kelly and his charges were more interested in betting on horse races at a nearby track than in winning baseball games. Kelly's managerial magic evaporated, and the Killers quickly sank to the bottom of the league. Perhaps Kelly's popularity did not extend far outside of Boston, for in August, after eight losses in a nine-game stretch before tiny crowds, Kelly's Killers disbanded. The King, suddenly a free agent, then joined his old Players League mates on the Boston Reds.

Selee's mixture of Irishmen and Germans kept the Beaneaters in the National League race, but the return of King Kelly in late August turned the tide for Boston. Kelly played only four games for the Boston Reds before switching teams again, abandoning the sinking Association for a triumphant return to the National League. Though he batted only .231 for the Beaneaters, Kelly's presence gave the team and fans an emotional lift. In September, an 18–0 streak, with one tie, vaulted the Beaneaters past Cap Anson's Chicago club and into the lead, which they retained until the end of the season. The 1891 pennant was Boston's first in the National League in eight years. The Reds of the Association, despite losing Kelly to the Beaneaters, won the AA pennant, the last in the circuit's history.

The Beaneaters grew even stronger in 1892, after the demise of the Association brought two Irish-American stars to Selee's team. Hugh Duffy, a native New Englander who captained the Reds in 1891, signed on to play center field, and the Boston-born Tommy McCarthy left the St. Louis Browns to play right for his hometown team. Duffy, one of the best young hitters in the game, had tied teammate Duke Farrell for the Association lead in runs batted in during the 1891 season. He brought a dash of power and fielding talent to the Boston lineup, while McCarthy, a fine base stealer and leadoff man, added much-needed speed to the attack.

Boston had an easier path to the pennant in 1892, when the National League played under a split-season arrangement. The league decreed that the winners of the first half of the season would face the winners of the second in a post-season series in October. Boston, led by Duffy, McCarthy, and 35-game winners Kid Nichols and Jack Stivetts, won the first half easily, then coasted through the next few months as the Cleveland Spiders won the second portion. So dominant were the Beaneaters that in mid-season, the club decided that it no longer needed two of its most celebrated Irish veteran stars, Mike Kelly and John Clarkson. In a cost-cutting move, the Triumvirs released both men, and though Kelly remained with the club after accepting a large salary cut, Clarkson's career in Boston was over. He signed on with Cleveland, where he spent two unhappy seasons before retiring at the age of 33.

Mike Kelly was still a popular presence on the club, especially with the Irish fans. However, his two-year absence from the National League had allowed Frank Selee to build the team in his own image, and the Beaneaters were now Selee's club, not Kelly's. The erstwhile "King of Ballplayers" batted only .189 that season, and with Charlie Bennett and Charlie Ganzel handling the catching chores, the aging Kelly had no position to play. Though only 34 years old, Kelly was finished as a player. He departed after the 1892 campaign, leaving the team in the hands of Selee and his group of young, aggressive Beaneaters.

Duffy and McCarthy, under Selee's direction, worked to devise new strategies and refine old ones. McCarthy brought his trap play, in which he would purposely drop a fly ball and force out the confused baserunners, to Boston, while he and Duffy resurrected the hit and run, which had been used in prior years but had fallen out of favor by the 1890s. Boston had traditionally employed the sacrifice bunt as a way to move runners along, but when hitting became easier in 1893 (after the National League moved the mound ten feet father from the plate), the Beaneaters turned to the hit and run. This maneuver, executed by speedy players with excellent bat control, moved the runners without giving up outs.

McCarthy, with Selee's support and approval, introduced additional new tactics. He played a short right field, so short that he often took part in infield rundowns. He would often pretend to miss a throw and turn around to hustle after it; the runner would then try to advance and be easily thrown out. Tommy probably invented the delayed steal, in which he would set out for the next base if the catcher lobbed the ball back to the pitcher too casually. Using his facility for sign stealing, he could tell what kind of pitch the opposing hurler was likely to throw, and communicate it to his teammates using whistles and code words. The fake bunt, in which McCarthy would square around to bunt and quickly draw his bat back for a full swing, was another weapon to intimidate opposing fielders. After most of the league's third basemen were victimized by the maneuver, infielders kept their distance and allowed McCarthy more room to drop real bunts. Tommy received so much positive press for his intelligent approach to the game that some papers referred to any especially clever play as a "Tommy McCarthy."

Selee had gathered a diverse mix of ethnicities. The Irish were well represented by Duffy, McCarthy, and Tucker, while the German presence was embodied by Lowe, Nichols, and Long, among others. The captain, Billy Nash, fell into neither group, as he was one of the few Jewish ballplayers in the major leagues at the time, and most of the other Beaneaters claimed English descent. They worked together with intelligence and drive, and while Tommy Tucker remained an old-style brawler, the Boston club gained renown for using more brains than brawn to win ballgames. They made the 1893 pennant chase a runaway, winning their third successive flag by five games over Pittsburgh in a race that was never really close. "The Bostons could have beaten any all-star nine the league could have put together this season," said Giants manager John Ward.[11]

Hugh Duffy, who "does nothing but play ball, save money, build houses, and go to church,"[12] according to *The New York Times*, was at the pinnacle of his game by 1893. He had long since proved his first major league manager, Cap Anson, wrong about his talent, and his partnership with Tommy McCarthy moved the Boston papers to dub the two Irish outfielders the "Heavenly Twins." Duffy was already maturing into an on-field leader with his eye on a future managing career. He and McCarthy became partners off the field as well when they opened a billiards parlor and bowling alley together in Boston's South End, not far from the ballpark, in 1894. The place became a popular hangout for players and fans, and the on-field success of the two ballplayers only added to the patronage. Despite his foray into bar ownership, Duffy rarely drank and

Left fielder and captain Hugh Duffy. By 1898, he and Jimmy Collins were the only two Irish-American stars left on the Beaneaters (Library of Congress).

remained a serious-minded individual. A direct, sometimes blunt man, Duffy explained his theory of hitting in simple terms. "It just comes natural," he insisted. "You just walk up there and hit it. That's all."[13]

Jimmy Bannon and Cozy Dolan were two more Irish ballplayers who proved popular with the Boston fans during the mid–1890s. Only 23 years old in 1894 (though, for some unknown reason, his nickname was "Foxy Grandpa"), Bannon was a native of Amesbury, Massachusetts, and a product of the College of the Holy Cross in Worcester. Bannon, an outfielder, had played briefly for the St. Louis Browns in 1893, batting .336 in 26 games, before arriving in Boston. Patrick Henry "Cozy" Dolan, a left-handed pitcher, joined the club in 1895 to provide support for stars Kid Nichols and Jack Stivetts. He was a product of the Irish-American baseball scene in Cambridge, Massachusetts, which had already sent Tim Keefe, the Clarkson brothers, and several other fine players to the major leagues.

At five feet and five inches in height, Bannon seemed too small to be a ballplayer, even in that era, but his hustle and fine hitting made him a particular favorite of the Irish fans in the bleachers. On Opening Day, in his first game for Boston, he belted two hits and scored three runs, "but showed that he had much to learn to cover right field ... in the face of the sun" after he committed two errors, according to one of the local newspapers.[14] He was part of an all–Irish outfield with Hugh Duffy and Tommy McCarthy, and although Bannon was the weakest fielder of the three, his popularity rivaled theirs during the next few seasons. Dolan, larger than Bannon at five feet and ten inches, became the third starter on the club. When he was on the mound, he gave the Beaneaters an Irish majority on the field with the three outfielders, first sacker Tommy Tucker, and himself.

Some believed the Beaneaters to be invincible, but Boston's title run ended in 1894 in a season filled with tragedy, disaster, and disharmony in the clubhouse. In January of that year, the Beaneaters lost catcher Charlie Bennett to a railroad accident that left the veteran wheel-chair-bound for the rest of his life. In May the Boston ballpark (which the Triumvirs had not adequately insured) burned, necessitating a scramble to find a place to play and causing more turmoil for a club that was already struggling to stay in the pennant race. The season was noted for great performances, including Hugh Duffy's record .440 batting average and a 25-game hitting streak by Jimmy Bannon, but injuries and mediocre pitching behind aces Kid Nichols and Jack Stivetts spelled trouble for Selee's team. Boston held first place as late as August 20, but a subsequent losing streak dropped the club to third at season's end.

Missing out on the championship after winning three in a row damaged Boston team morale, and tensions between the Irish Catholics and the non–Irish Protestants began to escalate during the 1895 season. One target of player criticism was Tommy McCarthy, once renowned for his speed, who reported to camp so overweight that his teammates nicknamed him "Pudge." A leg injury, probably exacerbated by his weight, slowed McCarthy down and kept him on the bench during the early part of the season, much to the disgust of several of his teammates. The Beaneaters fought mightily to stay above the .500 mark in the early going, as internal strife and bickering became more heated with each passing week. The team, despite Selee's efforts, divided into two camps based on ethnic lines, and the teamwork that had defined the Beaneaters during the pennant-winning years disappeared. Hugh Duffy, who harbored aspirations for the captaincy that could not be fulfilled as long as third baseman Billy Nash held the position, began to snipe at Nash, while Nash and his infield partner, shortstop Herman Long, stopped speaking. The fans could hear the bickering on the field, and though Selee fought to keep these highly competitive ballplayers from turning on each other, the effort proved futile.

Tensions came to a head on a road trip in late May, when an on-field argument between McCarthy and pitcher Jack Stivetts led to a bloody fistfight in a Louisville hotel room. The incident made the papers, both locally and nationally, as the 1895 campaign turned sour for the former champions. As if that were not bad enough, the "Heavenly Twins," Duffy and McCarthy, began to argue on and off the field. Duffy was still a rising star, while McCarthy was fading quickly, and their different career trajectories likely added to the tensions between them. It is also possible that the strain of running a business together put pressure on their friendship. Whatever the cause, the magic between the "Heavenly Twins" was gone, and the club struggled to stay in the first division all season long. The finished in fifth place, 16 and a half games behind pennant-winning Baltimore.

Selee recognized that the team needed a quick overhaul, and went to work immediately after the 1895 season ended. Tommy McCarthy could no longer provide the speed Selee desired at the top of his lineup, so in November of that year the Beaneaters sold McCarthy to Brooklyn for $6,000. Happily, McCarthy and Duffy worked out their differences, and apparently decided that their business partnership was interfering with their friendship. McCarthy bought out Duffy's share of the bar and bowling alley in late 1895 and renamed the place "McCarthy's." He operated the establishment for another 14 years, and he and Duffy remained close friends for the rest of their lives.

To replace McCarthy as a base-stealing threat, Selee traded his aging third baseman and captain, Billy Nash, to Philadelphia for the speedy center fielder, Billy Hamilton. Selee then moved his new field captain, Hugh Duffy, from center to left to make room for Hamilton. The 30-year-old Hamilton, a Scotsman from New Jersey, was every bit as aggressive on the bases as McCarthy had been, and Selee gave him free rein on the basepaths. This trade turned out to be one of the most successful in Boston history, as Nash soon entered the decline phase of his career, while "Sliding Billy" added needed energy to the Beaneaters. Nash, who was appointed manager of the Phillies upon his arrival, was replaced in Boston by rookie third baseman Jimmy Collins.

Collins, like several other Beaneaters, was the son of Irish immigrants. He was born in Niagara Falls, New York, and grew up in Buffalo, where his father worked as a railroad policeman. Jimmy starred as a shortstop and third baseman on the Buffalo sandlots as a young man, but also attended business school and worked for the Lackawanna Railroad. When the Buffalo Bisons of the Eastern League offered Jimmy a contract in 1893, he agreed to sign only after his supervisor at the railroad promised to hire him back if he failed to make good. Two years later, Jimmy advanced to the National League and left the Lackawanna Railroad behind.

Jimmy made his debut with the Beaneaters early in 1895 as a right fielder, as the third base and shortstop positions were held by veteran stars Billy Nash and Herman Long respectively. Selee, disappointed with Jimmy Bannon's poor fielding, hoped that Collins would provide an improvement with the glove, but the rookie found it difficult to adjust to major league play. He batted and fielded poorly, drawing boos from the impatient fans who chanted "We want Bannon!" at Collins and Selee. After a few weeks, the Boston manager decided that Collins needed seasoning in a less stressful environment, so he loaned the youngster to last-place Louisville for the remainder of the 1895 campaign.

In Louisville, Collins developed the fielding technique that revolutionized third base play. He started his Louisville sojourn in the outfield, but on May 31, after the Orioles bunted the hapless Colonels to death for a 16–6 victory in the first game of a doubleheader, manager John McCloskey put young Collins at third base for the second contest. Some say that the veteran Dan Brouthers, a former Oriole who had been sold to Louisville several weeks before, suggested the move.

Collins had been waiting for this opportunity, for he had been practicing a new way to field bunts. When Baltimore's Hugh Jennings, taking pity on a fellow Irishman, clapped Jimmy on the back and promised that the Orioles would not bunt against him that afternoon, Collins replied, "That's all right, Hughie. Bunt 'em down to me and I'll show you something!"[15] The Orioles decided to take the rookie up on his offer. When Baltimore came to bat in the first inning, they saw Collins playing an extremely shallow third base. "I came to the conclusion there was only one solution to this bunting game," said Collins many years later. "A third baseman had to give himself a chance to get those fast guys. Once around the circuit, you knew who would bunt and who wouldn't. You knew McGraw and Keeler were bunters. So I played them on the edge of the grass."[16]

The first batter, John McGraw, dropped a bunt down the third base line. Collins swooped in, grabbed the ball with his bare hand, and threw underhanded to first, beating McGraw by a few steps. Willie Keeler, a faster runner,

Jimmy Collins, king of third basemen and hero to the Boston Irish (author's collection).

tried the same thing, but Collins threw Wee Willie out as well. "I had to throw out four bunters in a row before the Orioles quit bunting that afternoon,"[17] recalled Collins long afterward. Though Louisville lost the game, Jimmy Collins emerged as a star that day, and the Beaneaters were happy to bring him back to Boston at season's end. "Just one word of warning might not be amiss," wrote *Boston Globe* columnist Tim Murnane to team ownership that November. "Never lose your hold on young Collins."[18]

With Collins established at third and Hugh Duffy assuming the captaincy in place of the departed Billy Nash, the Beaneaters rose a notch to fourth place in 1896. Selee recognized that more new talent was needed if the team was to return to contention, especially after outfielder Jimmy Bannon, a .350 hitter in 1895, saw his average fall by 99 points in 1896. Bannon should have been entering his prime, but his production dropped off so quickly and inexplicably that at season's end the Beaneaters released him. Despite his .320 career batting average, Bannon never played again in the major leagues. Pitcher Cozy Dolan, who won 11 games in 1895, was another Irish Beaneater whose future in Boston looked bleak. He made only six appearances in 1896 while battling an arm ailment that threatened to prematurely end his career.

Once again, Frank Selee saw an opportunity to build Boston into a contender, and he decided to eschew the brawling style of baseball that had helped Baltimore win three pennants in a row beginning in 1894. The National League had already taken some small steps to curb on-field rowdiness, passing a rule in 1895 against "boisterous coaching," the steady stream of insults directed by coaches against opponents. Selee believed that future pennants could be won without street-fighting tactics, and sought to fill his roster with intelligent, focused men in the Hugh Duffy mold. Tommy Tucker, the veteran Irish first baseman, rebelled against this, complaining to the papers that "this lawn tennis business is killing baseball,"[19] but he was in the minority. In 1897 a 25-year-old product of Brown University, Fred Tenney, replaced Tucker at first for the Beaneaters. Tucker played only four games for Boston that season before Selee sent him to Washington.

The 1897 Beaneaters were less Irish than previous Boston teams, though Hugh Duffy hit .340 and Jimmy Collins emerged as a star with 132 runs batted in and a .346 average. Tenney took over first base, leaving Collins as the only Irishman on the infield, while the outfield consisted of Duffy and two non–Irishmen, Billy Hamilton and rookie Charles (Chick) Stahl. Cozy Dolan was released, though he returned to the club nine years later as an outfielder, and of the remaining pitchers, only Jim Sullivan, who won four games, was an Irishman. The rest of the staff was composed of Germans, Kid Nichols and rookie Fred Klobedanz, and the Welsh-born Ted (Parson) Lewis. A few of the minor players claimed Irish descent, but this edition of the Beaneaters was noticeably less Irish than any since the early years of Harry Wright's tenure as manager.

Still, the Irish fans of Boston loved their team, and in Jimmy Collins they found a new star to adulate. By 1897, the 27-year-old Collins was widely considered the best third baseman in the game, and by the end of the decade many were calling him the greatest third sacker of all time. Only Cleveland's Bobby Wallace, a converted pitcher, came close to Jimmy as a fielder, but Wallace was not in Jimmy's league as a hitter. In addition, Collins, a bachelor, was handsome and personable, and enjoyed the attention of the fans. Some said that only John L. Sullivan, a Bostonian who reigned as heavyweight champion of the world during the 1890s, surpassed Jimmy Collins as the idol of the Boston Irish.

The reconfigured Beaneaters were a well-behaved team in 1897, partly due to the absence of the bombastic Tommy Tucker. Another factor was team president Arthur Soden's decree early in the season that henceforth, Boston players would pay their own fines to the league. Soon afterward, the Beaneaters went on a 28–2 run that lifted them from fourth place to first. The defending champion Orioles chipped away at the Boston lead and pulled even by late August, setting the stage for one of the most thrilling two-team races yet seen in the National League. The Orioles and Beaneaters were never separated by more than one game during the season's final four weeks and were locked in a dead heat when they met in Baltimore on Friday, September 24, for a three-game series to decide the pennant.

Boston fans were thrilled with the renascence of their Beaneaters, and more than 100 vocal supporters made the trip to Baltimore by train. Led by John "Honey Fitz" Fitzgerald, a young Irish-American congressman who was destined for greater things in politics, these mostly Irish fans blew horns, drank heartily, and waved pennants while they cheered their heroes. They called themselves the "Royal Rooters," and would have a significant effect on the Boston baseball scene during the next two decades. Greatly outnumbered by more than 12,000 Baltimore partisans, the Royal Rooters saw the Beaneaters take the first contest by a score of 6–4. On Saturday, in front of 18,750 people, the Orioles evened the series with a 6–3 win. There was no Sunday ball in Baltimore in 1897, so the season came down to a single game on Monday, September 27.

More than 25,000 people, the largest baseball crowd ever assembled in Baltimore up to that time, stormed the gates for the deciding game. Kid Nichols, who had pitched a complete-game win on Friday, started for Boston, but gave up five runs in the early going. He settled down after that, and the game was close until the Beaneaters erupted for nine runs in the seventh. Nichols surrendered five more tallies in the late innings, but held on for a 19–10 win that was paced by Hugh Duffy, who crossed the plate four times, and Jimmy Collins, who scored three times. The race was not yet officially over, as the Beaneaters still had three games to play against tenth-place Brooklyn, but Selee's men had clinched the pennant for all practical purposes.

In a departure from prevailing practice, the deciding contest was played in a highly sportsmanlike manner, despite the presence of the noisy Bostonians and the Orioles' history of brawling and umpire-baiting. "The conduct of the players was admirable and the cordial reception of the Boston rooters and the popular ovation tendered to the victors were in keeping with true Maryland hospitality," wrote the Baltimore correspondent to *The Sporting News*. "They defeated us and we feted them. The strain on the players throughout the series was something fearful and their splendid conduct under such exciting surroundings was all the more commendable."[20] About 75 Royal Rooters followed the Beaneaters to Brooklyn, where one of their number waved a broom with a sign on it, declaring a "clean sweep for the Hub." The Beaneaters won two of three in Brooklyn, ending the season two games ahead of the Orioles.

The Royal Rooters had more reason to cheer in 1898, as Boston's Irish-American third baseman, Jimmy Collins, made a major leap to stardom. He batted .328, led the league with 15 home runs, and solidified his stature as the hero of the Irish fans of Boston. He and Hugh Duffy, who drove in 110 runs, were two of the main contributors, while Kid Nichols won 30 games for the seventh time and curveball specialist Vic Willis posted a 25–13 record in his rookie season. Selee's Beaneaters outclassed the rest of the league, rolling to the pennant by six games over the fading Orioles.

Paradoxically, the rise of the mainly Irish Royal Rooters coincided with the erosion of Irish influence on the ballclub itself. Boston, which had traditionally presented teams built around Irish-American names such as Kelly, Clarkson, McCarthy, and Morrill, now listed only Collins and Duffy in its starting lineup. The sole Irish pitcher on the club, Jim Sullivan, made only three appearances in 1899 before being released in May, and his departure left the fans to cheer a team with only two Irishmen among its major contributors.

Many historians regard the 1897–1898 Beaneaters as the greatest team of the 19th century, and it took a major upheaval in the sport to bring their reign to an end. In 1899, the owners of the Baltimore Orioles entered into an arrangement with the Brooklyn club in which the best players on both teams were combined in Brooklyn, with Ned Hanlon as manager. Almost all the Oriole stars, with the notable exceptions of John McGraw and Wilbert Robinson, joined the Dodgers in a new powerhouse that soon became known as the Superbas. With key Orioles such as Willie Keeler, Joe Kelley, and Hugh Jennings joined by Brooklyn holdovers Fielder Jones, Bill Kennedy, and others, Hanlon and his fellow owners had created a superteam. Another such aggregation coalesced in Missouri after Cleveland team president Frank Robison bought the St. Louis Browns and transferred Cy Young, Jesse Burkett, and all the Cleveland stars to the Mound City. They called it "syndicate baseball," and it allowed the richest teams to improve themselves by buying out the poorer ones.

The more conservative Beaneater owners stood pat, only to see the Brooklyn squad steamroll over the National League despite minor challenges from Boston and the Philadelphia Phillies. The Superbas took the league lead in May, then built an insurmountable margin with a 20–1 streak that lasted into late June. The Beaneaters were ill-equipped to meet the challenge, as Jimmy Collins slumped at the bat while Hugh Duffy's leg problems kept him on the bench for more than half the season. Boston's troubles and Brooklyn's dominance made for empty seats at the South End Grounds, and even the Royal Rooters were subdued as Brooklyn took the pennant by eight games over Selee's team. The Superbas dominated again in 1900, as the injury-plagued and aging Beaneater club dropped to fourth place.

Frank Selee might have built another champion, but events beyond his control soon ended his tenure in Boston. A new league, the American, began play in 1901 and targeted Boston as a likely location for a successful new franchise. The American League backers recognized that the Irish fans of Boston were theirs for the taking, with the decline of the Beaneaters and the absence of Irish players, except for Collins, Duffy, and a few minor contributors, on Selee's team. The new league envisioned Jimmy Collins as the centerpiece of a new Boston ballclub, and in February of 1901 Collins quit the Beaneaters and signed a deal to manage the American League entry in the Hub. The acquisition of Collins, still in his prime as a player, was a major coup for the new club, as well as a crushing loss for the Beaneaters.

Boston's other Irish star, Hugh Duffy, who had joined the Beaneaters in 1892 and starred on four pennant winning teams, was the next to leave. He had worked with the new league to establish its franchise in Boston, signing players for the upstart circuit and helping to select a site for a new ballpark, which became the Huntington Avenue Grounds. His efforts were rewarded with the field leadership of the Milwaukee Brewers. Duffy had long held managerial aspirations, and now, with his playing career winding down, he was ready to direct his own ballclub after five years as Selee's chief lieutenant. He chose to ignore the reserve clause in his contract. As Duffy explained, "Mr. Soden asserts that the Boston club has an option on my services, but I have just finished a two-year contract at Boston. The option is the usual National League reserve clause, and I received no bonus except for $600 for captaining the Boston team last season. I consulted my lawyer and was told to go ahead and better myself if possible. That, I think, I am doing."[21]

Surprisingly, the Beaneaters made no effort to keep Duffy. William Conant, one of the Triumvirs, sneered to the papers, "He's about through as a player. We'll let him go in peace."[22]

However, the Beaneaters could ill afford to lose both their Irish stars, and after the 1901 club fell to sixth place, both Kid Nichols and Billy Hamilton decided to call it quits. The Triumvirs fired Frank Selee at season's end, and the glory days of the Beaneaters were finished. Hired almost immediately by Chicago's National League club, Selee assembled a new group of young players, which the newspapers dubbed the "Cubs," and built another championship team. He left Chicago due to illness in 1905, but his Cubs won four pennants and two World Series later in the decade while his former club, the Beaneaters, floundered.

The Irish fans of Boston transferred their allegiance to the American League while the Beaneaters sank into irrelevance. The club changed its nickname several times before settling on the moniker Braves in 1913, but the tide had turned, and the National League played second fiddle to the

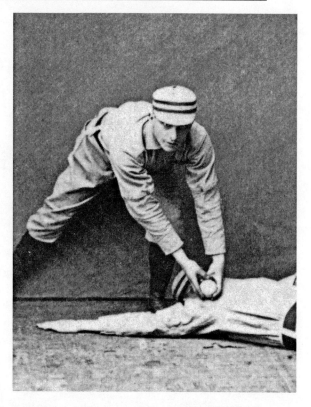

Tommy McCarthy, whom John Ward labeled the "chief schemer" of the Beaneaters (Library of Congress).

American for the rest of its existence in Boston. The Braves remained a perennial bottom-dweller, with only an unexpected World Series win in 1914 and a pennant in 1948 lifting the gloom, however briefly, of a franchise in decline. By the early 1950s, after five decades of poor performances, the team was ready to surrender. The franchise pulled up stakes and moved to Milwaukee in 1953 and to Atlanta 13 years later, where it remains to this day. In a ghostly repeat of times past, the Atlanta Braves won five pennants during the 1990s, as their Boston predecessors had won five flags in the 1890s, but few noticed the historical coincidence. The Boston Beaneaters are mostly forgotten today, their proud Irish-American heritage relegated to the history books.

9

The Umpires

The growing popularity of baseball during the late 19th century, on both the major and minor league levels, resulted in the formation of many new teams and leagues and led to a heightened demand for talented ballplayers. It also created new jobs for umpires to preside over the increasing number of games. Perhaps it was only natural that the Irish, having populated the ranks of players so thoroughly during the 1880s and 1890s, should also be drawn to the umpiring profession. Indeed, when the Baseball Hall of Fame, in 1946, decided to recognize non-playing personnel such as umpires, sportswriters, and executives by creating the short-lived "Honor Rolls of Baseball," the list of distinguished umpires was dotted with names such as Hurst, Kelly, O'Loughlin, Gaffney, and Sheridan. At a time when second-generation Irish-Americans dominated the playing field, umpiring was also largely Irish in character.

During the earliest days of amateur baseball, there was no such thing as a professional umpire. The arbiter was usually a respected and upstanding local citizen, selected before the game by agreement between the captains of the competing teams. Many of these designated umpires, mindful of their civic responsibility, wore top hats and Prince Albert coats to indicate their status. The umpire received no pay for his efforts, as the honor of serving in that capacity was compensation enough. He sat at a table or leaned on a stool at a safe distance from the action, rising at the end of a play to announce his rulings to the players and spectators. Arguments were rare, as it was considered unsportsmanlike to call the honesty or judgment of an honored citizen into question.

This custom began to change during the early 1870s, as professionalism entered the game. The National Association's first pennant winning team, the 1871 Philadelphia Athletics, were roundly criticized for bullying the umpire into calling plays their way. The Athletics were the "champion kickers" of the Association, and their tactics must have worked, as they boasted the best home winning percentage in the league. Disputes between players and game officials became more frequent, and fans entered the fray, booing and even physically threatening umpires who made decisions unfavorable to the home team. The elevated status enjoyed by the umpire a few short years before became a thing of the past. Perhaps the low point of umpiring in the Association came in 1873, when an argument between arbiter Bob Ferguson and New York Mutuals catcher Nat Hicks ended when Ferguson walloped Hicks with a bat, breaking the player's arm.

Harry Wright, manager of the four-time champion Boston Red Stockings, abhorred the increasingly rude treatment of game officials, but his soon became a minority view. Wright's star pitcher Al Spalding became manager of the Chicago White Stockings in 1876 and adopted a more aggressive approach in dealing with the game officials. Spalding was criticized for what was then called "crowding the umpire," but his club used such tactics to win the first National League pennant that season. Spalding's success convinced other managers to follow his example. Spalding's protégé, Adrian (Cap) Anson, became the field boss of the White Stockings in 1879 and expanded upon his mentor's example, using umpire intimidation and bullying as integral features of team strategy.

Baseball players were now thoroughly professional, and umpires followed suit. In 1878 the National League began paying its umpires the sum of five dollars per game, and in 1879 the league created a list of 20 men that it deemed qualified to serve as game officials. Team captains were required to choose an umpire from among the 20 names on the list. In 1883 the league went one step further, naming four men as full-time umpires at a salary of $1,000 per year. Only one lasted the entire season, as team owners could have an arbiter fired for any disputed call, but the umpiring profession had taken root. Its reach would expand during the next several years, populated mainly by Irish-Americans.

Perhaps the greatest umpire of the final two decades of the 19th century was John Gaffney, who was born in the Irish section of Roxbury, Massachusetts, in 1856. Gaffney, who grew up in Worcester, was a fine third baseman in the Boston area during the late 1870s, teaming with future stars Tim Keefe and Barney Gilligan on local amateur teams. Keefe and Gilligan soon graduated the major leagues, but Gaffney's career ended during the winter of 1880 when he hurt his arm while throwing a snowball. Disappointed, Gaffney left baseball and learned the printing trade, but could not resist the lure of the game. He started umpiring college contests in 1883, and gained so much positive notice for his game management skill that in August of 1884 Gaffney was invited to join the staff of the National League.

John Gaffney, the "King of Umpires" during the 1880s (Library of Congress).

Gaffney entered into a difficult situation. Competent game officials were scarce in 1884, and the emergence of a third would-be major league, the Union Association, added to the shortage. The two established major circuits, the National League and the American Association, were notorious for treating their umpires poorly, and were having a hard time retaining skilled arbiters. Gaffney, however, made an immediate impression on players and fans alike. His first assignment came in an important late-season match between pennant contenders Boston and Providence. The game lasted 11 innings, ending in a 1–0 Providence victory, and Gaffney drew praise for the efficient and professional way he handled the contest. By the end of the 1884 season he had staked his claim as the best umpire in the league, and before long he was routinely called "Honest John Gaffney" and the "King of Umpires."

His consistency and accuracy at calling balls and strikes earned Gaffney the respect of the players, and his thorough knowledge of the rule book enabled him to make correct decisions in the heat of battle. A fine athlete himself, he had played with or against many National League stars of the period and knew many on a personal basis. Also, as an Irishman, he could relate to the many Irish players in the league. His skill, experience, and personality combined to make him the most respected umpire in the game. Gaffney was so highly regarded for his baseball knowledge that the Washington team of the National League hired him as its manager in 1886. His honesty was so unquestioned that he sometimes umpired games involving his own team. In 1888 he left Washington and joined the American Association as its highest-paid umpire at a salary of $2,500 per year. Only a handful of star players earned more money than Gaffney.

In an era when many umpires responded to bullying and intimidation with more of the same, usually unsuccessfully, Gaffney relied on tact and diplomacy to control a game. "I have studied the rules thoroughly," explained the "King of Umpires" in 1891. "I keep my eyes wide open, and I follow the ball with all possible dispatch. With the players I try to keep as even tempered as I can, always speaking to them gentlemanly yet firmly. I dislike to fine, and in all my experience have not inflicted more than $300 in fines, and I never found it necessary to order a player from the field. Pleasant words to players in passion will work far better than fines."[1] Connie Mack, a young Irish-American catcher who played for Gaffney on the Washington club in 1886 and 1887, believed that his former manager was the greatest balls-and-strikes umpire in the game. "He was perfect," remembered Mack in 1943. "He would follow a ball all the way from the pitcher, and when he made his decision, he would say, 'That was one-eighth of an inch outside' or 'That was one-eighth of an inch too low,' and he was right. There has never been another umpire like him."[2]

Players and managers did their best to challenge Gaffney's authority, especially the "King of Kickers," Cap Anson of the Chicago White Stockings. During the 1886 season, in a key game between Chicago and Detroit, Gaffney declared a Wolverine runner safe at second on a close play. Several decisions had already gone against the White Stockings that day, and it was only a matter of time before Anson lost his temper. The umpire described the scene later for a newspaper reporter.

> "Not out!" cried I.
> "What?" exclaimed Anson, walking toward me, boiling with rage.
> "Anson, this will cost you $10."
> "Yes, and it will cost you your position, you — —."
> "Fifty dollars more! That makes it $60."
> "Why, you insignificant little Irish — —, what do you mean?"
> "Fifty more!" cried I; "that makes it $110 and I'll stay with you a week. If you can stand it I can."[3]

The enraged Anson vented his feelings after the game. "Will I pay [the fines]?" he replied to a question from a reporter. "Not I, not a dollar, not a penny. If Gaffney does not remit the fines I'll have him fired, or my name's not Anson."[4] However, league president Nick Young declared his support for Gaffney, and Anson, despite his protests, eventually paid the fine. "That ended the matter there," said Gaffney later. "Anson went back to his base, and I have not had any trouble with him since."

While Gaffney plied his trade in the National League, the American Association boasted its own Irish-American "King of Umpires." John Kelly, born in New York City in 1856, was a minor league catcher who reached the National League in 1879. A .155 batting average for Syracuse and Troy convinced young Kelly that he was not destined for success as a player. Instead, he became an umpire and worked on a substitute basis during the early 1880s, joining the National League staff as a full-timer in 1882. The Association hired him away in 1883, and his reputation grew during the next several years. Before long, "Honest John" Kelly was as highly respected in his league as John Gaffney was in the rival circuit.

Kelly and Gaffney shared many characteristics. Both were former players, second-generation Irishmen, and masters of the strike zone and the rule book. Both men ruled the field with their presence and personality, though Kelly may have had another angle working in his favor. An umpire's personal popularity played a key role in his success or failure during the 1880s, when fan rowdiness increased to alarming levels, and John Kelly proved highly popular with the crowds. Perhaps Kelly gained favor and kept the peace by being something of a "homer," for researchers have found that in 1884, the home team won more than two-thirds of the games over which Kelly presided.

Kelly, who was more than six feet tall, loomed over many of the players, and combined a forceful persona with physical presence to earn the respect of players and managers. In 1884, during the inaugural post-season "World's Series" between the champions of the National League and the American Association, John Kelly was chosen to officiate the first game. He presided over several of the October games during the next few seasons as well.

Like Gaffney, John Kelly was so highly respected that he was offered a managing position. In 1887 the Louisville club of the Association hired him as its field leader, and Kelly brought the formerly moribund team into the first division, finishing fourth in an eight-team league. He umpired a few games involving his own team with no apparent complaint, and at season's end he and Gaffney teamed up to work the 15-game World Series between Detroit and St. Louis. Kelly and Gaffney, the best in the business during the 1880s, comprised the first two-man umpiring crew in baseball history.

Other arbiters attempted to follow the example of Gaffney and Kelly, but few succeeded. Fergy Malone, the Irish-born former star player with the Philadelphia Athletics of the 1860s and early 1870s, joined the National League umpiring staff in 1884 and immediately ran into trouble. A Boston paper called him "a gentleman of preternatural stupidity [who] surpassed in this respect everything that has ever been known, or ever will be." Malone had difficulty moving the games along, as an unusual number of his contests lasted two hours or more, exhausting the patience of players and fans alike. After one such extended game, the *Providence Journal* noted the "frequent expressions of amusement at Fergy Malone's strenuous exertions to umpire the game intelligently and impartially. Perhaps it would be fair to say that his ignorance equally affected both teams, but as it was a sort of catch-as-catch-can operation, whatever preferences were given were unexpected, and hence all the more surprising and ludicrous." Malone was not asked back for a second season.[5]

Another ex-player of Irish heritage, pitching star Tim Keefe, also failed miserably as an umpire. Widely admired for his intelligence, demeanor, and honesty, Keefe pitched his last major league game in 1893. His sporting goods business, which had supplied balls and equipment to the Players League, had failed after the upstart league collapsed, so Keefe needed to find another line of work. He applied for an umpiring job and joined the National League staff in August of 1894. At the beginning of his tenure, it appeared that the league had made a good choice in hiring Keefe, who earned praise for his handling of the game and his knowledge of the rules.

However, not even Keefe, who was described by an opponent as "one of the most perfect gentlemen who ever played ball," could escape the brutal treatment of umpires so prevalent during that era. It did not take long for the former pitching star to be pilloried in newspapers and magazines, cursed on the field by players and managers, and jostled by the fans after the games. His reticent demeanor was ill-suited for the umpiring profession. One day Baltimore's John McGraw loudly accused Keefe of being drunk on the field. Keefe quietly protested that he'd taken some whiskey because he was sick, an admission that made McGraw and the Orioles roar with laughter. Once the pitching hero of New York, Keefe even drew boos from his former admirers at the Polo Grounds. Keefe tried his best to handle the pressure but reached his breaking point in St. Louis on July 7, 1896. After a series of vicious arguments with both the Giants and the Browns, Keefe walked off the field in the fifth inning and resigned his position.

"Baseball has reached a stage where it is absolutely disgraceful," complained the retired pitcher afterward. "It is the fashion for every player engaged in a game to froth at the mouth, and emit shrieks of anguish whenever a decision is given which is adverse to the interests of the club to which he belongs.... This continual senseless and puerile kicking at every decision has been infinitely trying to me, and I have been considering for some time whether I had not better resign. I can apparently please nobody."[6]

"I need the money," continued Keefe a few days later, "but I can't stay in a business that makes my friends abuse me and mistrust me. I can't have people whom I have had for associates for years pass me up when they meet me, and so I am going to resign."[7]

Indeed, the miserable working conditions for umpires during the 1890s drove baseball's finest arbiter, John Gaffney, from the game. He had shifted to the American Association for the 1888 and 1889 seasons, then joined the new Players League in 1890. Blackballed by the National League after the new circuit disbanded, he returned to the minors before rejoining the senior circuit in late 1891. Two years later, Gaffney complained about the National League's offensive explosion, a result of the relocation of the pitching rubber ten feet farther from the plate. The longer pitching distance made the ball easier to hit, and additional baserunners made the umpire's job more complicated. "I wish I had six eyes," sighed Gaffney, "and then I might be quick enough to see everything and even look around corners."[8]

Gaffney dealt with the increasing pressure and constant abuse by becoming a heavy drinker, and alcoholism soon derailed his career. Dismissed for drunkenness following the 1893 season, he made two attempts to regain his former status, but in 1900 he left the major leagues for good. He returned to umpiring minor league and college games before landing a job in New York City as a night watchman. After Gaffney died in 1913, Connie Mack, his former catcher, staged a benefit game to pay for a proper tombstone for the onetime "King of Umpires."

John Kelly also took leave of major league baseball, but for different reasons. Kelly was dismissed as Louisville's manager during the 1888 season, despite his success the year before, and although he returned to the umpiring profession he seethed with anger over his firing. Kelly did not need baseball, having built a fine reputation as a boxing referee, so he left baseball behind. He remained in the sporting world as a referee, officiating many championship bouts, and also grew interested in horse racing. In the early 1900s he turned to gambling, operating betting parlors in New York City that were admired for their honesty. "I don't know how I stood umpiring for so long," remarked Kelly. One of the nation's leading bookmakers, Kelly now vied for the title "King of Gamblers." He lived well on gambling proceeds and real estate investments until his death in 1926.

UMPIRE LYNCH
STRIKES DOYLE

Baltimore's "Dirty Jack" Doyle and umpire Thomas Lynch slug it out on August 6, 1897. This woodcut appeared in the *Boston Post* that evening (author's collection).

Thomas Lynch was one Irish-American umpire who lasted for more than ten seasons during the rowdiest era in baseball history. A forceful presence on the field, Lynch, a native of New Britain, Connecticut, reached the National League in 1888. Well respected for his honesty and integrity, Lynch's never-ending battles with teams such as the Orioles and Cleveland Spiders eventually wore him down. In August 1897 he was severely beaten on the field by Baltimore's "Dirty Jack" Doyle, and Lynch responded angrily by labeling the Orioles a "vile lot of blackguards" whose name-calling and threatening behavior would "bring a response in the shape of a bullet if they were off the field."[9] Lynch also declared that he would refuse to umpire games involving the Orioles in the future.

The league kept Lynch away from Baltimore as much as possible during the 1898 season, but a dispute the following year with New York Giants team owner Andrew Freedman brought his career to a close. Freedman publicly called Lynch a "robber" and a "cheat" after a particularly galling defeat, and Lynch decided that his reputation had sustained enough damage. He quit the game at season's end, taking a job as manager of a theater in his hometown.

Ten years later, after National League president Harry Pulliam committed suicide, the club owners were deadlocked in selecting a replacement. They needed to identify a man of integrity as a compromise candidate to break the stalemate, and remembered the umpire who had left the game a decade before. To the surprise of many, they called Thomas Lynch out of retirement and named him president of the league, a post he held for the next four seasons. Predictably, Lynch staunchly supported his umpires in confrontations with players, fans, and club owners during his term.

Oddly enough, Jack Doyle, the man who beat up Lynch in 1897, served as an umpire on Lynch's staff for one season. The Irish-born "Dirty Jack" had retired as a player, but remained in the game by umpiring in the minors for several years. In 1911 Lynch, who received good reports on Doyle's performance, hired him. He was teamed with the veteran Bob Emslie, who had also suffered at least one assault at Doyle's hands in the past. One day, when Doyle was playing for the Giants, he wrestled Emslie to the ground and tried to strip off the umpire's wig. Emslie was sensitive about his baldness, and Doyle could not resist showing the arbiter up before the crowd. Doyle lasted only one year in the National League, but he and his old enemy Emslie worked together surprisingly well. "Emslie and he got along like Damon and Pythias," said Christy Mathewson. "This business makes strange bed-fellows."[10]

Perhaps the prototypical Irish-American umpire of the 1890s was a cocky, temperamental son of immigrants from the Pennsylvania coal mining country named Tim Hurst. Five feet and five inches tall, Hurst relied upon his pugnacious nature and quick fists to control the game, though his willingness to fight often inflamed a situation. Still, Tim Hurst was a great umpire who knew the rule book, always hustled, and never backed down from a decision.

Hurst was a professional race-walker (a pedestrian, as they were called then) during the mid–1880s, and made the acquaintance of the noted baseball umpire and sporting referee Honest John Kelly. Inspired by Kelly's example, Hurst built a reputation as a fair and competent official for foot races, bicycle tourneys, and boxing matches before turning his attention to baseball. In 1888 he umpired in the Eastern League, and after managing the Minneapolis team of the Western Association in 1890, signed on with the National League as an umpire in 1891. He continued his career as a boxing referee, much to the displeasure of league officials who demanded that he focus solely on baseball. The National League dismissed him in 1894, but Hurst was so skilled an umpire that he was rehired the following August and allowed to continue his boxing duties.

Hurst used his quick wit and pugnacity to control a game. He took no abuse from anyone, and when threatened by a player or manager, Hurst would offer to settle the matter with his fists, challenging the offender in his rich Irish accent. They called him "Sir Timothy" for his bearing and "Terrible Tim" for his temper, and few players elected to punch it out with him. Hurst had learned to fight as a youth in Ashland, Pennsylvania, where he worked as a slate-picker in the coal mines before his teen years. The miners staged boxing matches during lunch breaks, for their own entertainment and to prove their mettle to each other. Tim Hurst had learned to hold his own with his fists against the toughest Irish coal miners, and was not afraid of any ballplayer.

During the 1890s, the life of an umpire was a difficult one, and Hurst was determined to succeed no matter the odds. Accosted after a game by an angry fan in 1892, Hurst flattened his assailant with his mask, then did the same to a policeman who attempted to intervene. In 1897 he invited Pittsburgh's Jake Stenzel, Pink Hawley, and Denny Lyons to meet him under the stands to settle a dispute with their fists. Hurst took on all three at once and whipped them soundly, stopping only when National League president Nick Young happened by and asked what was going on. "Somebody dropped a dollar bill, Uncle Nick," replied Hurst innocently, "and I said it was mine."[11] One day, New York infielder Kid Elberfeld shoved Tim during an argument, so the umpire picked up the catcher's mask and walloped his assailant, knocking Elberfeld unconscious. Hurst was fined $100 and suspended for a week for his actions, but he refereed a few boxing matches during his time off and came out ahead financially.

Hurst was undeniably tough, and his fighting skill earned respect, and sometimes outright fear, from the players. In 1896, St. Louis Browns pitcher Ted Breitenstein told the *Washington Post* about an incident between Hurst and manager Lew Phelan. Said Breitenstein, "Phelan yelled from the bench, 'Say, Hurst, if any of those decisions are close make them in our favor, and if you don't you'll hear from it through Nick Young.' Tim trotted over to Phelan with that funny little pigeon-toed walk of his, and fanning his finger under Phelan's nose said, 'See here, you big stiff, if you make any more cracks like that I'll give you a punch in the nose.' Phelan turned white, and apologized, and afterward addressed Tim as Mr. Hurst."[12] Many players, however, found Hurst's quick wit and colorful Irish brogue so entertaining that they purposely baited him every now and then, just to hear him argue.

Player rowdiness and fan violence worsened during the 1890s, mainly due to the indifference of the National League magnates, who believed that well-publicized disruptions and disturbances increased interest in the games. Most club owners agreed with Al Spalding, the president of the Chicago club, who stated, "Fans who despise umpires are simply showing their democratic right to protest against tyranny."[13] Few umpires were able to survive in this environment, but Tim Hurst's reputation grew with each passing year. He often wore a cap with the letter B on the front. When asked why, Hurst invariably replied, "Because I'm the best."[14]

Hurst managed the fans as well as anyone, but even he lost control now and then. In 1897, a Cincinnati supporter threw an empty beer mug at Hurst, nearly hitting the umpire in the head. Hurst picked it up and hurled it back into the stands, injuring a fan (not the one who threw it) and getting arrested for his trouble. Still, despite his temper, Hurst was able to maintain command of the game and its players. Connie Mack, who managed the Pirates during the 1890s, said, "Hurst lost his head at times, and this was eventually his undoing, but he did more to stamp out rowdyism than any other official I have known. He was fearless and one of the gamest men who ever handled an indicator."[15]

Hurst took a break from umpiring in 1898 to manage the moribund St. Louis Browns, but his combative style was not appreciated there. Hurst's quick temper and sharp tongue made him unpopular with his players, many of whom openly plotted against him as the season progressed, and his public battles with bankrupt team owner Chris von der Ahe turned the fans against him. The Browns were a poorly behaved lot, and some say that Tim fought each of his charges at least once during the season. The Browns finished in last place, and Hurst left baseball for a year, popping up again as a National League umpire in 1900. By this time, the Cincinnati and New York clubs had refused to let him umpire their games, probably because he was too honest and incorruptible for their tastes, so the disgusted Hurst quit the sport again, spending the next few years as a boxing referee. He returned to the National League late in the 1903 campaign, umpired only one game the following year, then moved to the American League for the 1905 season.

The game was changing, but Tim Hurst refused to change with it. He was still the same brawling, feisty umpire who had relied on his fists to survive, and league president Ban Johnson, widely praised for driving rowdiness from the game, despaired of his newest arbiter's behavior. In May of 1906 New York Highlanders manager Clark Griffith stomped on Hurst's feet during an argument. Hurst always wore dress shoes, not spikes, on the field, and a few innings later, after he noticed that his patent leathers were full of spike holes, the umpire called time and went to the New York dugout for a drink of water. He took his drink, put the cup down, then suddenly belted the unsuspecting Griffith in the head with a right cross, knocking the manager unconscious. Hurst was suspended for five days for the assault.

The feisty Irishman's major league career finally came to a close in 1909. An on-field argument with a group of Philadelphia Athletics ended when Hurst spit into the face of second baseman Eddie Collins. Johnson demanded an apology, but Hurst refused with the simple statement, "I don't like college boys." Though Hurst reportedly voiced his regrets to Collins privately, he was too stubborn and proud to do so in public, so Johnson fired him. Hurst spent his remaining years as a boxing referee and real estate investor before succumbing to pneumonia at the age of 50 in 1915.

The 20th century saw the birth of a new major league and the ascendance of a new crop of Irish-American umpires. One was Hank O'Day, a lefthanded pitcher of the 1880s who made an impression as a substitute umpire during the 1888 and 1889 seasons, while was still pitching for the New York Giants. His record as a pitcher is mediocre, with 73 wins and 110 losses, although he was a 22-game winner in his final season with the Players League in 1890. O'Day proved to be a much better umpire than player, and joined the National League crew on a full time basis in 1895. He lasted until 1927, with two years off to manage the Cincinnati Reds in 1912 and the Chicago Cubs in 1914. He was the only man who served as a player, manager, and umpire in the National League during the 20th century.

O'Day belied the stereotype of the garrulous, jovial son of Erin; instead, umpire Bill Klem called him a "misanthropic Irishman." He was a loner, with no family or hobbies and appeared to live totally for his career. "Look at O'Day," said fellow arbiter Frank (Silk) O'Loughlin. "He is one of the best umpires, maybe the best today, but he's sour. Umpiring does something to you. The abuse you get from the players, the insults from the crowds, and the awful things they write about you in the newspapers take their toll."[16] O'Day holds a unique place in baseball history as the only umpire to eject Connie Mack from a game. An argument between the usually agreeable Mack, then managing the Pirates, and O'Day in 1895 ended with a group of policemen dragging Mack from the field. It made no difference to O'Day that he and Mack had been teammates and friends with the Washington club several years before. Mack, who remained in baseball as a manager until 1950, was never again ordered out of a game by an umpire.

Still, thorny personality aside, O'Day served as an umpire for an astounding 33 years, officiating in 10 World Series. He made his calls and stuck to them no matter how poorly his decisions were received, as shown during the famous "Merkle boner" game between the Cubs and Giants on September 23, 1908. In the ninth inning, with darkness approaching, O'Day ruled New York's Fred Merkle out for failing to touch second base, negating the winning run and turning an apparent Giant victory into a tie. The two teams ended the season in a dead heat for the pennant, resulting in a playoff game which the Cubs won. Giants manager John McGraw believed for the rest of his life that O'Day's decision in the Merkle affair cost his team the 1908 pennant on a technicality. The game remains a source of controversy to this day, more than 100 years later, but O'Day never wavered in his belief that Merkle was out.

It would have done little good for the Giants to protest anyway. "O'Day cannot be reasoned with," complained Christy Mathewson in his book, *Pitching in a Pinch*. "It is as dangerous to argue with him as it is to try to ascertain how much gasoline is in the tank of an automobile by sticking down the lighted end of a cigar or a cigarette."[17]

Frank (Silk) O'Loughlin was a much more sociable individual, as well as one of the best arbiters in his circuit during the years before the first World War. O'Loughlin, who got his nickname in his youth from his fine blond hair, was born in Rochester, New York, in 1870. His father was an immigrant railroad fireman who died when the future umpire was five years old, leaving a wife and six children. Silk, the youngest of the brood, dreamed of playing ball but turned to umpiring when his playing career stalled. He learned his trade in the Eastern League before joining the American League in 1902.

O'Loughlin owned a loud voice, and became famous for his deep, bellowing "Strike Tuh" and "Heee-ee-zz out!" calls. "The patrons of the game like to hear an umpire," said O'Laughlin. "I think, too, that it enlivens the game to have the decisions given in a sharp, brisk way." He also knew that a good umpire was a firm, decisive one. "A man is always out or safe, or it is a ball or a strike," he said. "The umpire, if he is a good man and knows his business is always right. I am always right." He also made the statement, "The holy prophets for religion and O'Loughlin for baseball, both infallible."[18]

One day in Philadelphia, O'Loughlin found a creative way to eject a player when Detroit's Donie Bush put up a vehement argument over a strike call. O'Loughlin began walking down the first base line, and Bush followed him, spewing vitriol every step of the way. The two men did not stop until they reached a gate in the right field fence, just beyond the dugout. The umpire opened the gate, which led to the clubhouse, and ordered Bush through it. "Keep going, son," said O'Loughlin. "You're done for today."[19]

O'Loughlin was a convivial sort off the field, but never allowed a friendship to get in the way of his duties. He was on good terms with the mercurial Detroit star Ty Cobb, but in May of 1912, when Cobb charged into the stands at the Polo Grounds and beat up a heckler, O'Loughlin was the umpire who restored order and ejected Cobb from the game. Three years earlier, an interference call by Silk's partner Tommy Connolly cost the Philadelphia Athletics a game in a hotly contested pennant race with the Tigers. O'Loughlin saw no interference on the play, but the call was Connolly's to make, and Silk refused to intervene despite the pleadings of Connie Mack, the Philadelphia manager. Mack, a friend as well as a fellow second-generation Irishman, refused to speak to O'Loughlin for years after the incident.

Silk O'Loughlin might have made the Baseball Hall of Fame had his career lasted longer. He umpired in the American League for 17 seasons, appeared in five World Series, and called a record seven no-hitters, including Addie Joss' perfect game in 1908. Only his death at age 48 during the influenza epidemic of 1918 kept O'Loughlin's name from gracing a plaque in Cooperstown.

Jack Sheridan was another American League umpire whose fine career was cut short by illness, but some called him the best in the game. Sheridan was so thoroughly Irish in speech and manner that many people assumed that he was a native son of the island, but he was a Chicagoan who grew up in San Jose, California. A small, prematurely balding man with a bushy mustache, Sheridan debuted in the Players League in 1890. He umpired in the National League in 1892, making headlines on May 6 of that year for canceling a game on account of sunlight. Pitchers John Clarkson of Boston and Elton Chamberlain of Cincinnati carried a scoreless tie into extra frames that day, and by the 14th inning the sun began to set on the horizon past the outfield fence. It was so bright that the batters could not see the ball on its way to the plate, so Sheridan made the unprecedented decision to call off the contest.

Sheridan was roughly handled in the National League and spent only one year there, returning to the minors for the next few seasons. He served in the Western League, under league president and founder Ban Johnson, for several years, except for a brief return to the

National in 1896 and 1897. Sheridan was the Western League's best umpire, and when Johnson created the American League he hired Sheridan for his umpiring staff.

Sheridan was an innovator. He may have been the first umpire to crouch behind the plate and peer over the catcher's shoulder to see the pitch; arbiters before him stood straight up and missed low pitches. He also refused to wear a chest protector, because he was agile and quick enough to avoid foul tips. Billy Evans, who joined the umpiring corps at age 22 in 1906, teamed with Sheridan for the first several years of his career. "I immediately adopted Sheridan's style, as well as many other Sheridan theories," said Evans. "I imitated Sheridan in every way. He was about ten years ahead of the rest of us as to umpiring." However, Sheridan's strike three call was totally his own. He would make an exaggerated gesture with his arms and bellow, "Strike three! San Jose, California! The garden spot of America!"[20]

Sheridan had battled with noted umpire-baiter John McGraw in the National League, and when McGraw joined the American in 1901 as playing manager of the Baltimore Orioles, the two men resumed their feud almost immediately. In May of that year, Sheridan officiated a game between the Orioles and Tigers at Detroit and expelled pitcher Harry Howell for abusive language. Orioles outfielder Mike Donlin picked up the game ball and threw it at Sheridan, barely missing him, so Sheridan ejected Donlin as well. McGraw refused to remove the players from the field, so Sheridan forfeited the game to Detroit. A year later, after McGraw had incited the Baltimore fans to riot against one of Sheridan's decisions, the umpire took his revenge. Boston hurler Bill Dinneen hit McGraw with pitches five times in one game, but Sheridan refused to let the batter take first base, claiming that McGraw had not tried to get out of the way. Ban Johnson supported his umpire against the Oriole troublemaker, and a few months later, McGraw gave up on the American League and returned to the National as manager of the New York Giants.

McGraw may not have liked Jack Sheridan personally, but he respected an umpire who stood up to him. The Chicago White Sox and New York Giants staged a round-the-world baseball tour during the winter of 1913–1914, and the main promoters, Charles Comiskey of the White Sox and John McGraw of the Giants, hired the two best umpires in the game to accompany the teams. They chose two men with a long history of confrontations with McGraw, Bill Klem from the National League and Jack Sheridan from the American. Two Hall of Fame umpires, Klem and Billy Evans, later called Sheridan the greatest arbiter in the game.

Like Silk O'Loughlin, Jack Sheridan's career, and life, ended prematurely. After suffering an attack of sunstroke during a game in Chicago in August of 1914, he never fully recovered. He returned a few weeks later to finish the season and then, against the advice of friends and family, umpired the Chicago city series between the White Sox and Cubs in October. Exhausted, he went home to California, where he died in November of that year at age 52.

The stereotype of the "feisty Irishman" began to disappear from American life during the first half of the 20th century, but several new men carried on the tradition of the tough, scrappy Irish umpire. George Moriarty, a Chicagoan whose immigrant father had been a childhood friend of Charles Comiskey, was a fine ballplayer who reached the major leagues in 1906 as a third baseman with the New York Highlanders. He had cut a swath through the minors as a brawler who never backed down from a fight. During a game in Toledo, Moriarty soundly thrashed Indianapolis manager Ed Barrow, a tough customer himself, and his reputation grew. Boston catcher Bill "Rough" Carrigan once spit on Moriarty at home plate, starting a fight that ended with Moriarty knocking Carrigan out. When Moriarty joined the Detroit Tigers in 1909, Ty Cobb challenged him to a fight. Moriarty handed Cobb a bat. "A fellow like you," said the young third baseman, "needs a bat to even things up when fighting an Irishman." Cobb wisely backed off.

In 1917, his playing career at an end, Moriarty became an American League umpire, and here found his true calling. His toughness and courage served him well, and although he had dropped out of grade school, he was intelligent and well versed in the nuances of the rule book. His booming voice was perfect for an umpire and conferred instant authority. In 1935 a poll of players conducted by *The Sporting News* rated Moriarty the best umpire in the league by a wide margin. He remained on the

Detroit infielder George Moriarty tags a runner sliding into third at Cleveland's League Park. Moriarty later became an outstanding American League umpire (Library of Congress).

American League staff until 1940, with a two-year break (1927 and 1928) to serve as manager of his old team, the Tigers, succeeding Ty Cobb.

Though Moriarty was a devout Catholic who attended church every Sunday, he never backed down from an altercation. In 1932, after the White Sox rode him mercilessly in a game at Chicago, the angry umpire offered to fight the entire team. Three White Sox players and manager Lew Fonseca promptly attacked the 48-year-old arbiter, and although the players were barely half his age, Moriarty battled the four men to a draw, suffering a broken hand in the process. "Mr. Moriarty must be slipping," said newspaper columnist Joe Williams. "I can remember when he used to take on whole ball clubs as a warmup." Moriarty took no nonsense from anyone. During the 1935 World Series, he ordered the Chicago Cubs to stop their relentless anti–Semitic heckling of Detroit first baseman Hank Greenberg. The Cubs ignored the umpire, and during Game 3 Moriarty ejected three Chicago players. No other post-season contest in baseball history has featured even two expulsions in a single game. Commissioner Kenesaw M. Landis fined and reprimanded Moriarty for his actions, as ejections from World Series games were supposed to be approved by the commissioner in advance.

As Moriarty's career drew to a close, another Irishman entered the umpiring profession almost by accident. John (Jocko) Conlan was a 36-year-old reserve outfielder for the White Sox in 1935, when illness sidelined umpire Red Ormsby one hot afternoon in Chicago. Conlan was not in the lineup that day, so he volunteered to serve as a substitute arbiter. He liked the work so much, and was so intent on remaining in the game in some capacity, that he opted to quit playing and follow a new career path. After a minor league apprenticeship, he joined the National League in 1941 and remained for 24 years.

Conlan, born in Chicago in 1899, was a throwback to previous Irish-American umpires such as Hurst, Gaffney, and O'Loughlin. Not a physically imposing man at five feet and seven inches in height, Conlan hustled every minute on the field, made quick and accurate decisions in an Irish brogue, and stuck by them. He related well to players, having been one himself, but allowed no backtalk from them. In 1941, his first full season as an arbiter, he led the league with 26 ejections. "You've got to have a thick skin and a strong heart," said Conlan. "You've got to have and command respect. Without them, you're nothing."[21] In 1961, Jocko ejected Los Angeles Dodgers coach Leo Durocher, who kicked at the ground in anger and struck Conlan in the shins instead. Conlan kicked Durocher in return, and the two men took turns booting each other until Leo realized that Conlan, the home plate umpire, was wearing shin guards and steel-toed shoes. Durocher limped back to the dugout in defeat.

Ethnic solidarity had not completely disappeared from the game during Conlan's career. Danny Murtaugh, the Pittsburgh second baseman, got into an argument with Conlan over balls and strikes one day in St. Louis and drew an ejection. Murtaugh appealed to Jocko's sense of Irish pride. He pointed out that the Cardinals had Polish players (Stan Musial and Whitey Kurowski) at first and third, a German (Red Schoendienst) at second, a French pitcher in Howie Pollet and an Italian catcher in Joe Garagiola. As for shortstop Marty Marion, "I don't even know what he is," confessed Murtaugh. "But there are only two Irishmen on the field, and you want to throw half of us out!" Conlan, duly impressed, let Murtaugh stay in the game.[22]

Conlan was a personable chap, but had little patience for players and managers who questioned his judgment. One day he tired of hearing Richie Ashburn complain about his decisions, so Jocko invited the Phillies center fielder to call his own balls and strikes. The next pitch dove into the dirt, but Ashburn, for some reason, called a strike on himself. "Richie," said Conlan, "you have just had the only chance a hitter has ever had in the history of baseball to bat and umpire at the same time. And you blew it. That's the last pitch you call. I'm not going to have you louse up my profession."[23] On one rainy afternoon in 1941, Conlan's first season, he ejected Pittsburgh manager Frankie Frisch for demanding that the game be called. Frisch had embarrassed Conlan by opening a large umbrella to make his point, and Jocko made sure to finish the game no matter how much rain fell on the field.

Jocko Conlan was the last of a breed. Elected to the Hall of Fame in 1974, Jocko was only the fourth arbiter so honored. He lived to a ripe old age, unlike many of his umpiring forebears such as Silk O'Loughlin, Tim Hurst, and Jack Sheridan, none of whom made it to their 55th birthdays. Jocko was nearly 90 years old when he died in 1989, and the image of the dapper, quick-witted umpire with an Irish brogue disappeared with him, never to return.

10

Comiskey and the White Sox

Charlie Comiskey, who led the St. Louis Browns to four pennants during the 1880s, introduced the brawling, fighting style of baseball that proved to be the dominant mode of play during the 1890s. However, while the Baltimore Orioles won three successive pennants from 1894 to 1896 using such tactics, Comiskey himself fell into obscurity. He tried, but failed, to lead the Cincinnati Reds into contention, spending three unsuccessful years in the Queen City and never finishing higher than fifth place. He put some of his old Irish team-mates from St. Louis, such as Tip O'Neill, Tony Mullane, and Curt Welch, in Reds uniforms, but the largely German-American fans in Cincinnati never warmed to Comiskey and his men. The Reds finished tenth in the 12-team National League in 1894, and Comiskey relinquished his post at season's end. He then bought the Sioux City, Iowa, franchise in the Western League, moved it to St. Paul, Minnesota, and settled into his new role as owner, manager, and part-time player for a minor league team.

The St. Paul club spent the latter half of the 1890s in the middle of the Western League standings, but Comiskey and his older brother Patrick, who served as team treasurer, drew praise for their well-run operation. Charlie also eyed a return to major league status, aided and abetted by Western League president Ban Johnson, a former Cincinnati sportswriter whom Comiskey had befriended while managing the Reds. Both men decried the dominance of the bloated, arrogant National Legaue, and both dreamed of turning the Western League into a major circuit and competing with the National on an equal footing.

Several attempts to establish new major leagues were made during the late 1890s, including an abortive try at reviving the old American Association under the leadership of Cap Anson. This proposed circuit was organized late in 1899 and drew interest from star players such as Ed Delahanty, Napoleon Lajoie, and John McGraw, who was slated to own and manage a team in Baltimore, where the National League had recently disbanded the Orioles. Anson, president of the new Association and owner of the Chicago franchise, proclaimed that the circuit would be ready to take the field in 1900, but time ran out on the effort, and the league collapsed in March of that year. Billy Barnie, the former Baltimore Orioles manager, also planned a new league, based in the eastern states, that never got off the ground. Not one of these proposed new circuits succeeded, mainly because none of them had an organizer like Ban Johnson at the helm.

Following the 1899 season, Johnson changed the name of the Western League to the American and began to relocate several of the circuit's teams to larger cities. He first replaced the team in Grand Rapids, Michigan, with a new aggregation in Cleveland, a city recently abandoned by the National League. The new Cleveland club, variously called the Blues and the Lake Shores, was managed by a popular former Cleveland player, the veteran center fielder Jimmy McAleer. The second move was even more important. Charlie Comiskey, after much negotiation, received permission from the National League to take his St. Paul club into Chicago, Comiskey's hometown and the city in which he had managed the short-lived Pirates of the Players League ten years before.

Since the infant American League was still considered a minor circuit at the time, Comiskey was required to obtain the approval of Chicago's long-established National League club before planting his new team there. For this reason, Comiskey could not afford to be too picky about the circumstances surrounding his venture. Al Spalding, the main owner of the Chicago National League franchise (the one now known as the Cubs), drove a tough bargain with the upstart new league. Spalding agreed to let Comiskey's team play on the South Side of the city, an area more famous for the smell of its stockyards during the hot summer months than for the quality of life to be found there. He also enjoined the new club from using the name "Chicago," an edict that the local papers ignored. Perhaps more importantly, the National League reserved the right to draft players off American League rosters during the 1900 season, a right it enjoyed with other minor circuits as well. Comiskey and his fellow club owners hated to see some of their best players leave for the National in mid-season, but they had no choice in the matter, at least temporarily.

Comiskey plowed ahead with preparations for the ballclub. His National League rivals had abandoned the name "White Stockings" years before, having been known during the 1890s as "Anson's Colts." After the longtime captain was dismissed after the 1897 campaign, they were dubbed the "Orphans." Comiskey appropriated the traditional White Stockings name for his new club, though he shortened it to "White Sox" for the convenience of the headline writers of the city's many newspapers. He then built a wooden grandstand on a site on 39th Street, where a cricket team had given exhibitions as part of the 1893 Chicago World's Fair. This field, called South Side Park, was located near the heavily Irish Bridgeport neighborhood, which Comiskey astutely saw as a potentially fertile market for new fans. The park served the team for more than a decade and eventually grew large enough to hold 15,000 people.

Comiskey managed the new White Sox himself in 1900, winning the pennant by four games over the second-place Boston club, then turned the field leadership over to pitcher Clark Griffith for the following season. Griffith, who claimed Welsh descent, had begun his major league career as a rookie under Comiskey ten years earlier on the St. Louis Browns. Griffith was one of Chicago's most popular athletes, having been a star pitcher and perennial 20-game winner for Cap Anson's Colts during the 1890s before quitting the National League and joining the White Sox after the 1900 season. Comiskey signed many other fine players who were willing to cast their lot with the new circuit during the winter of 1900–1901, and with Griffith as his manager and pitching ace, the White Sox won the 1901 pennant, the first for the American League as a major circuit.

The White Sox fell to fourth in 1902, but Griffith was still widely regarded as one of the best young managers in the league, and his success drew the eye of league president Ban Johnson. Johnson was building a team in New York and wanted it to be a success, so he prevailed upon Comiskey to allow Griffith to manage the new club in New York, then called the Highlanders and now called the Yankees. Comiskey agreed to release Griffith, and hired Jimmy Callahan to manage the White Sox for the 1903 season.

Comiskey had a penchant for hiring second-generation Irishmen like himself, and in Jimmy Callahan he found a perfect example of a brainy Irish player and manager. The son of Irish immigrants, Callahan was born in the mill town of Fitchburg, Massachusetts, in 1874. After losing his father at a young age, he went to work in a cotton mill, and later served an apprenticeship as a plumber, as had Comiskey himself many years before. Callahan, whose childhood nickname "Nixey" followed him into adulthood, disliked plumbing as much as had Comiskey, so he turned to the diamond, entering the major leagues as a pitcher with the Phillies in 1894. In 1897 he landed in Chicago, where Cap Anson used him on the mound, in the outfield, and on second base to take advantage of his many talents. Callahan and Clark Griffith had been teammates on Anson's Colts, and after the 1900 season they jumped together to Comiskey's White Sox.

In 1901, the multi-talented Callahan won 15 games on the mound and batted .331 for the pennant-winning White Sox, and on September 20, 1902 he threw the first American League no-hitter against Detroit. Intelligent and inquisitive, he had learned much from both Comiskey and Griffith, and when Griffith left for New York at the conclusion of the 1902 season, Callahan was the logical choice to replace him. Callahan's arm had given out by this time, so in 1903 he moved himself to third base, where he batted .292. He was still a good player, but not yet a success as a manager. Injuries and weak starting pitching caused Callahan's 1903 team to drop to seventh place. It appears that the loss of Griffith and the permanent move of Callahan to the infield hurt the White Sox in the pitching department.

To complicate things further for Callahan, Comiskey proved to be a hands-on owner, full of suggestions on running the team. Having won five pennants himself as a manager, Comiskey felt entitled to sit in the stands behind home plate at each game, make notes on the team's performance, and share his observations with his field leader. He was also an impatient man, and when the White Sox stumbled out of the gate in 1904, he fired Callahan as manager in early June and appointed outfielder Fielder Jones to the post. Callahan remained on the team for two more seasons before quitting to form his own semipro team on Chicago's South Side. For this he was blacklisted by the American League, but the clever Callahan discovered that he could make more money as owner of his own club than by remaining with the White Sox. Always on the lookout for a money-making opportunity, Callahan also took to the stage during the winter months, telling Irish stories in a colorful brogue that entertained his audiences and enhanced his popularity in Chicago.

Callahan's two seasons as a manager were unsuccessful, but in 1904 he did the team a favor in spring training when he roomed a rookie pitcher named Ed Walsh with veteran hurler Elmer Stricklett. Walsh, a 23-year-old who had not yet pitched in the majors, noticed that the 36-year-old Stricklett threw a spitball, which Walsh had never seen before. Stricklett taught Walsh how to throw the wet pitch, and the right-hander used it to become not only one of the greatest pitchers in White Sox history, but one of Charles Comiskey's favorite players as well.

Ed Walsh, the son of an Irish immigrant shoemaker and his Welsh-born wife, was born in Plains, Pennsylvania, in 1881. Plains was situated in the middle of coal country, and at age 12 Ed went to work in a mine as a slate picker and mule driver. Baseball saved him from a life in the mines, and by 1904 he was ready for the major leagues after Comiskey bought his contract from Newark of the Eastern League for $750. Walsh did not throw the spitball in earnest during his first two seasons with the White Sox, but in 1904 he posted a 6–3 record as a spot starter and reliever. He pitched more often after Fielder Jones became manager, and in 1906 Walsh started to throw the spitter full-time. The spitball was all the rage in the major leagues during this era, but nobody threw a better one than Ed Walsh. "I think that ball dis-integrated on the way to the plate and the catcher put it back together again," said Detroit outfielder Sam Crawford in *The Glory of Their Times*. "I swear, when it went past the plate it was just the spit went by."[1]

The spitball rocketed Walsh to stardom, making him a key component of the league's best pitching staff. Walsh contributed 17 wins to a starting corps that included 20-game win-ners Frank Smith and Nick Altrock, and 18-game winner Doc White, offsetting an offense that finished last in the league in batting average and had earned the appellation "Hitless Wonders." Despite their .230 team batting average in 1906, the Sox finished fourth out of eight American League teams in runs scored. No regular batted higher than .279 that season and the team hit only seven home runs in 154 games. Pitching and defense, which helped mediocre hitting teams in St. Louis win pennants for Comiskey 20 years before, fueled the rise of the White Sox, and the ascendance of Ed Walsh may have been the final piece of the championship puzzle. The White Sox won the pennant by three games over second-place New York, and Walsh's two complete-game wins in the World Series, one a two-hit shutout with 12 strikeouts, led the Sox to an unexpected victory over their greatest rivals, the National League Cubs.

Comiskey, after years of effort, had finally bested his National League rivals and claimed the top rung on the ladder of Chicago baseball, though his stay there was short-lived. His White Sox failed to repeat as champions in 1907, finishing third, while the crosstown Cubs won the first of two consecutive World Series titles over the Detroit Tigers that October. Still, Comiskey could be proud of the prosperous baseball franchise he had created in his home-town, the place where his Irish immigrant father had risen from the ranks of laborers to respect and admiration as an alderman. His only regret was that "Honest John" Comiskey, who died in 1900, did not live to see his son Charlie's greatest success.

The Irish still played an important role in baseball, though their numbers were not as great as they had been a decade earlier. Ed Walsh, the workhorse spitball hurler, was the most familiar, but Comiskey's 1906 champions featured other important contributors who shared their owner's ethnic heritage. Patsy Dougherty and Jiggs Donahue are little-known today,

Spitball king Ed Walsh, one of Charlie Comiskey's favorite players. Walsh was the last major league pitcher to win 40 games in a season (author's collection).

but they were key performers on Comiskey's first world champi-onship team.

Patrick (Patsy) Dougherty was a tall, muscular outfielder whose fair skin and bright, curly red hair made him look like the stereotype of the Irish ballplayer. His parents were born in Ireland and fled the famine like so many of their coun-trymen. After settling in Allegany County, New York, they built a prosperous farming business and later found oil on their land. His family was well off, with invest-ments in banking and real estate, but Patsy was intent on a baseball career. He bounced around the minors for several years before Boston manager Jimmy Collins saw him play in a California winter league contest and signed him for the 1902 season. Within two years, Dougherty became one of Boston's best hitters, batting .331 and leading the Boston Americans (later called the Red Sox) to victory in the first World Series in 1903.

Dougherty was so valuable that league president Ban Johnson, intent on building a strong team in New York, engineered his transfer to the Highlanders (now called the Yankees) in mid-season of 1904. The trade was loudly criticized in the Boston papers, and although the Americans won the pennant again, Dougherty's bat helped keep the Highlanders in the race until the final day of the season, when Jack Chesbro's wild pitch gave Boston the flag by one game. Dougherty was unhappy in New York, slumping at the bat in 1905, and in June of 1906 he and Highlanders manager Clark Griffith traded punches in the clubhouse after a particularly tough loss. Shortly thereafter, Dougherty was dealt to Chicago, where his resuscitated bat gave a boost to the "Hitless Wonders" in their pennant race.

Like Comiskey, John (Jiggs) Donahue, a native of Springfield, Ohio, was a second-generation Irishman whose defensive skill at first base made up for his mediocre hitting. Though Donahue was one of only three starters on the 1906 championship team to bat above .250 (shortstop George Davis and second baseman Frank Isbell were the others), he was better known for his glove work. In 1908 he set a record by handling 21 putouts without an error in a nine-inning game. Still, he could rise to the occasion on offense when needed, and White Sox fans long remembered his seventh-inning single which broke up Ed Reulbach's quest for a no-hitter in Game 2 of the 1906 World Series. Donahue had the only hit off Reulbach that day, saving his team the embarrassment of being no-hit on baseball's biggest stage by their bitter rivals, the Cubs. Another 50 years would pass before Don Larsen of the Yankees became the first man to pitch a hitless game in the Series.

Donahue was a valuable player, but an undisciplined one. His late-night escapades kept manager Fielder Jones on his toes, and a series of fines levied by Comiskey appeared to have little effect on the red-haired first baseman's behavior. Donahue loathed spring training, and Comiskey could always count on his first baseman to hold out for more money every March and report late even after he had signed his name to a contract. Still, Donahue solidified the infield defense and helped the White Sox pitchers allow the fewest runs in the league in 1906.

Ed Walsh won 24 games in 1907 and became the workhorse of the Chicago staff. He pitched 422 innings and started 46 games, cementing his status as Comiskey's favorite player. In 1908 Walsh, at age 27, put together one of the finest seasons ever by an American League pitcher. He won an astounding 40 games, becoming the last major leaguer to win that many in one season, and his 464 innings pitched set a post–1900 record that has lasted for 100 years. "Big Ed" nearly pitched the White Sox to the pennant by himself, and on October 2, 1908, he struck out a record 15 Cleveland Naps in perhaps the most important game of the season, allowing only one run in nine innings. Unfortunately, his Cleveland mound opponent, Addie Joss, threw a perfect game against Chicago that afternoon, all but knocking the White Sox out of the pennant race. The 1908 Sox, an even weaker-hitting aggregation than the 1906 crew, finished in third place behind Detroit and Cleveland.

At season's end, manager Fielder Jones decided to step down as manager. He may have been tired of Comiskey's meddling, though some reports say that he was troubled by health problems. Rumors flew that he wanted an ownership stake in the ballclub, a demand that Comiskey was unwilling to meet. For whatever reason, Jones relinquished the manager's post, despite appeals from both Comiskey and league president Ban Johnson to stay on for one more year. In the spring of 1909, after Comiskey was finally convinced that Jones was not returning, the team owner hired another Irish-American manager when he appointed catcher Billy Sullivan, another of his favorite players, to the position.

Most Irish immigrants settled in the larger cities of the East and Midwest, but others, having been farmers in Ireland, decided to pursue the same occupation in their new country. Billy Sullivan's parents were among those who left Ireland and opted for the rural life, settling in the farming community of Oakland, Wisconsin, where Billy was born in 1875. He starred in high school as a shortstop before moving to the catching position, then played independent ball before his climb up the professional baseball ladder brought him to the National League with the Boston Beaneaters in 1899. After two solid years, he jumped to the White Sox of the American League for the 1901 season. He claimed the starting catcher's job for the pennant-winning Sox that season, and held it for the rest of the decade.

Sullivan was, to put it bluntly, one of the worst hitters in baseball history. His .213 career batting average is the second lowest of all players with more than 1,000 times at bat, and in five different campaigns his average failed to reach the .200 mark. However, he was also one of the greatest defensive catchers in the game's annals, and his work behind the bat and stellar game management skills won many contests for the White Sox. Ty Cobb praised Sullivan as the best catcher "ever to wear shoe leather," and stated that "no man in the business [knew] more about getting the best work from a pitcher and holding an infield together."[2] The Chicago hurlers always seemed to pitch better with Sullivan behind the plate, and Comiskey, himself a great defensive player and below-average hitter, valued Sullivan highly. By 1909, Sullivan and first baseman Frank Isbell were the only remaining members of both the 1901 and 1906 White Sox pennant-winning teams.

The new manager faced a daunting task. Comiskey had always built his teams with pitching and defense as priorities, but the "Hitless Wonders" tag was even more deserved in 1908 than it had been two years earlier. None of the four starting infielders batted above .217 that season, and Sullivan, the regular catcher, contributed a .191 average. Moreover, first baseman Jiggs Donahue was fading rapidly, due to age and his undisciplined lifestyle. Comiskey could no longer tolerate Donahue's curfew-breaking and alcohol-feuled escapades, so he sold the first sacker to Washington in May of 1909. Within a year Donahue was out of the majors and faced a demotion to the Minneapolis team of the American Association. Instead, Donahue bought Cap Anson's semipro team with the intention of managing his own club in the Chicago city league, but the effort failed, leaving Donahue penniless. Three years later, he contracted a disease, reportedly syphilis, and died only six days after his 34th birthday.

Billy Sullivan, a poor hitter but a top-notch defensive catcher, managed the White Sox in 1909 (Library of Congress).

Sullivan did his best, but a punchless offense, combined with a rapidly aging roster, caused the White Sox to drop to fourth place in 1909. Ed Walsh's record-setting workload of the season before caused arm problems for the spitball specialist, and his win total fell from 40 in 1908 to 15 in 1909. Sullivan himself batted only .162 as the regular catcher and was unable to establish discipline, being too amiable a man to enforce team rules on players who had been his teammates the year before. At season's end, Comiskey decided that Sullivan was not cut out to manage after all. The owner promised him a place with the White Sox for the rest of his life if he wanted it, but replaced him as manager with another Irish-American veteran, Hugh Duffy.

Duffy and Comiskey knew each other well, having performed together on the Players League team in Chicago in 1890. Duffy had captained Boston's pennant winning clubs in the National League during the 1890s, and had spent two years as field leader of the Phillies. He also served as owner and manager of the Eastern League club in Providence, in his home state of Rhode Island. He had passed his 40th birthday, but still batted well over .300 as a part-time player in 1907 and 1908. Duffy was eager to return to the majors, and agreed to manage the White Sox in 1910 for his old teammate and manager Comiskey.

The 1910 season saw the opening of a new ballpark, which the optimistic owner labeled the "Base Ball Palace of the World," on Chicago's South Side. Comiskey asked his favorite pitcher, Ed Walsh, for advice on the layout of the field, and Walsh made sure that the new edifice (which became known as Comiskey Park) was one of the worst hitter's parks in the major leagues. He suggested that Comiskey set the fences at 362 feet down the lines and 420 feet to center. Comiskey needed no prodding to make the field dimensions especially large, as he believed that batters should earn their hits, and that defense and pitching win games. True to the owner's Irish heritage, Comiskey laid a cornerstone, painted green, on St. Patrick's Day. The new ballpark, which seated 29,000 people, was completed in only three and a half months, and opened for business on July 1, 1910. The distant outfield fences and spacious foul area proved helpful to the pitchers, and Walsh led the league in earned run average that season despite his 18-20 record. The layout also depressed batting averages, and the already low-hitting White Sox finished last or next to last in the league in scoring during four of the next five seasons.[3]

Hugh Duffy was unable to elevate the White Sox above fifth place during his two seasons as manager, so in 1912 Comiskey brought in a familiar face to lead his ballclub. Jimmy Callahan, fired by Comiskey as manager eight years before, had impressed the Chicago team owner by operating his own profitable semipro team, the Logan Squares, in the Chicago City League. With a few former major leaguers on his roster, Callahan's club may have been the best "outlaw" team in the nation at the time. The Logan Squares won the Chicago city championship over clubs headed by other famous names, including former Chicago National League stars Cap Anson and Jimmy Ryan. In the fall of 1906, Callahan's team defeated both major league pennant winners, the Cubs and White Sox, in exhibition games. The popularity of the Chicago semipro scene had abated by the end of the decade, so Callahan sold the Logan Squares and returned to the White Sox as a player under Hugh Duffy for the 1911 season. Before signing Callahan to a contract, Comiskey had to get his name removed from baseball's ineligible list, on which he had been placed after quitting the White Sox in 1905. After a round of negotiations with league president Ban Johnson, Callahan paid a fine of $700 and was restored to the league's good graces. Comiskey, the founder and sole owner of his own successful ballclub, may have seen something of himself in his former manager, so in 1912 he hired Callahan to succeed Duffy.

The 37-year-old Callahan was still a good player, having batted .281 with 45 stolen bases as Chicago's regular left fielder in 1911. As a manager, however, he was subject to the same obstacles faced by all of Comiskey's field leaders. Comiskey was a hands-on boss, always ready with a stream of suggestions that were uncomfortably close to direct orders. The Chicago offense was still as poor as ever, and Callahan proved no more successful than his predecessor had been, ending up in fourth, fifth, and sixth place in his three seasons at the helm. He played for only one more year, hitting .272 in 1912. Thereafter, he managed from the bench, appearing in only six games in 1913.

During the winter of 1913-1914, Comiskey and Giants manager John McGraw staged a round-the-world baseball tour in imitation of the famous trip conducted in 1888 by Al Spalding, Cap Anson and a team of National League all-stars. The trip was filled with interesting sights, and the Irish Catholics on the excursion were thrilled to meet Pope Benedict in Rome. However, World War One broke out not long after the conclusion of the tour, and the resultant goodwill and publicity were quickly forgotten. Moreover, the two teams were exhausted when they returned home after six months abroad, just in time for the 1914 baseball season. The White Sox fell to sixth place that year, while the Giants, winners of the previous three National League championships, lost the pennant by ten and a half games to the Boston Braves.

Comiskey's White Sox had not won a pennant since their World Series victory of 1906, so the owner decided to shake things up. At the conclusion of the 1914 season, he dismissed Jimmy Callahan and appointed a virtual unknown to manage his club. Clarence (Pants) Rowland, the first non–Irishman to lead the Sox since Fielder Jones left in 1908, came to the White Sox from Dubuque, Iowa, which was Mrs. Comiskey's home town and the scene of the owner's professional debut more than 30 years before. Rowland, as a major league novice, was eager to make a good impression, and did not mind listening to and acting upon Comiskey's advice. Though many around the American League called Rowland "the busher" in a sneering tone, it appeared that Comiskey had finally found his ideal manager, even though Rowland's ancestry was English, not Irish.

Despite their mediocre showing in the standings, Comiskey's ballclub finished first or second in attendance each season during this era, making the White Sox the most profitable team in Ban Johnson's circuit. By this time, Comiskey had recognized that the White Sox could not compete with their usual anemic offense, so he decided to use his checkbook to upgrade his lineup. Following the 1914 season, he bought Eddie Collins, a high average hitter and the premier second baseman in the game, from the Philadelphia Athletics for $50,000. In August of 1915, taking advantage of the impending bankruptcy of Cleveland Indians owner Charles Somers, he set his sights on one of baseball's top hitters, Shoeless Joe Jackson. Comiskey gave his secretary, Harry Grabiner, a blank check. "Go to Cleveland," ordered Comiskey, "watch the bidding for Jackson, [and] raise the highest one made by any club until they all drop out."[4] Twenty-four hours later, Grabiner informed Comiskey that he had purchased Jackson from the Indians for $31,500 in cash and four players who represented a total value of $34,000. The deal for Jackson was the most expensive, in terms of cash and player value, in the history of baseball up to that time.[5]

Thus fortified, the White Sox jumped to third place in 1915 and second in 1916. Collins and Jackson added a much-needed dose of hitting skill to the lineup, and a pitching staff headed by Red Faber, Eddie Cicotte, and Claude (Lefty) Williams boosted the club into the ranks of contenders. Comiskey's latest aggregation of talent ran away with the pennant in 1917, ending Boston's two-year reign on top of the American League. A six-game victory over McGraw's Giants in the World Series put Comiskey's White Sox once again at the pinnacle of the baseball world.

Comiskey, who was usually something of a sentimentalist, nevertheless cut his ties with two of his favorite Irish veterans during this period. In early 1915, he fired Billy Sullivan, the longtime catcher and former manager who had served as a coach for the team for the previous few seasons. The decision shocked Sullivan, who had counted on Comiskey's long-ago promise of lifetime employment with the team, and confused many Chicago fans and sportswriters. Perhaps the owner wanted to give his new manager, Pants Rowland, free rein to hire his own assistants, and maybe Comiskey believed that having a former manager on the coaching staff would distract the new field leader. At any rate, Comiskey never explained why he made the move. After spending one year in the minors and another with the Detroit Tigers, Sullivan retired to a fruit farm in Oregon and never returned to the game. Years later, Billy Sullivan Junior, a catcher like his father, played for the White Sox for three seasons of his 12-year major league career.

The other Comiskey favorite to leave the employ of the White Sox was Ed Walsh, the spitball king and perennial workhorse of the pitching staff. Walsh had won 27 games for Chicago in both 1911 and 1912, but years of pitching from 350 to 460 innings per season caught up to him. In 1913 "Big Ed" won only eight games in limited action. The sore-armed Irishman tried for several years to salvage his career, but managed to pitch in only nine games from 1914 to 1916, whereupon Comiskey decided to release his former ace. After another comeback attempt with the Braves in 1917, Walsh called it quits at the age of 36. Like Billy Sullivan, Walsh also had a son who pitched for the White Sox many years later, though the younger Ed Walsh won only 11 major league games, 171 fewer than his famous father.

Walsh and Sullivan were gone, but the White Sox of this era were not without an Irish presence. Outfielder John (Shano) Collins, no relation to Eddie, was the son of an immigrant laborer from the heavily Irish Charlestown section of Boston. Shano, so called because the Irish equivalent of his first name was Sean, had joined the White Sox as a first baseman in 1910 before switching to right field. Never a star, he was still a valuable outfielder who delivered the game-winning hit on September 21, 1917, when the White Sox clinched their first pennant in 11 years. By this time, Shano was the senior member of the team in length of service, and though he was only a part-time player during the latter part of the decade, he was a solidly dependable member of the ballclub. Eddie Murphy, from Hancock, New York, had played briefly at Villanova University and for Jack Dunn's Baltimore Orioles before Connie Mack acquired him in 1912 to play for the Athletics. He had been Mack's right fielder on Philadelphia's 1913 and 1914 championship clubs before Comiskey bought his contract from Mack for $13,500 in July of 1915. Murphy, like Shano Collins, was a reserve outfielder whose veteran presence was much appreciated by Comiskey and manager Rowland.

The coaching staff, too, had its own Irish character, and some say that Pants Rowland owed his success to the baseball acumen of one of his coaches. Kid Gleason, hired by Comiskey in 1912, was an Irishman who had been in the game for nearly three decades, first as a pitcher with Harry Wright's Philadelphia Phillies in the late 1880s, then on the infield with John McGraw and the battling Orioles of the 1890s. Gleason was a colorful character, perhaps the best pound-for-pound fighter in the game, and a multitalented player who enjoyed a 22-year career in the major leagues. His sharp tongue and endless supply of witty observations made him popular with the Chicago sportswriters. He was also the team's unofficial trainer. "The Kid was as good a man with tape and bandages, pills and ointments, as he was with the quick retort," wrote newspaperman Warren Brown, who described the new manager as "a belligerent little man."[6] John J. Ward, in *Baseball Magazine*, described him as "intensely active and even fidgety with suppressed energy. His eyes sparkle when he talks and he seems to find it difficult to sit still for any length of time."[7]

Gleason had built an enviable reputation in the baseball world since leaving Ned Hanlon's

Orioles after the 1895 season. He spent five years with the New York Giants, jumped to the new American League's Detroit Tigers for two years, then switched leagues again to play for the Phillies in his adopted hometown of Philadelphia. He was still a battler, though by 1905 he was the oldest active player in the National League. One day a New York Giants rookie named Moose McCormick, not knowing of Gleason's tough-guy reputation, offered to trade punches with the Kid at second base one day. Giants manager John McGraw fairly leaped off the bench and charged onto the field to save his young player from a severe beating at Gleason's hands. "Don't you hit him!" he screamed at Gleason. "You keep your hands off him!"[8] Despite McGraw's agitation, McCormick rashly challenged Gleason to meet him outside the clubhouse after the game.

Fortunately for McCormick, Gleason admired the rookie's aggressive attitude. "Don't get excited," said Gleason to his old Oriole teammate McGraw. "I'm not going to hurt him. I just think he's a game kid, and I like him and want to take him out to dinner." In later years, McCormick was relieved with the outcome of the incident. "I wasn't game," said McCormick. "I was just dumb. After I found out how tough he was I realized what a narrow escape I had had from a terrific beating."[9]

Many observers figured that Gleason, assisted by captain Eddie Collins, was the real brains behind the White Sox, with Rowland merely a figurehead, and such suspicions gained credence when Gleason sat out the 1918 season after a pay dispute with Comiskey. Rowland's defending world champions fell to sixth place without Gleason, though all of baseball was turned upside down by the military draft. Star pitchers Red Faber and Jim Scott enlisted in the armed services, while other White Sox (pitcher Lefty Williams and outfielders Joe Jackson and Happy

Felsch among them) left the team to work in war-related industries such as steel mills and shipyards. The White Sox roster was in a state of flux all year, and without Gleason's steadying presence, the club floundered in the second division.

The success of the White Sox, culminating in the 1917 world championship, had come at a price. Comiskey's franchise was perhaps the most profitable in the game at the time, but many of the players grumbled about their salaries. Jackson, one of the most prolific hitters in baseball, was earning only $6,000 a year, the same amount that Comiskey himself had received from the St. Louis Browns nearly 30 years before (though Comiskey was both a player and the manager of the Browns). Collins, however, drew a salary of $14,500 per season, a fact which aroused the jealousy of some of his teammates. It appeared that the college men on the club, especially Collins and pitcher Red Faber, were favored with larger paychecks than the less-educated country boys who were led by first baseman Arnold (Chick) Gandil. The World Series win over the Giants had calmed the bad feelings, but

Charles Comiskey in his heyday as owner of the Chicago White Sox (author's collection).

not eliminated them, and by 1918 the White Sox were divided into two bitterly opposed camps, led by Collins and Gandil.

The 1918 campaign ended, at the government's request, on Labor Day, and Pants Rowland decided that he had taken the White Sox as far as he could. The Collins and Gandil factions had bickered and fought all year long, making the manager's job, as Warren Brown described it, like "getting room and board in a den of jaguars, with a hyena or two and a few wolves tossed in for good measure."[10] Rowland, tired of the discord, opted to leave the Sox and join the minor league Milwaukee team as president and part owner. His departure gave Comiskey the opportunity to hire his favorite type of manager, the brainy Irishman, once again. On New Year's Eve, the club announced that Kid Gleason would return to the team and manage it for the 1919 season.

Gleason's appointment was well received by fans and players alike, and the end of the war in November 1918 made it possible for Comiskey and his new manager to reassemble the most talented team in baseball. The 1919 White Sox, with almost all of the same players who had won the world title two years before, breezed to the pennant, Comiskey's fifth (counting the 1900 flag) as a team owner. The club was still torn by factions and backbiting, especially between the Collins group, who came mostly from the northern states, and the rougher Gandil followers, mainly from the South. The divisions can be illustrated by the fact that Collins, the captain of the ballclub, was not on speaking terms with any of his fellow infielders. When the White Sox threw the ball around between innings, none of the other infielders would toss Collins the ball. Instead, he warmed up with catcher Ray Schalk. However, Kid Gleason was a stronger personality than Pants Rowland, and led the team to the flag despite the ongoing clubhouse turmoil. "I think they're the greatest ball club I've ever seen. Period," said Gleason later.

However, not even a forceful presence like Kid Gleason could avert the disaster that occurred in the 1919 World Series against the Cincinnati Reds. First baseman Chick Gandil, driven by his hatred of Eddie Collins and his resentment at what he considered a paltry salary, saw an opportunity to turn the upcoming post-season match into a financial windfall, as well as a way to exact revenge for his perceived ill-treatment. Acting in concert with a bevy of gamblers and other shady characters, Gandil convinced several of his teammates to join him in throwing the World Series in exchange for amounts of cash that, on the best available evidence, ranged from $5,000 to $35,000 per man. The October series against the Reds was a distressing display of poor hitting and bad fielding, and though Kid Gleason raged at his players, the Reds defeated the favored White Sox in eight games to win their first world championship.

The 1920 campaign was a nightmare for the Sox, though they battled the Yankees and Indians for the pennant until the final week of the season. Kid Gleason, Eddie Collins, and the honest White Sox were convinced that several of their teammates had lost the Series on purpose. Although conclusive proof was lacking, the suspected members of the Gandil faction kept to themselves all year, fearing the exposure that was no doubt inevitable under the circumstances. When a grand jury investigation made the particulars of the scandal public in the last few days of the 1920 season, Comiskey suspended seven of his White Sox for their apparent involvement in the scheme (Gandil, the mastermind of the plan, had retired before the campaign began). None of the "Black Sox" ever played major league ball again, and the White Sox team, shorn of much of its talent, dropped all the way to seventh place in 1921, with only the inept Philadelphia Athletics preventing the once-powerful Sox from falling to rock bottom.

The World Series fiasco profoundly affected both Charles Comiskey and Kid Gleason, two tough Irishmen who were heartbroken by the betrayal of many of their star players.

Gleason remained as manager until 1923, but observers noted that his heart was not really in his work during his last several seasons. After five years at the helm, Gleason quit the team and spent two years out of baseball, returning to the game only after his good friend and fellow Philadelphia native, Connie Mack, talked him out of retirement to coach for the Athletics. He helped Mack build the Athletics into a championship ballclub, then retired after the 1931 World Series due to failing health. He died in Philadelphia on the day after New Year's in 1933.

As for Charlie Comiskey, his final years were colored by the events of the 1919 Series and the resultant banishment of Shoeless Joe Jackson and seven other White Sox. The Sox never climbed above fifth place during the remainder of Comiskey's life, and in 1924, the year after Gleason left, the Sox finished last in the American League for the first time. Comiskey tried to replace Gleason with other Irish managers, including Johnny Evers, Eddie Collins, and, briefly, his longtime favorite Ed Walsh, but nothing worked, and the White Sox sank into the doldrums as the 1920s progressed. Comiskey's health began to fail as his team's prospects dimmed, and in October of 1931, the founder and sole owner of the White Sox died at his vacation home in rural Wisconsin. Eight years later, on May 2, 1939, Comiskey was one of six men named by a special committee to the Baseball Hall of Fame. Cap Anson, his longtime rival for Chicago baseball supremacy, was one of the other five.

Charlie Comiskey, the son of an Irish immigrant, had won four pennants as a manager during the 1880s, then built one of the most storied franchises of major league baseball, one that prospers to this day. However, the events of the 1919 Series scandal brought him down, and though family members carried on as owners after he died, the remaining Comiskeys sold the team to Bill Veeck in 1959. Comiskey Park, the "Base Ball Palace of the World," lasted until 1990 when it was replaced by a new stadium, originally called New Comiskey Park and now known as U.S. Cellular Field. The Comiskey name is no longer a part of the team Charlie built, and not until 2005, 74 years after his death, would his Chicago White Sox win another World Series.

11

McGraw and the Giants

John McGraw was a man in a hurry. At the age of 26, he took a decimated Baltimore club in 1899 and led it, through hard work and sheer will, to a respectable fourth-place finish in a 12-team league. He was a major participant in the effort to revive the dormant American Association and create a new circuit, but when that dream failed, he reluctantly spent the 1900 campaign playing for Patsy Tebeau with the St. Louis Cardinals. However, he had agreed to go to St. Louis in return for unrestricted free agency at season's end. He was already plotting his next move, which turned out to be, to the surprise of no one, a return to Baltimore with a new edition of the Orioles.

Byron (Ban) Johnson, a former Cincinnati sportswriter, had founded the Western League in 1894. This circuit, the best-run minor league in the nation, was centered in the Midwest, hosting teams in cities such as Detroit, Indianapolis, and St. Paul, Minnesota. Johnson, however, was not content with a mere minor league. He had long planned to move into larger cities, especially in the eastern part of the country, and create a second major circuit on a par with the established National League. In 1900 Johnson renamed his circuit the American League, moved Charlie Comiskey's St. Paul team to Chicago, and placed a new team in Cleveland with Jimmy McAleer as manager. In 1901, Johnson made his biggest move. He declared his American League a major circuit, and placed teams in Boston and Philadelphia as direct rivals of the older league. He also scored a coup in convincing John McGraw, the most sought-after young manager in the game, to create a new franchise from scratch in Baltimore.

McGraw, once again in charge, rose to the challenge. Several of his old Oriole teammates and friends, such as Willie Keeler, Joe Kelley, and Hugh Jennings, could not be pried away from their National League contracts, but "Iron Man" Joe McGinnity, his most reliable pitcher on the 1899 Orioles, signed on happily for a salary of $2,800. The 37-year-old veteran Wilbert Robinson also followed McGraw back to Baltimore, serving as a backup catcher and chief assistant to his much younger manager. Predictably, the new Orioles had a distinct Irish flavor, enhanced by young stars such as Roger Bresnahan and Mike Donlin.

Roger Bresnahan was totally Irish in character and manner, and did not bother to correct people who naturally assumed that he was born on the Emerald Isle. In fact, his parents, Michael Bresnahan and the former Mary O'Donoughue, came from Tralee in County Cork. They arrived in America in 1870 and settled in Toledo, Ohio, where Roger was born in 1879. The seventh child of the family, Roger starred on the Toledo sandlots, and at age 17, he began his pro career in the Ohio State League with the Lima club. One year later, Roger signed with the Washington Senators and pitched in six games late in the 1897 season, posting a 4-0 record and batting .375. Deacon McGuire, the veteran catcher, told the papers that Roger "comes of the right stuff; good, old gamey Irish blood in that lad,"[1] but a salary dispute the following spring sent Roger back to Toledo. A two-game tryout in Chicago in 1900 ended in his release, but McGraw liked what he saw in the 20-year-old. He signed Bresnahan to play for Baltimore in 1901, beginning a lifelong friendship between the two men.

Bresnahan, like his fellow second-generation Irishman McGraw, was small in stature, highly intelligent, and maniacally combative when a ballgame was on the line. He was "highly strung and almost abnormally emotional," said one reporter, but was a winner with a talent for playing many positions on the field. He had spent the bulk of his professional career on the mound or behind the plate, but McGraw recognized his versatility. Accordingly, Bresnahan shared the catching duties with Wilbert Robinson in 1901, but saw action at second base, third base, pitcher, right field, and left field as well. He batted only .268 that year, in a season in which the league as a whole hit .277, but his flexibility made Roger one of the most valuable Orioles.

Another new Oriole, outfielder Mike Donlin, was feisty like Bresnahan, with an added touch of volatility in his makeup. Donlin, too, was an Irishman, having been born to immigrant parents in Peoria, Illinois in 1878. The Donlins moved to Erie, Pennsylvania, where John Donlin found work as a railroad conductor, but tragedy struck when Mike's parents were killed in the collapse of a railroad bridge. Orphaned at the age of eight, Mike moved in with another Irish family, the Murphys, who treated him as their own. However, Mike was sickly from then on, suffering from consumption and a weak constitution. He moved to California as a teenager, and playing baseball in the mild climate eventually restored his health. He was only five feet and nine inches tall, but his strength and quickness afoot made up for his lack of height.

Mike Donlin rose quickly through the California minor leagues, aided by a keen sense of self-promotion. While pitching for Santa Cruz in 1898, he handed a photo of himself to a San Francisco newspaper artist and said, "If you put a picture of me in the paper, I know I'll get a break. I know I'm going to be great."[2] He attracted more notice by painting his bat red, white, and blue to commemorate the nation's victory in the Spanish-American War. He was "the typical wild Irish kid," complained one opposing manager, but his campaign for attention paid off. He batted .402 for Santa Cruz in 1899, then made his National League debut with St. Louis later that year. In 1900, still with St. Louis, he became a teammate of John McGraw, who saw in Donlin his ideal of the scrapping, hustling Irish ballplayer. Although not much of a fielder, he played passably in the outfield and batted .344 for Baltimore in 1901.

Donlin was an outgoing, personable chap, but his love for nightlife and alcohol often outweighed his commitment to baseball. They called him "Turkey Mike" for the way he strutted, on the field and off, brashly displaying his confidence to opponents and fans alike. He could not be counted upon to follow team rules, especially those regarding curfew in hotels on the road. Even when he was present for bed check late at night, Donlin was known to climb out a window and down a drainpipe for another round of partying. Still, McGraw believed that Donlin's talent was worth the trouble he would inevitably cause. McGraw never shied away from a disciplinary challenge and was convinced that he could control his star outfielder's behavior.

With Joe McGinnity and McGraw himself added to a solid, largely Irish core of talent, the Baltimore club expected to contend for the first American League pennant. However, McGraw had assembled a team that was perfectly suited to battle in the wild and untamed

National League of the previous decade. American League founder and president Ban Johnson was a crusader for "clean baseball," meaning that the unfettered rowdiness and umpire abuse that flourished in the National League would not be allowed in his circuit. "My determination," said Johnson in an interview many years later, "was to pattern baseball in this new league along the lines of scholastic contests, to make ability and brains and clean, honest play, not the swinging of clenched fists, coarse oaths, riots or assaults upon the umpires, decide the issue."[3] Given McGraw's history, one wonders how anyone thought that McGraw and Johnson could coexist. Both men soon regretted their partnership, which lasted less than two seasons.

McGraw's Orioles ran into trouble with the league president almost immediately. They bullied, threatened, and raged at umpires, following McGraw's dictum that "it's the prospect of a hot fight that brings out the crowds ... namby-pamby methods don't get much in results."[4] Ban Johnson, however, would not tolerate such tactics. In May he suspended McGraw for five games after a running battle between the Baltimore manager and the arbiters in Philadelphia, and later that month a near-riot ensued in Detroit when umpire Jack Sheridan ejected pitcher Harry Howell for obscene language. McGraw refused to take Howell off the field, Mike Donlin threw a baseball at Sheridan, and Sheri-

"Turkey Mike" Donlin in 1905. He quit baseball in 1908 and spent the next two years on the stage before returning to the Giants (1906 Spalding Guide).

dan forfeited the game to the Tigers. That June, Johnson blocked Hugh Jennings, McGraw's old National League teammate and close friend, from joining the Orioles, insisting that the Philadelphia Athletics had a prior claim on Jennings' services. Jennings then refused to join the Athletics and remained in the National League, and the relationship between Johnson and McGraw continued to deteriorate.

Baltimore finished in fifth place in 1901, and the next year McGraw received a new infusion of Irish talent. Joe Kelley, perhaps the best player on the Oriole pennant winners of 1894 to 1896, and Dan McGann, who played with McGraw in Baltimore and St. Louis, arrived and bolstered the lineup for another run at the pennant. Kelley and his father-in-law, a powerful Baltimore political figure named John J. Mahon, bought stock in the team, with Mahon becoming president of the club. However, McGraw's own playing career virtually ended in May of that season, when Dick Harley of the Detroit Tigers slid into the manager with his spikes high, inflicting a deep gash in McGraw's left knee. The resulting infection incapacitated McGraw for weeks, and his knee never fully recovered. Mike Donlin, too, was unavailable, having accosted a woman on the street and punched her in a drunken rage in March of 1902. He was sentenced to spend six months in the Baltimore County jail, after which Ban Johnson expelled the troubled player from the American League.

McGraw and Johnson continued to snipe at each other, and rumors soon reached Baltimore that Johnson planned to drop the Orioles from the league after the 1902 season in favor of a new franchise in New York. Such a move would give the young league a presence in the nation's largest city, and would also rid the circuit of McGraw and his raucous crew of combative Orioles. McGraw, however, was determined to leave the league on his own terms. "Someone would be left holding the bag," said McGraw years later, "and I made up my mind it wouldn't be me."[5] In June of 1902, he hatched a plan that would not only pave his return to the National League, but might also damage the American, and Ban Johnson, irreparably.

McGraw, Wilbert Robinson, Joe Kelley, and John J. Mahon all owned stock in the Baltimore team. Mahon bought up the shares held by the three players and then set to work buying out enough of the other stockholders to give him majority ownership in the franchise. Once that task was accomplished, McGraw demanded, and received, a release from his contract. On July 8, he abruptly quit the Orioles and signed a deal to manage the New York Giants of the National League. Eight days later, Mahon shocked the baseball world when he sold the Orioles to Andrew Freedman, owner of the Giants. A National League team now owned an American League franchise outright, and the destruction of the Orioles began immediately. Freedman, following McGraw's advice, released Kelley, McGann, Bresnahan, McGinnity, and other stars from their Baltimore contracts, making them free agents and available to sign anywhere they wished.

Most of these new free agents enthusiastically followed McGraw to the Giants, though Joe Kelley did not. Kelley had long nurtured aspirations to manage, but his path had always been blocked by either Ned Hanlon or John McGraw. As a reward for his part in the scheme, Kelley emerged from the deal as the new playing manager of the Cincinnati Reds. As it turned out, one of the Giants' co-owners, John T. Brush, also held most of the stock in the Cincinnati club, and had coveted Kelley for some time. As part of the deal worked out among Brush and Freedman on one side and Kelley and his father-in-law, John J. Mahon, on the other, Kelley was allowed to go to Cincinnati and take pitcher-turned-outfielder Cy Seymour with him. This transfer provided a needed talent infusion to the moribund Reds, a team that had not won a pennant since 1882.

Wilbert Robinson remained in Baltimore, his adopted home town, but when the dust settled, the decimated Oriole club was left with only five players on its roster. Ban Johnson quickly gained control of the wrecked franchise, borrowed players from the other seven American League teams, and, with Robinson as manager, kept the Orioles afloat for the rest of the season, though the team sank quickly to the bottom of the standings. In 1903, as predicted, Johnson dropped Baltimore from the league and created a franchise in New York, one that would eventually become the Yankees. Baltimore would not host major league baseball again, except for a two-year membership in the short-lived Federal League, until 1954.

John McGraw now faced his greatest challenge in reviving the New York Giants, once one of the premier teams in the National League. They had been virtually dormant since their victory over the Orioles in the 1894 Temple Cup series. Andrew Freedman, a prominent Tammany Hall politician and a key figure in the national Democratic Party hierarchy, had been a disaster as a club owner, hiring and firing managers on a whim and driving talented players away from the Polo Grounds. By 1902 the Giants were a perennial second-division team with poor attendance, and looked to McGraw to turn the franchise around. He did so in spectacular fashion, following his tried-and-true formula of filling his roster with tough, scrappy Irishmen like himself.

At McGraw's direction, Freedman released six players from the New York roster to make room for the mostly Irish contingent from Baltimore. Joe McGinnity, Roger Bresnahan, Dan McGann, and pitcher Jack Cronin signed contracts with the Giants, and no one doubted that Mike Donlin would do the same after his release from jail in the fall. One Irishman who had already received his walking papers from the Giants was McGraw's old teammate and enemy, Jack Doyle, who had managed the club seven years before and had bounced around the league ever since. McGraw wanted no part of Doyle, so "Dirty Jack" was free to continue his nomadic career elsewhere.

The Giants finished in last place in 1902, but began their climb up the standings the following year under McGraw's leadership. Christy Mathewson, the best young pitcher in the game, had preceded McGraw to New York. He teamed with Joe McGinnity to form a formidable pitching duo, with Mathewson posting a 30-13 record and McGinnity a 31-20 mark. The versatile Bresnahan batted .350, spending most of his time in the outfield while filling in occasionally at catcher. The Giants finished in second position and led the league in attendance, making the franchise the premier team in the National League once more. However, McGraw was not done remaking the Giants. The left side of the infield, with Charlie Babb at shortstop and Billy Lauder at third, was weak, so McGraw upgraded both positions in early 1904. He made a trade with Chicago to acquire veteran shortstop Bill Dahlen, and signed a former Georgetown University player named Art Devlin to play third.

Art Devlin, like Bresnahan, Donlin, McGinnity, and McGraw himself, was a quick-tempered second-generation Irishman who never hesitated to use his fists when called upon. Born in Washington, D.C., in 1879, his immigrant father Edward worked as a harness maker and locksmith. The family must have been prosperous, for Edward Devlin sent his son to Georgetown University beginning in 1899. Art did not complete his degree, but starred on the baseball and football teams before leaving school after two years to play professional ball. A good season at Newark in 1903 brought him to the attention of John McGraw, who signed the youngster to a contract.

Devlin was one of the biggest Irish Giants, standing six feet tall and weighing about 175 pounds. Some of the veterans wanted to test "McGraw's college boy" upon his arrival, but Devlin proved as tough as any of them. He was superstitious about teammates humming, whistling, or singing on the bench, believing that music drove base hits away, and threatened to belt anyone who

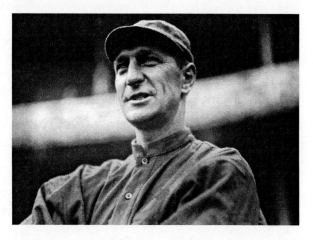

Art Devlin, a Georgetown University product who manned third base for McGraw's Giants from 1904 to 1911 (author's collection).

did so. Of course, some of his mates wanted to find out if he was serious, and after a few fierce battles they stopped producing music when Devlin was around. In 1910 he went into the stands at the Polo Grounds to beat up a fan who had called him either a "dog" or a "yellow dog." This action resulted in a brawl, a league suspension, and the threat of a lawsuit which, fortunately, never came to pass. Devlin fit in well with McGraw's Irishmen, and solidified the third base position for the rest of the decade.

It took McGraw only two and a half seasons to put the Giants back on top of the National League. With Mathewson and McGinnity heading the pitching staff, Devlin and Dahlen firming up the left side of the infield, and Roger Bresnahan in center, the Giants won 106 games in 1904 and cruised to the pennant by 13 games over the second-place Chicago Cubs. McGraw, still seething over his treatment by American League president Ban Johnson, refused to meet the junior circuit champion Boston club in a post-season World Series, but the season was a resounding success nonetheless.

Though John McGraw was as tough as nails on the outside, he held a soft spot in his heart for old ballplayers. To give the New York fans a nostalgic thrill in the final days of the 1904 campaign, McGraw put two Irish stars from the past in uniform for the Giants. Dan Brouthers, already a veteran when he performed with McGraw on the first Baltimore pennant winning club ten years before, joined the Giants at age 46 and played in two contests. The 53-year-old "Orator Jim" O'Rourke donned a chest protector and caught all nine innings of one game, 32 years after his 1872 debut in the National Association. Brouthers went hitless, but O'Rourke belted a single and scored a run in his final major league appearance. Many years later, McGraw assisted old Irish stars such as Brouthers, Mickey Welch, and Amos Rusie by giving them jobs as press box attendants and night watchmen at the Polo Grounds.

The 1905 club repeated as pennant winners, then (after the club dropped its objections to playing the American League in post-season action) defeated the Philadelphia Athletics four games to one in the World Series to give McGraw the first of his three world championships. However, the arrogant Giants were not popular in other league cities, and when McGraw decked out his players for the 1906 season in new white uniforms with "World Champions" instead of "New York" in bold black letters across the front, fans across the country reacted angrily. A ride to the ballpark was an adventure in many cities, with showers of rocks and garbage hitting the carriages transporting the Giants. Roger Bresnahan and Mike Donlin, refusing to cower before the barrage, often loaded their carriages with rocks and returned fire. Post-game travel was even more dangerous, especially if the Giants brawled with the opposition that day, but McGraw did not seem to mind. He had built the best team in the National League, and believed that the Giants had earned the right to boast and strut.

Through it all, McGraw remained loyal to Irish ballplayers. Though the percentage of Irish-Americans in baseball fell during the first decade of the 20th century, the Giants, like the Baltimore pennant winners of the previous decade, were dominated by Irishmen. New York's greatest rival during this period was the Chicago team, managed first by Frank Selee and then, beginning in 1905, by Frank Chance. Almost all of the Cubs' stars were Germans, bearing names like Reulbach, Tinker, Steinfeldt, Schulte, and Pfeister, to name but a few. Only second baseman Johnny Evers upheld the tradition of the brainy, scrappy Irish ballplayer in Chicago. McGraw used the ethnic rivalry between the two teams as a rallying point. During the 1906 season, he reportedly held a closed-door team meeting and indignantly asked his charges if they intended to allow a bunch of "Dutchmen" to beat them out for the pennant.[6]

The Cubs, led by its German-American stars, took the flag in 1906 with a league record

116 wins, while the Giants finished in third place as injuries and complacency crippled the team. Some of McGraw's old Irish standbys, such as Joe McGinnity and Dan McGann, were aging quickly, while Roger Bresnahan resented sharing the catching position with Frank Bowerman. Bresnahan, an ambitious sort, openly pined for a managing career of his own, perhaps as the eventual successor to McGraw. Mike Donlin, who had married the popular vaudeville star Mabel Hite, began to lose interest in baseball and wanted to become an actor, especially after a broken ankle suffered in May of 1906 ended his season and threatened his baseball career. The Giants needed new blood, especially on the infield, where shortstop Bill Dahlen and second baseman Billy Gilbert could no longer cover enough ground. McGraw retained Dahlen, but signed an Irish player he had long admired, the veteran Tommy Corcoran, to replace Gilbert. Corcoran's arrival gave the Giants three-fourths of an Irish infield, with Art Devlin at third and Dan McGann at first.

"Tommy the Cork" was a field leader of the first rank, but was also 38 years old and nearing the end of a career that had begun with Ned Hanlon's Pittsburgh team in the Players League 17 years before. He had spent a decade as shortstop and captain of the Cincinnati Reds, where he was managed by McGraw's close friend and former teammate Joe Kelley, and later by Hanlon, who took over for Kelley as manager of the Reds in 1905. Smart and aggressive, he was most famous for sniffing out a sign-stealing operation conducted by the Phillies in 1900. Corcoran, who thought it strange that Philadelphia third base coach Pete Chiles stood in exactly the same position all the time, dug into the coaches' box with his spikes and uncovered an electronic buzzer system, connected by a long wire to a spy with binoculars in the outfield stands. The spy stole signals from the Cincinnati catcher and relayed them through the wire to Chiles, who then whistled to tell the batter what pitch was coming. Corcoran tore the apparatus out of the ground, though the Phillies, who had won nearly two thirds of their home games that season while posting a losing record on the road, won both ends of a doubleheader that day anyhow.

To mollify Bresnahan, McGraw named him assistant manager and gave him the catching job on a full-time basis. Catchers had always been susceptible to leg injuries from missed pitches, foul tips, and sliding runners, but on Opening Day of 1907, Bresnahan appeared on the field at the Polo Grounds wearing a pair of shin guards, adapted from equipment worn by wicket-keepers in the sport of cricket. This equipment was widely ridiculed, but enabled Bresnahan to remain in the lineup nearly every day. His innovation was soon copied by other major league catchers, and remains a standard piece of catching regalia to this day.

Bresnahan enjoyed a fine season in 1907, but the rest of the club needed work. Donlin did not play at all that year, having quit the team in spring training after insisting upon a $600 contract bonus for staying sober, a demand that Giants management regarded as blackmail. Donlin then abandoned baseball to pursue a stage career, while McGann slumped at bat and found trouble off the field with dismaying regularity. McGinnity was losing his effectiveness, and the aging Corcoran covered even less ground than the departed Billy Gilbert. In July of 1907, McGraw released Corcoran and replaced him with a youngster who would soon be called the "Hibernian Slugger" in the New York newspapers. The Giants paid $4,500, a record sum for a minor leaguer, to the Springfield, Illinois club of the Three-I league for a 20-year-old third baseman named Larry Doyle.

Doyle's parents had fled Ireland after the famine and settled in Caseyville, Illinois, a town in coal mining country about 40 miles east of St. Louis. Larry, born there in 1886, eventually followed his father into the mines, working beneath the earth during the week and playing ball on weekends. He quit mining in 1906 to pursue a baseball career, which was fortunate, for shortly afterward a cave-in at the mine where he had worked killed several men. Larry played well at Springfield in 1907, and McGraw dispatched Dan Brouthers to have a look at the young third baseman. Brouthers gave a favorable report, so McGraw outbid several other teams for Doyle's services.

With Art Devlin firmly entrenched at third base in New York, McGraw put Doyle at second, a position he had never played. Though error-prone in his first months with the Giants, Doyle progressed so well that by 1912 columnist Hugh Fullerton could write, "Doyle is easily the best ball player on the Giants, a hustling, aggressive, McGraw style of player, full of nerve, grit and true courage. I think he is gamer than his manager, and in some respects a better baseball general."[7] McGraw recognized Doyle's leadership qualities and made him team captain in 1908, his second season with the Giants. Called "Laughing Larry" for his enthusiastic attitude, Doyle's greatest claim to fame may have been his oft-quoted declaration, "It's great to be young and a Giant!"

Larry Doyle was a rising star, but Dan McGann's career was fading quickly. A broken wrist, suffered during spring training in 1907, kept him out of the lineup until mid-season, and he returned to the Giants overweight and out of shape. He and McGraw had been fighting all year long over McGann's behavior both on and off the field, and McGann's lack of conditioning convinced the manager that it was time to find another first baseman. At the conclusion of that season, McGraw began an overhaul of his team. He sent McGann, short-

Laughing Larry" Doyle, the second baseman who said, "It's great to be young and a Giant" (Library of Congress).

stop Bill Dahlen, and three other Giants to Boston for first baseman Fred Tenney, shortstop Al Bridwell, and catcher Tom Needham. When someone pointed out that Tenney, a veteran who first played in the National League in 1894, was the same age as McGann, McGraw replied testily that Tenney had taken better care of himself. Such comments deepened the animosity between the highly emotional McGann and his former manager.

McGann was gone, and the aging Joe McGinnity was relegated to the status of a reliever and spot starter, but Larry Doyle, Art Devlin, and Roger Bresnahan kept the Irish influence alive on the Giants during the 1908 season. However, John McGraw had not seen the last of Dan McGann. McGraw, still seething over his former first baseman's poor play and disciplinary troubles of the year before, went out of his way to taunt McGann when the Giants played in Boston early in 1908. He shouted "damned ice wagon" when McGann grounded into a double play in the ninth, and after the game McGraw explained to reporters, "That's how the Giants lost a lot of games last season ... there isn't a regular on my team now who wouldn't have beaten the ball that cut McGann off at first and ended the game."[8] McGann heard about McGraw's comments and went to the Copley Square Hotel, where the Giants were staying, to confront his former manager. Though Christy Mathewson tried to keep McGraw and McGann apart, the two hot-tempered Irishmen met in the hotel's billiard room and began to throw punches, with McGann then chasing McGraw up a staircase and down the hall to the manager's room. McGraw dashed into his room and locked the door just ahead of the irate first baseman.

Tragically, Dan McGann lived for only three more years after his departure from the Giants. Released by Boston after the 1908 campaign, he played for Milwaukee of the American Association during the next two seasons. His batting average fell to the .220 level in 1910, and it was obvious that McGann's playing days were over. Despondent over the end of his baseball career and haunted by the violent deaths of several family members, he shot himself in a Louisville hotel room on the night of December 13, 1910. He was 39 years old.

Mike Donlin, on the other hand, was welcome to rejoin the Giants in 1908 after spending the previous season on the vaudeville circuit with his wife Mabel. Donlin won the home opener with a home run, and batted .334 with 106 runs scored that year. However, the Donlins had been working on a play called "Stealing Home," which opened in New York in October of 1908. It was generally well-received, and a critic from *Variety* wrote, "Mike Donlin as a polite comedian is quite the most delightful vaudeville surprise you ever enjoyed."[9] Others were less enamored of his talents, but he remained with the show as it toured the country for the next two years. Donlin, claiming that he made more money on the stage than on the baseball field, sat out the 1909 and 1910 seasons at what should have been the peak of his career.

The Giants were a team in transition in 1908, but nearly won the pennant anyway. Joe McGinnity won only 11 games in his final major league season, but Christy Mathewson posted 37 wins, Roger Bresnahan caught a record 139 games, and Larry Doyle batted .308 in his first full season as the Giants battled the defending champion Cubs down to the wire. Only the famous "Merkle boner" on September 23, in which rookie Fred Merkle's failure to touch second on Al Bridwell's run-scoring single in the ninth inning cost the Giants an important win over the Cubs, kept McGraw's men from reaching the World Series. The Giants and Cubs were obliged to replay the game on October 8, and the Chicagoans defeated Christy Mathewson and the Giants before more than 30,000 fans to clinch the pennant.

Though the influence of Irish-American players had lessened by 1908, several Irishmen played pivotal roles in denying the Giants the win in that fateful game of September 23. The first, Chicago infielder Johnny Evers, noticed that Merkle had not touched second base and called for the ball as his teammates ran off the field. New York's Joe McGinnity, sensing that something was up, intercepted the ball and heaved it into the outfield among the surging crowd that had swarmed the field. After much confusion, Evers somehow retrieved the ball (or, more likely, procured another from the Cubs bench area), stepped on the second base bag and appealed to umpire Hank O'Day, who called Merkle out and declared the game a tie.

McGraw knew that the Giants needed fresh blood, and at season's end two of his favorite veteran Irishmen, Bresnahan and McGinnity, left the team. The 37-year-old McGinnity's major league career was finished, but he returned to the minors as pitcher and manager with Newark of the Eastern League. He was still an "Iron Man" on the mound, winning 29 games in 1909 and 30 more in 1910 while pitching more than 400 innings in each season. McGinnity pitched minor league ball until he was 54 years old, finally hanging up his glove after a 6-6 season in the Mississippi Valley League in 1925. As for Bresnahan, he finally got his chance to manage when McGraw traded him to the St. Louis Cardinals for three players. The Cardinals had finished last in the National League in 1908, but Bresnahan whipped the team into shape, using lessons he had learned from McGraw. In 1911, Bresnahan's third season in charge, the Cardinals finished above the .500 mark for the first time in ten years.

Until the early 20th century, baseball managers performed all the managing, teaching, and coaching tasks themselves and were responsible for scouting and player evaluation as well. The New York franchise, however, was the most profitable in the game, and could afford to hire people to carry out some of these tasks. Accordingly, McGraw employed several old teammates and opponents as assistants, creating the first true coaching and scouting staff in the major leagues. He had already utilized Dan Brouthers, his old Baltimore teammate, for scouting expeditions, and in 1909 hired his close friend Wilbert Robinson to assist the Giant pitchers at spring training. Robinson, the avuncular old catcher who by this time was called "Uncle Robbie" by players and sportswriters, had remained in Baltimore after McGraw decamped to New York seven years before. Robinson briefly managed an Orioles franchise in the Eastern League, then quit the game and ran a butcher shop for several years until McGraw came calling. Robinson eventually sold his business and spent the remainder of his life in baseball.

McGraw also signed an old St. Louis Brown, Arlie Latham, as baseball's first full-time coach for the 1909 campaign. Apparently McGraw believed that Latham, a notorious practical joker during his playing days, would keep the Giants loose and entertained during the season, though some of his charges objected to their new coach's presence. Giants outfielder Fred Snodgrass once called Latham "probably the worst third base coach who ever lived,"[10] while Cy Seymour, a veteran outfielder, took exception to one of Latham's pranks one day and beat up the older man in a hotel lobby.

Latham did not stay with the Giants for long, but in future years McGraw hired many old ballplayers, many of them Irishmen, to assist him. Wilbert Robinson helped McGraw with the pitching staff at spring training in 1910 and 1911, and then signed on as a full-time coach, traveling with the team and coaching on the base lines. His influence and advice helped the Giants return to the top of the league, as the team won three pennants in a row from 1911 to 1913. Sadly, the long friendship between McGraw and Robinson began to unravel during the 1913 season, and ended after that year's World Series, which the Giants lost to Connie Mack's Philadelphia Athletics. At a reunion of the old Orioles that October, McGraw, who had been drinking, blamed Robinson for mistakes on the coaching line that cost the Giants in the Series. Robinson responded angrily, and McGraw promptly fired him. "This is my party," snarled McGraw. "Get the hell out of here." Robinson complied, but only after dumping a pitcher of beer over McGraw's head.[11] Robinson then accepted a position as manager of the Brooklyn Dodgers, and, except for necessary team-related communications, the two former friends did not speak for 17 years.

McGraw's most loyal assistant was gone, but the Giants manager found no shortage of former teammates to help him. Jesse Burkett, the old Cleveland Spiders star who reacted so negatively to McGraw's presence on the 1900 St. Louis club, nonetheless knew the game and was dependable, so McGraw hired him as a scout during the early 1920s. Later, the manager entrusted Burkett with the care of Phil Douglas, a talented pitcher with an alcohol problem. Burkett, a non-drinker, was assigned to watch Douglas around the clock, keeping him out of bars and curbing his penchant for getting into fights. The effort eventually failed, as Douglas went on a bender during the 1923 season and foolishly wrote a letter to a former teammate, offering to lose games on purpose to keep McGraw from winning the pennant. This misstep caused Douglas to be expelled from baseball for life, and Burkett's employment with the Giants ended soon after.

Burkett's scouting career was also undistinguished. He recommended against signing a minor league catcher from Worcester, Massachusetts named Charles (Gabby) Hartnett, because Burkett claimed that the youngster's hands were too small. The Chicago Cubs signed Hartnett, who went on to a Hall of Fame career while the catching position remained a perennial weakness for the Giants. Another former Irish teammate of McGraw's from the Baltimore days, Sadie McMahon, was more successful, serving the Giants as a scout for 14 years. Other old stars of the 1880s and 1890s, including Dan Brouthers, worked in various capacities at the Polo Grounds. "Dan's getting old," wrote McGraw in his 1923 autobiography, "but will always have a job."[12]

Three more National League pennants in a row from 1911 to 1913 cemented McGraw's reputation as a baseball general, though the Giants failed to win the World Series during this period. The former "Muggsy" was now the "Little Napoleon," a clever baseball strategist whose tactics were studied and copied by other managers. Though his behavior occasionally caused trouble for his club, as evidenced by his assault upon umpire Bill Byron after a game in 1917, McGraw stood at the pinnacle of his profession. Another pennant in 1917, only two years after the Giants collapsed to last place, added to his legacy. "We'll win the pennant if my brains hold out!"[13] McGraw told his men, and the Giants believed it. Only Connie Mack, the Philadelphia Athletics manager who defeated McGraw in the 1911 and 1913 World Series, was as respected a field leader and team builder as was John McGraw during this era.

In 1921, McGraw hired another old Oriole teammate and friend, Hugh Jennings, as coach with the title of assistant manager. Jennings had spent 14 seasons leading the Detroit Tigers, winning three pennants, and it was probably no coincidence that the Giants finished first in the National League in each of Jennings' first four seasons with the club. During the late 1920s, after Jennings left the game due to ill health, Roger Bresnahan assumed the same role and managed the club when McGraw was away due to illness or suspension. Many observers believed that Bresnahan would succeed McGraw someday as Giants manager, but the veteran was reluctant to let go, so Bresnahan moved on to the Detroit Tigers in 1929.

Larry Doyle, the onetime "Hibernian slugger" of the Giants and one of McGraw's favorites, also coached and performed front-office duties during the 1920s. Doyle's job description was always nebulous, and most observers simply figured that McGraw liked having Doyle around. Though McGraw was aging as his 30th season with the Giants approached, he made no plans to retire. Surrounded by old friends and teammates and lionized by the New York press, he was comfortable in his role, though his Giants never won another pennant after 1924.

"I'm sort of a permanent fixture, like home plate or the foul pole," the old manager said.[14] He also never forgot his Irish roots, donating the proceeds of a game against the Cardinals on May 12, 1921, to the Irish Relief Fund.

The coaching staff remained thoroughly Irish throughout McGraw's tenure at the helm of the Giants, but the Irish presence on the field had noticeably lessened by the 1920s. The stars were mostly men of German or Scandinavian descent like Frankie Frisch, Art Nehf, and Fred Lindstrom, or Southerners like Bill Terry and Ross Youngs. Oddly enough, the one Giant with the nickname "Irish" was not descended from the Emerald Isle at all. Emil (Irish) Meusel, a strong-hitting left fielder who joined the club in 1921, came from French and German ancestry, but earned his nickname because people said that his red hair and unusually fair skin made him look like an Irishman. A few Giants (future Hall of Famer George Kelly among them) shared McGraw's heritage, but the ethnic makeup of baseball in general was more diverse that it had been a few decades before, at least within the Caucasian population. McGraw finally retired in 1932 after 31 seasons at the helm. He selected first baseman Bill Terry to succeed him, and three decades of Irish influence on the Giants franchise came to an end.

McGraw's former friend Wilbert Robinson, who managed the Brooklyn club for 18 years and won pennants in 1916 and 1920, also hired old teammates to assist him. In 1926 he brought two of his long-ago Irish friends from the Baltimore Orioles, Joe Kelley and Joe McGinnity, out of retirement to man the coaching lines, though both men were well past their primes. Kelley coached third base, even though he had trouble seeing balls hit to the outfield. "Without my glasses," he confessed to outfielder Babe Herman one day, "I can't even see who's pitching. But I won't wear glasses on a ball field."

"Why not?" asked Herman.

"Pride!" replied Kelley.[15] The old Oriole, who had drawn female fans to Baltimore games with his good looks and who reportedly carried a mirror in his uniform pocket during his playing career, was still concerned about his appearance. Kelley's day was long past, however, and his oft-expressed contempt for modern ballplayers made him unpopular with the young Dodgers. Both Kelley and McGinnity left the team after only one year, but Irish influence remained in the person of Robinson's Irish-born wife, the former Mary O'Rourke. During the 1920s, Mary was known as "Ma Robinson" to players, sportswriters, and fans. "Ma" traveled with the team, advised her husband, and acted as a sort of den mother for the Dodgers, offering advice to young players and their families.

The two unexpected pennants won by the Dodgers during Robinson's early years as manager cemented his popularity with the fans and made the lean years that followed more bearable. The Brooklyn supporters continued to back the man they called "Uncle Robbie," even though the team (called the Robins in his honor during the 1920s) finished above fourth place only once during Robinson's final 11 years in charge. Always a portly man, Robinson's weight ballooned to more than 250 pounds during the 1920s, giving him a grandfatherly appearance and making him almost a comical character at the head of a team that some labeled the "Daffy Dodgers." In truth, Robinson was always a fine strategist and teacher, especially skilled in handling pitchers, but the talent level of the club was low during this era. The Brooklyn club was an entertaining one, if not a good one, during these years, but not until 1941 would it win another pennant, long after Robinson had departed the scene.

Though Robinson and McGraw were not on speaking terms during these years, they were both responsible for the managerial career of one of baseball's most successful, and colorful, field leaders. Charles (Casey) Stengel was a half–Irish, half–German outfielder from

Kansas City (hence his nickname) who first played major league ball for the Brooklyn club in 1912. In 1916, the year Robinson won his first National League flag with the Dodgers, Stengel kept the team loose with funny stories and practical jokes. "Of course, Robbie was the manager," recalled catcher John (Chief) Meyers in Lawrence Ritter's work, *The Glory of Their Times*. "But Robbie was just a good old soul and everything. It was Casey who kept us on our toes. He was the life of the party and kept us old-timers pepped up all season."[16] However, Brooklyn's reign at the top of the National League was short-lived. The team fell to seventh place in 1917, and at season's end Robinson sent Stengel to the Pittsburgh Pirates.

Traded to the Giants in 1921, Stengel became the protégé of John McGraw, then entering his 20th season as manager of the Giants. Stengel toned down his clownish behavior in New York and often dined at the Pelham, New York, home of McGraw and his wife Blanche, talking baseball and strategy until the wee hours. In 1926, after five years of tutelage under McGraw, Stengel was hired to lead the Toledo Mud Hens of the American Association, a club owned and managed for the previous several years by McGraw's old catcher Roger Bresnahan. Toledo had a close working relationship with the Giants, with future stars such as Bill Terry, Fred Lindstrom, and Hack Wilson passing through on their way to New York. Stengel learned his lessons well, for in 1927 Toledo won the Junior World Series, the national minor league championship, for the first time. In 1934 Stengel began his major league managerial career with the Dodgers, three years after Wilbert Robinson's tenure in Brooklyn ended.

Stengel's leadership style was noticeably influenced by John McGraw. After his first decade with the Giants, McGraw stopped using the sacrifice bunt to any great extent, and Stengel chose to eschew that tactic as well. Both McGraw and Stengel insisted on using good defensive infielders who could turn the double play, and both men used platooning to take advantage of left-right matchups between pitchers and batters. Platooning had largely fallen out of favor after McGraw exited the game, but Stengel revived the practice when he became manager of the Yankees in 1949. "He kind of walked like McGraw," said Art Johnson, who pitched for Stengel on the Boston Braves during the early 1940s, "and every once in a while, he'd refer to him. When [Stengel] was telling you something, he would say, 'As Mr. McGraw told me ...' [or] 'When I was talking to Mr. McGraw, he told me ...'

"You could tell that McGraw was in the background all the time."[17]

When Stengel's 12-year tenure with the New York Yankees ended in 1960, his record had surpassed that of his mentor, John McGraw. Stengel had won 10 pennants, matching McGraw's production, with seven World Series titles to McGraw's three.

John McGraw and Wilbert Robinson finally patched up their feud and resumed their friendship before the 1931 season, but both men were nearing the end. McGraw was not an old man, but his health had been poor for several years, and his Giants had not met expectations since their last league title in 1924. In June of 1932, he abruptly resigned as manager, and never led a team on the field again, save for a special appearance at the helm of the National League squad at the first All-Star game in Chicago during the summer of 1933. After the game, asked by a sportswriter if he was interested in managing again, McGraw was characteristically blunt. "I'm through with it," he said with finality. "I have quit."[18] On February 25, 1934, he died of prostate cancer at the age of 60.

In the meantime, Robinson had been deposed as field leader of the Dodgers after a fourth-place finish in 1931. He managed the Atlanta Crackers of the Southern League for two years after that, but his health, too, was failing. In August of 1934 the 71-year-old Robinson fell in a hotel room, hitting his head on the bathtub and breaking his arm. He tried to laugh it off, telling his attendants, "This broken arm doesn't hurt me. I'm an old Oriole. Wrap it

This monument to John McGraw was erected in Truxton, New York, his hometown, in 1942 (photograph taken by the author in 2008).

up and let me stay here."[19] The injury was much more serious than Robinson let on. The blow to his head caused a brain hemorrhage, and "Uncle Robbie" died on August 8, 1934. The two teammates and friends, Wilbert Robinson and John McGraw, were buried not far from each other in New Cathedral Cemetery in Baltimore, the city in which both had achieved prominence in the baseball world.

Dozens of old teammates attended their funerals, but none were more conspicuous than Ned Hanlon and Joe Kelley. Hanlon, who had won five National League championships with Baltimore and Brooklyn more than 30 years before, had mentored both McGraw and Robinson as they grew from young ballplayers to respected veteran managers with 12 pennants between them. Kelley, the best player on Hanlon's Orioles, was a teammate of both men for many years before embarking on a managing career of his own. None of these four baseball icons — McGraw, Robinson, Kelley, and Hanlon — was born in Baltimore, but all were forever linked to the city by their presence on one of baseball's most storied teams, the Oriole champions of the 1890s. In 1937, Hanlon died at age 79, and six years later Kelley followed suit at age 71. They, too, were buried at New Cathedral Cemetery with their longtime friends and teammates.

12

Wild Bill, Whiskey Face,
and the Tall Tactician

By 1900, when the nascent American League became a major circuit and ushered in the so-called "modern era" of baseball, the traditional dominance of second-generation Irish ballplayers had abated. Other ethnic groups, especially the Germans, had staked their claim to roster spots at the highest level of competition, and though the 1890s are often considered the peak of Irish influence in baseball, the number of German players in the National League had surpassed the Irish by the middle of the decade. Scandinavians, Welshmen, Eastern Europeans, and one Native American, Cleveland outfielder Louis Sockalexis, also appeared in lineups during this era. Another group, the Italians, made their first appearance in the person of infielder Ed Abbaticchio of the Phillies. The game had become more diverse, though still entirely Caucasian except for Sockalexis, and the Irish would henceforth be only one of many immigrant groups vying for positions on major league teams.

Though no longer the dominant ethnic group in the playing ranks, Irishmen held more than their share of managerial positions during the first two decades of the new century. Many Irishmen made the transition from playing rosters to field leadership positions with varying degrees of success. John McGraw, who learned his baseball under Ned Hanlon in Baltimore and led the Orioles in 1899 after Hanlon decamped to Brooklyn, was one of the most notable, taking over the New York Giants in 1902 and managing them for 31 years. Connie Mack, who spent the 1891 season in Pittsburgh as a player under Hanlon, led the Philadelphia Athletics for half a century beginning in 1901. Another Hanlon protégé, Hugh Jennings, was the field leader of the Detroit Tigers for 14 seasons, winning three pennants, while other old Orioles, Joe Kelley and Kid Gleason, worked their way into management as well. Hugh Duffy, Jimmy Collins, Deacon McGuire, and Jimmy McAleer are only a few of the many Irish players-turned-managers of the 1900–1920 period.

Some baseball historians have overstated the dominance of the Irish-American manager during this era, though not by much. An oft-quoted statistic, one which probably originated in the work of historian Steven J. Riess during the 1970s, states that during the 1915 season, 11 of the 16 major league managers were Irish. An examination of the ethnic heritage of these 16 men shows that, at most, nine were second- or third-generation Irish-American, accounting for more than half of the total. In the American League, Bill Carrigan (Red Sox), Connie Mack (Athletics), Bill Donovan (Yankees), Hugh Jennings (Tigers), and Joe Birmingham

(Indians) were Irish, while the National League featured Pat Moran (Phillies), John McGraw (Giants), and Roger Bresnahan (Cubs). Miller Huggins, manager of the St. Louis Cardinals, had an Irish-born grandfather and perhaps should be included as well, though his father had emigrated from England.

Riess may have counted Brooklyn's Wilbert Robinson because of his Irish-born wife and long association with Hanlon and McGraw, though "Uncle Robbie" claimed English descent. Robinson's inclusion brings the total to 10, while the Chicago White Sox, led on the field by Clarence (Pants) Rowland, of Scottish and English extraction, were solely owned and controlled by the second-generation Irishman Charlie Comiskey. Whatever the true number of Irish-American managers may have been, the fact remains that the Irish dominated the managerial profession as completely as they had the playing ranks in previous decades.

The success of Irish-American managers during the 1901–1919 period can be measured by the number of pennants they won. John McGraw and Connie Mack each directed their teams to six league titles during those two decades, while Hugh Jennings won three, Jimmy Collins two, Pat Moran two, Bill Carrigan two, Fred Mitchell one, and Kid Gleason one. These accounted for 23 of the 38 pennants won during those 19 seasons. The Irish managerial presence was more pronounced in the American League. Between 1902 and 1916, Irish-American managers Mack, Jennings, Collins, and Carrigan won 13 flags in 15 seasons. Mack and McGraw continued their winning ways into the 1920s, while the part–Irish Miller Huggins teamed with owners Jacob Ruppert and T. L. Huston to build a long-lasting American League dynasty in New York, leading the Yankees to six pennants and three World Series titles beginning in 1921.

Ban Johnson, founder of the American League, relied heavily on second-generation Irishmen when he created the franchises that made his league a major circuit in 1901. Charlie Comiskey had moved his Western League club into Chicago and given birth to the White Sox the year before, while Connie Mack not only built a new team, the Athletics, in Philadelphia, but also did much of the preparatory work for the creation of the Boston club that would later become the Red Sox. Jimmy McAleer was the first manager of the Cleveland team, then moved to St. Louis after the 1901 season and built the Browns as a rival to the National League Cardinals. Johnson chose Hugh Duffy to lead the Milwaukee Brewers, while John McGraw's Baltimore team would have been one of the flagship franchises of the new league had not McGraw and Johnson clashed over disciplinary issues, resulting in McGraw's quick departure from the circuit. Baseball at this time was still heavily Irish in character, and for many years after the birth of Johnson's league, half or more of its managers were Irish.

Though he never won a pennant, one of the more colorful individuals to manage a major league team during these years was a former pitching star named "Wild Bill" Donovan. His father Jeremiah, a carpenter, and mother Mary were the children of immigrants, making Bill a third-generation Irish-American. The future ballplayer was born in Lawrence, Massachusetts, in America's centennial year of 1876. The Irish were the first major immigrant group to settle in Lawrence, but by the time of Bill's birth, the city was home to Germans, English, and French Canadians as well. Most of them came to work in the textile mills that dotted the shores of the Merrimack River. The Donovans, however, did not remain, but moved to Philadelphia when Bill was young. A curveball specialist with a friendly manner that hid a quick temper, Bill pitched in Philadelphia's competitive semipro leagues as a teenager, then entered the professional ranks and landed in the National League in 1898 with the Washington Senators.

It was in Washington that the young righthander earned the nickname "Wild Bill." He

posted a 1–6 record in 17 games, with 69 walks in only 88 innings, for the perennially hapless Senators, and his penchant for losing his temper on the mound made his nickname seem
fitting. Signed by Brooklyn for the 1899 season, he mostly rode the bench until manager Ned
Hanlon sent him to the minors in 1900 to play for Hartford of the Eastern League. Wild Bill,
disappointed with his demotion, seemed fated to live up to his moniker. One day he showed
his displeasure with team management by walking nine batters in a row. He displayed little
self-control on the field and off, and news of his after-hours escapades in Hartford traveled
quickly back to Brooklyn. Hanlon, who saw great talent in his undisciplined pitcher, decided
to bring Donovan back to the majors to keep better tabs on his progress. Hanlon was rewarded
when Donovan blossomed into a star in 1901 with a 25–15 record for the second-place Brooklyn club. After one more good season for Hanlon, he jumped to the American League in 1903,
signing with the Detroit Tigers shortly before the war between the American and National
leagues ended.

   Though Donovan could give the umpires fits with his volcanic displays of temper on the
field, he was a popular fellow out of uniform. As sportswriter Bill Slocum put it, "There is
no credit for you if you like Bill Donovan. Everybody does. But you can take credit if he likes
you. Then you must be all right."[1] He became a leader on the Detroit team, heading the committee that bought a diamond-studded watch for departing manager Ed Barrow in 1904, and
reportedly leading a player revolt in 1906 against Barrow's successor, Bill Armour. In 1907,
owner Frank Navin hired the former Baltimore Oriole shortstop, Hugh Jennings, as manager,
and Donovan compiled his best season for the pennant-winning Tigers with a stellar 25–4
record. Jennings, who learned his baseball under Ned Hanlon and formed a lifelong friendship with John McGraw in Baltimore, managed the previously underachieving Tigers to three
consecutive pennants from 1907 to 1909.

   The Irish dominance of baseball, so pronounced during the previous two decades, had
abated by 1907, but Jennings managed several Tigers, including Donovan, who shared his ethnic heritage. Shortstop Charley O'Leary and left fielder Matty McIntyre came from Irish
immigrant stock, while the Dublin-born catcher Jimmy Archer batted only .119 and was
released at season's end. Archer signed on later with the Chicago Cubs and spent the next
decade in the National League. The three main pitchers for Detroit were a German, Ed Kil-
lian, and two Irishmen in Donovan and "Wabash George" Mullin. Mullin, born in Toledo,
Ohio, but a resident of Wabash, Indiana, holds second place on the all-time win list for the
Detroit franchise, but was an unlucky pitcher in 1907, posting a 20–20 record. Two years
later, Mullin, whose weight had fluctuated his entire career, decided to concentrate on his
conditioning during the off-season. He reported to spring training 40 pounds lighter and compiled a 29–8 record in 1909. Not until 1968, when Denny McLain won 31 games, would
another Detroit pitcher surpass Mullin's team record for wins in a season.

   Bill Donovan performed well again in 1908, despite two suspensions for run-ins with
umpires, but in the following year he suffered from a sore arm, which soon ended his playing career. He went to Providence of the Eastern League as manager, part owner, and occasional player for the 1913 and 1914 seasons, and drew praise for his leadership skill. In 1914,
after the Providence club entered into a working agreement with the Boston Red Sox, Wild
Bill helped develop future pitching stars Carl Mays, who won 24 games for Providence that
year, and Babe Ruth, who won nine games in the two months he spent with Donovan's team.
Donovan led Providence to the International League pennant, and in 1915 he returned to the
American League as manager of the New York Yankees.

   At the time, the Yankee franchise was one of the least successful in the league. The former Highlanders had finished the 1904 and 1910 seasons in second place, but had not yet won a pennant despite the presence of otherwise accomplished managers such as Clark Griffith, George Stallings, and Frank Chance. The team had closed the 1914 season under the direction of Roger Peckinpaugh, a 23-year-old shortstop and the closest thing the club had to a star. When two new owners, beer baron Jacob Ruppert and construction magnate T. L. Huston, bought the club in January of 1915, they announced their determination to build the Yankees into a winner. They returned Peckinpaugh to the playing ranks and hired Donovan as their manager.

Some say that the Yankees hired the personable Donovan to compete with a fellow Irishman, John McGraw, whose New York Giants were the number one team on the New York baseball scene. Donovan, indeed, was a popular man with the local sportswriters, and his presence gave the Yankees a boost in the battle for newspaper coverage. Still, the team was lacking in the talent department, and though Ruppert and Huston strengthened the club by buying such stars as third baseman Frank "Home Run" Baker and first sacker Wally Pipp, the Yankees did not improve immediately. Donovan did his best to jump-start his club by playing aggressive baseball and arguing with the umpires at every opportunity, but a fourth-place finish in 1915 was his best in three years at the helm.

By 1917, Ruppert and Huston had run out of patience, and Ban Johnson, still trying to build a winning team in New York, was ready to give Wild Bill Donovan the boot. In a move widely criticized in the newspapers, the popular manager was released following a sixth-place finish in 1917. He was succeeded by a former National League infielder and St. Louis Cardinals manager, Miller Huggins, who was only partly Irish and not nearly as personable as Donovan had been. However, Huggins was an inspired choice. He led the Yankees to six pennants and three World Series titles during the 1920s and turned the club into a dominant force in the American League, a distinction it held for decades thereafter.

Wild Bill coached for Hugh Jennings in Detroit in 1918, then managed at Jersey City for the next two years while awaiting his next opportunity to lead a major league team. That chance came in the National League in Philadelphia in 1921, but the Phillies were even more talent-starved than Donovan's Yankees had been. The new manager harshly criticized his men for their losing ways, and the players took the disparagement badly. By mid–season the Phillies were locked into last place and were in a state of open revolt against Donovan. Outfielder Casey Stengel, nursing a sore leg, was on the trainer's table one day when he received a telegram stating that he had been traded to the Giants. Stengel jumped off the table and immediately began dancing across the room. "I thought your leg hurt," remarked the trainer. "Not any more!" said Stengel with glee. "I'm going to the Giants!"[2]

Wild Bill's tenure in Philadelphia ended quickly and badly. Team owner William F. Baker fired Donovan in late July, refusing to pay the rest of his season's salary. To make matters worse, Baker accused Donovan of peripheral involvement in the 1919 "Black Sox" scandal, in which eight Chicago players were banned for life for throwing the World Series. Fortunately for Donovan, he was one of Commissioner Kenesaw M. Landis' favorite players, and Landis cleared Wild Bill of any wrongdoing. Judge Landis also ordered Baker to retract his charges and issue a public apology, restoring Donovan's good name and allowing the former pitching star to continue in baseball. In 1922 and 1923 Donovan managed at New Haven in the Eastern League and waited for another major league position to open up.

Like Bill Donovan, Pat Moran was a well-respected major league manager who was born in Massachusetts and came from Irish stock, though Moran was a second-generation Irishman and Donovan was of the third generation. They were born in the same year, and both had been valuable players, Moran as a catcher and Donovan as a pitcher, though they built their careers in different leagues and did not compete against each other except in exhibition play. Both men were outgoing, popular with the press, and highly acclaimed for their skill at developing pitchers. The primary difference between them was that Donovan never won a major league pennant, while Moran won two with two different teams.

Patrick Joseph Moran was born on February 7, 1876, in Fitchburg, Massachusetts, a mill town in the northern part of the state near the New Hampshire border. Like so many others in Fitchburg, Patrick's parents were Irish refugees who settled in the town to work in one of its many cotton and textile mills. Pat labored with his father in the local woolen mill, earning about $3 a day, and played baseball for the local town team in his spare time. Pat was the star of the team, and in 1897, at age 21, he joined the Lyons club in the New York State League. He was an average hitter, but a fearless, durable catcher with a strong throwing arm. In September of 1900, the Boston Beaneaters of the National League bought his contract. He played the first season of his major league career under Frank Selee, whom he later credited for teaching him how to play the game.

Moran, a hard drinker who earned the nickname "Whiskey Face," played for Boston until 1905, then joined the Chicago Cubs to back up starting catcher Johnny Kling on three pennant-winning teams. Sold to the Phillies in 1910, Moran's playing time dwindled, but he was already earning a reputation as a smart strategist and leader. He spent much of his time guiding young pitchers like Grover Alexander, who joined the club in 1911, and Eppa Rixey,

John McGraw (Giants) and Pat Moran (Phillies) in 1916. These two Irish-American managers were good friends as well as rivals (author's collection).

who arrived in 1912, and soon became a part-time catcher and full-time pitching coach. "It was Pat who made a pitcher out of me and I was fortunate to play under him in both Philadelphia and Cincinnati," Rixey recalled many years later. "Few men that I've ever known in baseball knew the fine arts of pitching as did Moran."[3]

Mickey (Red) Dooin, another Irish-American catcher, was the playing manager of the Phillies at the time, but Dooin began to cede more authority over the pitching staff to Moran. By 1913 Moran, not Dooin, would decide which pitcher would start each game, though Dooin always announced the choice to the media. The arrangement worked for a while, and the Phillies, a team that had not yet won a National League pennant, finished in second place behind the New York Giants in 1913. However, Dooin appeared to resent the credit Moran earned in the newspapers for his handling of the pitching staff, especially after Grover Alexander blossomed into one of baseball's biggest stars. Dooin reportedly wanted Moran dismissed, but when the 1914 team fell four notches to sixth place, team management fired Dooin and appointed Moran as manager.

Dooin had trouble controlling his players' behavior, but Pat Moran was a tough, no-nonsense "red-faced Irishman," as the papers usually described him. He demanded discipline and concentration, as the Phillies soon learned. One day Moran ordered Eppa Rixey, sitting idly on the bench, to study the opposing pitcher. Rixey chose to ignore his new manager, so Moran whacked the pitcher on the toes with a bat to get his attention. "As leader, it is my business to give orders," explained Moran to the newspapers, "and these are always carried out. Not by the 'mailed fist' method, as I do not believe in that style, but as one friend to another. The players carry them out because they have confidence in me."[4] Perhaps they feared him as well, but Moran's leadership skills and strategic acumen earned the respect of his charges, many of whom considered him the best manager they ever played for. In the National League of that era, perhaps only John McGraw was more esteemed as a leader and strategist than Pat Moran.

The new manager made trades to fill some of the holes on the ballclub. Sherry Magee, the team's best hitter, was a disciplinary nightmare who had nonetheless expected to be named manager after Dooin's dismissal. When the unhappy Magee threatened to jump to the new Federal League, Moran traded him to Boston for two players. Dooin, still a valuable catcher, could not remain on the club after his dismissal as field leader, so Moran sent him to Cincinnati for second baseman Bert Niehoff. Moran also installed rookie Dave Bancroft, a future Hall of Famer, at shortstop, and traded veteran third baseman Hans Lobert to the Giants for three players, all of whom proved helpful to the Phillies. This new edition of the Phillies, with stars such as Alexander and outfielder Gavvy Cravath supported by Moran's trade acquisitions, was now ready to contend for a pennant.

Moran worked his usual magic with the pitching staff, as Grover Alexander compiled the first of three consecutive 30-win seasons and Eppa Rixey matured into a dependable left-handed starter. With Cravath leading the league in home runs and right-hander Erskine Mayer winning 21 games, the Phillies took advantage of a poor year by the perennial champion Giants to win their first National League pennant. "Nobody ever did a better job than he did with the Phillies in 1915," said Bobby Byrne, a reserve infielder on the club, "when he won the pennant on a team with only one .300 hitter, Fred Luderus, and one great pitcher, Grover Alexander; a team that was fifth in batting and fourth in fielding."[5] The Phillies lost the World Series to the Boston Red Sox (managed by another tough Irish-American catcher, Bill Carrigan) in five games, but thanks to Pat Moran, the future looked bright for National League baseball in Philadelphia.

Under Moran's tutelage, Eppa Rixey blossomed in 1916 with his first 20-win season. The Phillies battled down to the wire for the pennant, eventually losing by two and a half games to the Brooklyn Dodgers. Early in the 1917 season, before the Phillies opened a series against the Giants at the Polo Grounds, a reporter asked the Philadelphia manager if he thought his team would win the pennant. "No, I don't," he replied. "I think the Giants will win. They finished fourth last year, but you know as well as I do they were the best club in the league when the season ended and would have won if the race had lasted a couple of weeks more. They're just as good today as they were then and we aren't as good as they are." The Philadelphia sportswriters, and team owner William F. Baker, were shocked, but Moran was simply too honest to give a misleading answer. "That's what I think," he insisted. "Why shouldn't I say so? You wouldn't want me to kid anybody, would you?"[6] Moran's prediction was correct. The Giants won the pennant, and the Phillies came in second once again.

Pat lasted only one more season in Philadelphia. Baker traded star pitcher Grover Alexander and catcher Bill Killefer to the Cubs at season's end, mostly because both men were due to be drafted by the military during World War One, and the Phillies fell all the way to sixth place in 1918. Baker then dismissed Moran, who signed on to coach for John McGraw and the Giants for the 1919 season. Moran was still in demand as a manager, however, and the Cincinnati Reds asked McGraw for permission to hire him. McGraw, a longtime friend and admirer of Moran, agreed, and the Reds took on Pat as their manager, succeeding Christy Mathewson.

The Reds, like the Phillies, had not yet won a National League pennant when Pat Moran arrived; in fact, the team had never finished higher than third place since it entered the league in 1890. The club had some talent, with future Hall of Famer Edd Roush in centerfield and fine players in third baseman Heinie Groh and pitcher Hod Eller, and had finished a distant third in the league in 1918. Moran moved to strengthen the pitching staff, acquiring Ray Fisher from the Yankees and Slim Sallee from the Giants via the waiver wire. He solidified first base by trading Hal Chase to the Giants and receiving Jake Daubert, a two-time batting champion, from Brooklyn in another transaction. Bill Rariden, who came to the Reds in the Chase trade, joined Ivey Wingo in a strong catching tandem, while pitchers Sallee, Fisher, Dutch Ruether, Jimmy Ring, and Hod Eller gave the Reds five solid starters. Not a man to hold grudges, the new manager decided to retain Sherry Magee, with whom he had quarreled in Philadelphia four years earlier, as a pinch-hitter and substitute outfielder. After Moran made all his moves, the Reds were suddenly a contender in the National League for the first time in many years.

Moran had built his reputation in Philadelphia as a developer of pitchers, and pitching was the key to the Reds' success in 1919. No other club could match Cincinnati's solid starting five, and after a spirited race with the Giants through the first two-thirds of the season, the Reds pulled away in August and September and won the flag by nine games over McGraw's club. Perhaps McGraw wished he hadn't let Moran out of his coaching contract after all.

The Reds faced the American League champion Chicago White Sox, managed by Moran's fellow Irishman Kid Gleason, in the World Series that October. This was the Series in which several Chicago players were suspected of throwing games, and after the Reds won four of the first five contests (the Series was a best-of-nine affair that year), rumors of a Chicago sellout gained credence. After the White Sox won games 6 and 7 to narrow the Cincinnati margin to four games to three, the Reds bombed Chicago pitcher Lefty Williams in the first inning of Game 8, winning the contest by a 10–5 score and taking Cincinnati's first World Series title.

Though eight members of the White Sox were later banned from the game as participants in a plot to lose the Series intentionally, Moran and the Reds always maintained that they would have won anyway. "If they threw some of the games they must be consummate actors, and their place is on the stage," said Pat defiantly after news of the Chicago players' confessions became public, "for nothing in their playing gave us the impression that they weren't doing their best.... It is an astonishing thing to me that [they] could get away with that sort of thing and us not know it."[7] News of the scandal put a damper on Cincinnati's first world title, and Moran was determined to win the Series again to prove that the victory against the White Sox was not a fluke. However, the pitching staff began to age, and by 1921 only one (Hod Eller) of Moran's five World Series starting pitchers remained with the team. Moran acquired one of his old Philadelphia pupils, Eppa Rixey, after the 1920 season, but the Reds dropped to sixth place in 1921.

Moran overhauled the team once more, trading third baseman Heinie Groh to the Giants, who had been pursuing Groh for several years, in exchange for two players and $150,000 in cash. Pat built a new pitching staff around Rixey, right-hander Pete Donohue, and a Cuban star, Adolfo Luque, who had pitched mostly in relief for the 1919 world champions. The 1922 Reds jumped to second place, and in 1923, when Rixey, Luque, and Donohue all won 20 games or more, Cincinnati finished second again, ending the season only four and a half games behind the pennant-winning Giants. With a strong pitching staff, good team defense, and centerfielder Edd Roush in the prime of his Hall of Fame career, the Reds were favored by many to defeat the Giants for the National League flag in 1924.

Both Bill Donovan and Pat Moran were successful Irish-American managers who might have risen to greater heights in 1924 had not fate intervened. Donovan, who probably would have been hired for another major league managerial position, was killed in December of 1923 in a train crash while riding the famous Twentieth Century Limited from New York to Chicago. He was 47 years old. Moran, who had always been a heavy drinker, reportedly hit the bottle harder than ever after the 1923 season, and by 1924 was a sick man, with liver and kidney problems draining his strength. Hospitalized in Florida during spring training, Moran died of Bright's disease, a form of kidney failure, on March 7, 1924, at the age of 48.

While most major league clubs changed managers regularly during the first two decades of the 20th century, one American League team employed only one field leader during that time, and well beyond it. In 1901, when Ban Johnson decided to place a team in Philadelphia to do battle with the established Phillies of the National League, he chose a respected, experienced Irish-American to manage the new club. At Johnson's request, Connie Mack, a former National League catcher and field leader of the Pittsburgh Pirates for three seasons during the 1890s, moved over from the Western League's Milwaukee Brewers to lead the new Philadelphia franchise, which became the Athletics.

The new manager's real name was Cornelius McGillicuddy, but friends and neighbors in East Brookfield, Massachusetts, had always known his family as the Macks. Con, or Connie, was born in that New England mill town on December 23, 1862. His father, Michael McGillicuddy, left County Kerry in 1846 at the height of the first wave of famine, and found work as a laborer in his new town. Connie's mother, the former Mary McKillop, was born in Scotland but grew up in Belfast, now part of Northern Ireland. Her family arrived sometime during the late 1840s, and in 1857 she married Michael McGillicuddy. Cornelius, named after his paternal grandfather, was the third child of the union.

Michael enlisted in the 51st Massachusetts Volunteer Infantry in August of 1862, more than a year after the outbreak of the Civil War. He came home from his nine-month tour of duty a sick man, weakened by malaria and dyspepsia, and never really regained his health. He worked as much as he could, but young Connie was obliged to find summer employment at an East Brookfield cotton mill at the age of 9 to help feed his family. He left school for good at age 14, when his father's many illnesses and advancing alcoholism made Connie the main breadwinner of the family.

Connie Mack was a tall, thin youngster, nicknamed "Slats" by his neighborhood friends, and though he did not look much like an athlete, he fell in love with baseball. He was a born leader, and though he sometimes pitched for the East Brookfield town team, he found his natural position at catcher. In 1882, when Connie was 19 years old, the Worcester Brown Stockings of the National League came to town and played against Connie and the local club. Though the professionals defeated East Brookfield by a score of 23 to 9, Connie pounded out three hits and began to believe that he could make good at the highest levels of competition.

A visit later that same year by the defending National League champions, the Chicago White Stockings, made him even more determined to make baseball his profession. Connie recalled many years later that Cap Anson, star slugger and manager of the Chicago club, sized him up at the plate and remarked, "I've looked at a lot of catchers, and I don't think I ever saw one built as high as you."[8]

Connie sought employment as a catcher with various New England minor league teams in early 1884, but found no takers for his services. He cut leather in a boot factory in East Brookfield until Will Hogan, a former pitcher for his town team, invited him to try out for the Meriden club of the Connecticut State League. Hogan was having trouble with his catcher in Meriden and convinced the manager that his friend Connie Mack could handle his deliveries. Connie went to Meriden, made good, and began an association with professional baseball that would last for nearly 70 years. In September of 1886, Connie made his first appearance in the major leagues, catching for Washington of the National League.

The 23-year-old Mack, who carried only about 150 pounds on his tall frame, learned his trade under a succes-

Connie Mack as a young catcher with Washington in 1887. John Gaffney, the former "King of Umpires," was his manager (Library of Congress).

sion of Irish-American managers in Washington. Mike Scanlon, an immigrant from County Cork, had started the 1886 season as the Washington manager, but soon lost his job. He was replaced by "Honest John" Gaffney, the former "King of Umpires" who left the ranks of arbiters to try his hand at managing. Gaffney lasted until 1888, when he was succeeded by Ted Sullivan, who led the St. Louis Browns earlier in the decade and was one of the premier organizers in the early game. However, the club, known popularly as the Senators by this time, was a poor one, and in early 1889 former Boston manager John Morrill took over. All these men, who shared Connie's ancestry and spoke in terms that he could understand, left their mark on the young ballplayer.

Most of the Washington players, Mack included, bolted to the Buffalo team of the new Players League in 1890, and although Connie invested his entire savings of $500 in the club, the circuit collapsed after only one season. Connie wound up in Pittsburgh, where another Irish-American manager, Ned Hanlon, found a willing pupil in the tall, thin catcher. "I took particular interest in drilling [Mack] in the finer points of the game. He assimilated and added to it," said Hanlon proudly many years later.[9] Mack, unlike many of his teammates, was neither a drinking man nor a carouser, and was more interested in learning baseball from the veteran field leader Hanlon than in keeping late hours on the road. Hanlon's season-long fight against drunkenness in the ranks made him unpopular with most of the Pittsburgh players, though not with Connie Mack, and later that year the team rebelled against his strict rule, prompting his ouster. Bill McGunnigle, like Hanlon a son of Irish immigrants, took over for the remainder of the campaign.

The club, which in 1892 became known as the Pirates, went through several more leadership changes until late 1894, when the team owners invited Connie to take charge. He had learned much from his predecessors. Ned Hanlon, who was unafraid to enforce his rules no matter how loudly his charges objected, had made an impression on young Connie, as did Bill McGunnigle, a stickler for fundamentals who used a tin whistle to get his players' attention at practice. One of Mack's most important lessons came after his first National League game, when he and several other new Washington players powered the team into a come-from-behind win at home over the Phillies. Mack and the other rookies were whooping it up in the dressing room when John Gaffney stuck his head in the doorway. "Here, you young fellers," snarled the manager, "don't get swell-headed because you happened to win."[10] The season was a marathon, not a sprint, and Mack soon learned not to get too high or too low over the outcome of a single game.

Connie Mack led the Pirates for two full seasons, spending much of his energy fighting the meddlesome Pittsburgh team management and finishing seventh and sixth in the 12-team National League. Released after the 1896 campaign, Mack was immediately snapped up by Ban Johnson of the Western League, who installed the 35-year-old in Milwaukee as manager and part owner of the Brewers. Four years later, when the Western circuit became the American League, Johnson convinced Mack to move to Philadelphia and lead the new franchise there. Mack decided to let the local press select a nickname for the new ballclub, and the sportswriters revived the name "Athletics," a moniker that had been carried by Philadelphia baseball teams since before the Civil War. Mack showed his approval by designing uniforms with a script "A" on the front.

Unlike other second-generation Irishmen such as Charlie Comiskey and John McGraw, Mack did not intentionally fill his roster with Irish ballplayers. His Athletics won pennants in 1902 and 1905 with a diverse collection of ethnicities, with Irishmen (Danny Murphy), Germans (Ossee Schreckengost, Topsy Hartsel), Englishmen (team captain Harry Davis), and others sharing the field with a Native American pitcher (Charles "Chief" Bender). Mack also signed Luis Castro, one of the few Latin-American players of the era, who played second base briefly during the 1902 campaign. His best player was a French-Canadian from Rhode Island, Napoleon Lajoie, who jumped to the American League from the crosstown Phillies and hit an astounding .422 in 1901. Mack's club took a severe hit when its two biggest stars, Lajoie and slugging outfielder Elmer Flick, were traded to Cleveland in mid–1902 after the National League went to court to prevent the two men from playing for Mack's club. The Athletics won the pennant that year anyway, the first of nine league titles for Mack.

Labeled the "Tall Tactician" by sportswriters, Mack showed a clear preference, not for players who shared his ethnicity, but for college men. Many of his charges had attended college at some point before arriving in Philadelphia, and Mack, who had little formal education himself, believed that such players were more self-disciplined and more receptive to instruction. Though Mack could not resist signing the occasional talented problem child such as pitcher Rube Waddell, most of his Athletics were focused and sober. They eschewed the brawling, battling style of play that typified the 1890s in favor of a serious approach to the game. Baseball was now a profession, not a mere pastime, and Connie Mack did much to raise the stature of the game and its players during the first few decades of the 20th century.

Though Mack, unlike John McGraw (who famously labeled the Athletics franchise a "white elephant" during the war between the leagues), cultivated a diverse group of ballplayers, some of his key men were the sons of Irish immigrants. One of these was Danny Murphy, who was born in Philadelphia during the centennial year of 1876 and moved to New England as a youngster. Murphy, a second baseman who stood about five feet and seven inches tall, entered pro ball in the New England League in 1897 and enjoyed a brief stay in the National League with the Giants in 1900 and 1901. Dropped by that club, he joined Norwich of the Connecticut State League and was batting .462 when he came to Mack's attention in June of 1902. Napoleon Lajoie had been traded to Cleveland a short time before, and Mack, who desperately needed a new second baseman, bought Murphy's contract from Norwich for $600. Murphy solidified the fractured Philadelphia infield, batted .313, and helped the Athletics to the 1902 pennant despite the loss of future Hall of Famers Lajoie and Flick. Though largely forgotten today, Murphy was one of the key performers of the Philadelphia ballclub that won American League pennants in 1902 and 1905.

Another important player arrived in late 1906, when a 19-year-old from Millerton, New York, named Eddie Collins joined the Athletics and struggled to find a place on the team. Collins, too, claimed Irish descent, but his family had arrived in America decades before the famine, so he had little in common with the second- and third-generation Irishmen who still represented a significant presence in baseball. Collins came from a well-to-do family, and while most of the Irish in the game were Catholics (as were Mack and Murphy), the members of the Collins clan were Episcopalians of long standing. This new player, whom the other Athletics dubbed "Cocky" Collins, had been an outstanding multi-sport athlete at Columbia University, and exuded supreme confidence in his talent.

Collins, a fine hitter and speedy baserunner, was a poor shortstop, and a failure in the outfield as well. Mack recognized that the talented Collins was the kind of leader that he could build a championship team around, but only if he could find a position for the youngster to play. Finally, in mid–1908, Mack decided to move the versatile Danny Murphy to right field and install Collins at second base. Murphy worked with Collins on the nuances of infield play, and before long both right field and second base were strong points for the Athletics. Though many fans, and even a few of the Athletics, objected to the popular Murphy being shunted off to another position to make room for the much younger Collins, Murphy himself did not mind. As Collins recalled many years later, "When I replaced him in the infield, and he took over in right field, it didn't sit too well with the A's followers.... Murphy wasn't resentful of the shift. In fact, unlike many players of that era, he willingly cooperated with me. I took to the position naturally and really found myself there, but Murphy played a great part in helping mold me into a good infielder, or rather a good second baseman."[11] Collins blossomed into a star, while Murphy became one of the best right fielders in the league.

The Detroit Tigers, managed by former Baltimore Orioles shortstop Hugh Jennings, won three straight American League flags from 1907 to 1909, but by 1910 Mack's Athletics were ready to mount a challenge for the pennant. With Eddie Collins as its anchor, Mack built a new infield, one that would gain fame as the "$100,000 infield" that some still regard as the greatest of all time. Collins manned second base, while a right-handed slugger from Maryland named Frank "Home Run" Baker took the third base slot and John (Stuffy) McInnis, a Massachusetts lad, played first. The shortstop position was held by Jack Barry, a young college man of Irish descent who batted only .243 during his 11-year career, but played a major role in bringing four pennants in a five-year period to Philadelphia.

Born in 1887 in Meriden, Connecticut (where Connie Mack had made his professional baseball debut a few years earlier), Jack Barry was the oldest child of Patrick Barry and the former Mary Doohan, both natives of County Cork, Ireland. Patrick was a saloon owner who had a barn on his property, and Jack developed his speed and throwing ability by hurling baseballs over the barn roof, then running around the structure to catch the ball on the other side. At Meriden High School, Jack, though small in stature, was the star of a team that won the state championship in both his junior and senior years.

Like many fine Irish Catholic athletes in New England at the time, Jack made his way to the College of the Holy Cross in Worcester, Massachusetts, where he became captain of the baseball team and played every infield position. Holy Cross was a proving ground for future major league ballplayers; among its products were pitcher Andy Coakley, a starter on Mack's early Philadelphia teams, and Mike (Doc) Powers, who served as a valuable, though weak-hitting, backup catcher on Mack's 1902 and 1905 pennant winners. Powers, a son of Irish immigrants from the cotton mill town of Pittsfield, Massachusetts, had captained the Holy Cross team during the late 1890s and kept in touch with the baseball program at his old school. Barry impressed everyone who saw him, including Powers, who recommended him to Connie Mack. The Philadelphia manager outbid several other teams for Barry's services, and Barry joined the Athletics in the spring of 1909.

Tragically, Mike Powers, nicknamed "Doc" because he had attended medical school during the off-seasons and earned his degree, did not live to see his fellow Irishman and Holy Cross product, Barry, become a star. On April 12, 1909, Powers slammed into a railing while chasing a foul ball during the Athletics' home opener. After the game, Powers complained of severe abdominal pain and was taken to a hospital, where surgeons discovered an intestinal blockage. They operated and removed much of his intestine, but peritonitis set in, and on April 26, Mike Powers died. No one knows if his malady was caused by the collision with the railing or existed beforehand, but some say that Powers was the first on-field fatality in major league history. His death stunned the Athletics, and the team stumbled in the early part of the season before mounting a pennant charge that fell short in September.

Jack Barry, who became the starting shortstop for the Athletics in 1909, was exactly the kind of player that Connie Mack wanted on his roster. Barry was a quiet, studious non-drinker who went to Mass every day and practiced diligently, even after he became a star. He and Eddie Collins, who became lifelong friends, developed new strategies for playing the infield, and Barry's wide range allowed Collins and third baseman Frank Baker to play closer to first and third respectively. Though Barry never hit more than .275 in a season, he earned a reputation as a tough hitter with a game on the line. "Barry is the weakest hitter of the quartet," wrote Edgar Wolfe of the *Philadelphia Inquirer*, "but his hits are always timely and his sensational fielding is something that cannot be computed in cold, soulless figures."[12]

The Athletics had strong starting pitching and timely hitting, but the "$100,000 Infield," anchored by Jack Barry at short and Eddie Collins at second, was the linchpin of Connie Mack's first world championship team. The Athletics won pennants in 1910 and 1911, running away with the flag in both seasons, and defeated the Cubs and Giants respectively in the World Series. After an unexpected third-place finish in 1912, the Athletics regrouped for two more flags in 1913 and 1914, with another World Series win over John McGraw's Giants in 1913 giving Mack his third world title in four seasons.

Danny Murphy, the second-generation Irishman who not only switched positions to make way for Eddie Collins, but also helped Collins improve at second base, was one of Mack's favorite players during this era. However, by 1912 Murphy was 36 years old and nearing the end of a fine career, especially after suffering a broken kneecap while sliding during a game in June of that year. He remained with the Athletics through the 1913 season, which ended with the team's third World Series victory in four years. Many believed that Mack was preparing the trusted Murphy for a career as a coach or, perhaps, as the eventual manager of the team. Murphy, on the other hand, insisted that his playing career was not yet finished. In March of 1914 Mack released Murphy to the minor-league Baltimore Orioles, but Murphy signed instead with Brooklyn of the upstart Federal League. This move not only strained the close relationship between Mack and his longtime player, but would spell the end of the Athletics as a baseball dynasty as well.

The Federal League backers believed they could entice stars of the established major circuits to join up with them, and the popular and personable Danny Murphy became one of their main recruiting agents. Murphy knew that the players on Mack's championship teams had not been highly paid, and when Murphy made lucrative offers to his former teammates, he found many of them willing to listen. Mack seethed with anger, knowing that not only would the powerful team that he had built would soon collapse, but also that Murphy was the main instrument of his ballclub's destruction. "The Philadelphia club was split into two groups," recalled Mack many years later. "One was for sticking with me; the other was for jumping to the big money."[13] After much discussion, several of the key players on the team decided to remain with Mack's club till the end of the 1914 season, but prepared to move to the Federal League and higher paydays in 1915.

The 1914 Athletics swept to the pennant for the fourth time in five seasons, but the general mood was tense and unhappy all season long. Some of the players felt underpaid and unappreciated, while others condemned their teammates for running out on Mack, the man who made them into champions, for bigger money in the new league. Mack had to endure the knowledge that his carefully-built championship team was on the verge of falling apart, mostly because he could not compete with the Federal League's salary offers. Attendance had fallen off in Philadelphia, perhaps because the fans were sated with success, and Mack could not afford to pay his players top dollar. "Murphy offered my players three times what they were getting from me," complained Mack later.[14]

The Athletics lost the World Series in a stunning four-game sweep to the Boston Braves, and afterwards Mack released veterans Chief Bender, Eddie Plank, and others who had been in close contact with Danny Murphy. He then sold Eddie Collins, his greatest star, to the Chicago White Sox for $50,000, and in June of 1915 sent his prize shortstop, Jack Barry, to the Boston Red Sox for another outlay of cash. Mack's reign at the top of the league was over, and the Athletics fell to last place, where they would remain for the next seven years.

Murphy, once considered Mack's possible successor as manager of the Athletics, was now *persona non grata* with the club, but after several seasons the manager began to mellow toward his onetime protégé. Mack later said, "I was pretty sore at the time -awfully sore.... Today, over the perspective of the years, I feel a little differently. The players were taking advantage of a baseball war to get all they could, just as I took advantage of a baseball war to raid the National League when we first put a club in Philadelphia. I long have forgiven the players who gave me those 1914 headaches, and most of them have been back with me in some capacity."[15] By 1920 Mack had forgiven Danny Murphy, who rejoined the Philadelphia coaching staff and remained with his old mentor until 1925. The two men were friends again, and in 1948 Mack named Murphy as the right fielder on his personal Philadelphia Athletics all-time team.

Mack had built one championship team from scratch, and was determined to do it again. During the 1920s he scouted, signed, and developed young talent, once again relying on self-directed, intelligent players who could be counted on to play sound fundamental baseball and behave off the field. A few were Irish, including catcher Gordon (Mickey) Cochrane, a fine hitter and natural leader, but the Athletics of the 1920s came from all parts of the country and represented many ethnicities. Despite reported tension on the club between Northern and Southern players, Mack once again molded a group of youngsters into champions. Though the New York Yankees of the late 1920s were nearly invincible, Mack's Athletics won three more pennants in a row beginning in 1929. World Series victories in 1929 and 1930 gave Mack five world titles,

Connie Mack in 1911, the year he won his second of five World Series crowns (1912 Spalding Guide).

the most in baseball history up to that point and still the third-highest total of all time.

A few of Mack's Philadelphia players became managers themselves, but none could match the record compiled by Jack Barry. The shortstop of the "$100,000 Infield" led the Boston club to a second-place finish in 1917, then served in the navy while Ed Barrow led the Red Sox to the world title the following season. In 1921 Barry was appointed head coach at his alma mater, Holy Cross, where he remained for 40 years. He never had a losing season at Holy Cross, leading the Crusaders to the 1952 College World Series title and sending 25 players to the major leagues. Though his coaching career ended with his death in 1961, his all-time collegiate records for wins (616) and winning percentage (.802) stand to this day.

Connie Mack managed the Philadelphia Athletics for an incredible 50 years. By 1931, the year his last American League pennant winners lost the World Series to the St. Louis Cardinals, the era of Irish-American dominance of baseball was long past, but Mack, whose father fled the potato famine during the 1840s and fought in the Civil War, remained at the helm of the Athletics until 1950. His Athletics by then had become only a shell of the championship franchise it had once been, having finished in the second division in 16 of Mack's final 17 seasons. He was nearly 88 years old, the last major leaguer to manage his team from the bench in a suit and tie, when he finally gave up the reins, albeit reluctantly. "I'm not quitting because I'm too old," he insisted. "I'm quitting because I think the people want me to."[16] Four years later, his beloved Athletics abandoned Philadelphia for a new start in Kansas City, and in 1956, Connie Mack died at the age of 93.

13

Red Sox and Royal Rooters

Ban Johnson's Western League operated franchises in smaller Midwestern cities such as Grand Rapids, Michigan, and St. Paul, Minnesota, during the late 1890s, but in 1900 Johnson formed the American League and placed teams in larger metropolitan areas such as Cleveland and Chicago. Johnson's circuit was anchored to the Midwest during its first season of operation, and he recognized that if his organization was to succeed, it would need to compete with the National League in the eastern part of the country. To that end, in 1901 Johnson awarded franchises to Boston and Philadelphia in direct competition with the established teams in those cities. Two more moves, into St. Louis in 1902 and New York in 1903, would put the circuit on a firm footing as an equal partner on the major league scene, but Johnson's foray into Boston and Philadelphia may have been the most important step in his league's battle for equality.

The Boston Beaneaters, champions of the National League eight times between 1877 and 1898, had always been a largely Irish ballclub, with much of its popularity resting with the city's Irish fans. Men such as John Morrill, Mike (King) Kelly, and Tommy McCarthy were heroes to the Boston Irish, who had supported the club since the early 1870s when Andy Leonard, a native of County Cavan, roamed the outfield. Though the team had become more diverse during the late 1890s, with Irish stars Hugh Duffy and Jimmy Collins sharing the field with Germans (Herman Long, Kid Nichols, Bobby Lowe), Englishmen (Fred Tenney, Vic Willis), Scotsmen (Billy Hamilton), and Welshmen (Ted Lewis), the Irish made up the core of baseball fans in the Hub. Ban Johnson recognized that the viability of his new league depended in large part upon the success of its Boston entry, and that this club could only prosper by appealing to the city's Irish fans.

The American League's task was made easier by the fact that the Beaneaters were on the decline. After winning pennants in 1897 and 1898, they finished second to Brooklyn in 1899, then dropped to fourth in 1900 as many of their veteran stars aged. Kid Nichols suffered from a sore arm and fell to a 13–16 record in 1900, while outfielder Hugh Duffy was sidelined by various injuries and appeared in only 55 games that year. The team also lost catcher Marty Bergen in a shocking tragedy in January of 1900, when Bergen killed his wife and two children, then took his own life. Bergen was a fine defensive catcher and handler of pitchers, and his loss proved as devastating to the Beaneaters as was the railroad accident that ended Charlie Bennett's career six years before. The 1900 Beaneaters fell out of the pennant race early, and though manager Frank Selee tried his best to improve the club, attendance sagged, creating an opportunity for a new team to capture the loyalties of the Boston fans.

Jimmy Collins, the Irish third baseman of the Beaneaters, was the logical choice to lead the new American League entry in Boston. Collins had led the league in home runs in 1898 and revolutionized defensive play at his position, and was already being hailed in the national sporting press as the greatest third baseman of all time. An outgoing and friendly bachelor who played ball with a constant smile on his face, the 27-year-old Collins may have been the most popular athlete in the Hub at the time, save for former heavyweight boxing champion John L. Sullivan, another Irish lad who had risen to prominence in the sports world. Collins also held managerial aspirations that the new club was eager to fulfill.

Collins, like most of the other Boston stars, chafed at the stinginess of the Triumvirs, the three-man consortium that owned the Beaneaters. The National League had decreed a maximum player salary of $2,400 during the early 1890s, and while other clubs found ways around the pay ceiling, team president Arthur Soden was not inclined to give his players any more money than league rules allowed. This shortsighted policy, rigidly followed in the face of potentially powerful competition, made many of the Boston players interested in what the new league had to offer. Collins, an ambitious individual, met with Connie Mack and other American League emissaries during the early months of 1901 and liked what he heard. In February, he signed on as player and manager for the new Boston club at a substantial increase in pay, with an attendance bonus clause in his contract. The third baseman told the local papers that the Triumvirs "have always treated me nicely and paid every cent that their obligations called for, but I saw a chance to better myself and took it and I can name 50 others that will do the same thing."[1]

Collins set to work, choosing uniform colors (white with blue stockings and trim, in contrast to the Beaneaters' traditional red), negotiating for a site upon which to build a ballpark, and signing players. The biggest boost to Boston's new American League entry came with the arrival of pitching star Cy Young, winner of 286 major league games at the age of 34 and still in his prime. Young had spent the previous two years pitching in the summer heat of St. Louis, and preferred to return to the eastern states, closer to his farm in Ohio. Collins also convinced several of his old Beaneater teammates, such as first baseman Buck Freeman, pitcher Ted Lewis, and outfielder Chick Stahl, to join him in the new league. Their defections decimated the Beaneaters, who fell to the bottom of the standings and would not challenge again for the pennant for more than a decade.

The new Boston team, sometimes called the Invaders or Somersets (for part-owner and financier Charles Somers) but most widely known as the Americans, also captured the loyalty of Boston's most important fan group. The Royal Rooters were a loosely-organized collection of about 200 enthusiastic fans, almost all Irish, who attended every game and sometimes followed their heroes on the road. A vociferous bunch, they drank heartily and generally whooped it up on behalf of the local ballclub. The group had emerged in the late 1890s, supporting the Beaneaters at home and on the road during their pennant-winning seasons of 1897 and 1898. The Royal Rooters were headquartered at a popular bar, called "Third Base," owned by a local character and political fixer named Michael "Nuf Ced" McGreevey. "Nuf Ced" earned his nickname because he settled arguments among his patrons by delivering his opinion on the matter at hand, slamming his fist on the bar, and bellowing "Nuf Ced!" McGreevey was the leader of the Royal Rooters, although Congressman John (Honey Fitz) Fitzgerald, grandfather of the future President John F. Kennedy, was also a principal figure in the group. The Royal Rooters revered their fellow Irishman Collins and, with the decline of the Beaneaters, switched their allegiance to the new Boston Americans.

Collins, with the Royal Rooters firmly in his corner, brought the Americans home in second place in 1901, four games behind the pennant-winning White Sox. The new team proved popular with both Irishmen and non–Irishmen in the Hub, attracting around 300,000 fans that season. This support enabled Collins to earn an unprecedented $18,000 bonus due to the attendance clause in his contract. Immediately after the close of the 1901 season, Collins went to work to build a contender for 1902. Pitcher Ted Lewis, the number two starter behind the 33-game winner Cy Young, quit the game to attend divinity school, so Collins looked to the rival Beaneaters for another quality hurler to replace him. Vic Willis, the curveball specialist, decided to remain in the National League, but Bill Dinneen, a 27-year-old right-hander, abandoned the Beaneaters and signed on with the Americans.

Dinneen, like Collins, was born to Irish immigrant parents in New York state. Thomas and Katherine Dinneen had left Ireland and settled near Syracuse not long before the future pitcher's birth in 1876. Bill played semipro ball in the area before joining Toronto of the International League, where he spent two seasons before breaking into the National League with Washington in 1898. Sold to the Beaneaters in 1900 after the Senators disbanded, Dinneen won 20 games that year and 15 more the next for Frank Selee's club. Selee was dismissed after the 1901 season, and with future Hall of Famers Billy Hamilton and Kid Nichols also leaving the club, perhaps Dinneen recognized that the Americans were on the rise while the Beaneaters were fading quickly. Dinneen signed on with the Americans to fill the number two starter role behind Cy Young.

The Americans finished in fourth place in 1902, but the 1903 edition won the pennant, Boston's first in the American League. The Americans were strengthened by the addition of

Strike.

BILL DINNEEN

BOSTON.

Pitcher Bill Dinneen, who won three games for Boston in the 1903 World Series (author's collection).

yet another Irish lad from New York, outfielder Patrick (Patsy) Dougherty, whom Collins had scouted and signed the year before. Dougherty was a mediocre fielder, but a fine hitter who led the team with a .331 average. Several other Irishmen contributed to the pennant, with Collins batting .296, Dinneen winning 21 games, and veteran catcher Duke Farrell batting .404 in limited action. The Americans made a shambles of the pennant race, running away with the flag by 14 and a half games and making Jimmy Collins an even bigger hero to the Irish fans of Boston.

By this time, the war between the leagues was over, and the champions of the American and National circuits agreed to meet in a post-season World Series that October. Collins was enthusiastic about the matchup with the Pittsburgh Pirates, three-time defending champions of the older circuit. "I should not be surprised to see post season games each fall," said the Boston manager, "as long as there are two big leagues.... They give the public a high article of base ball and enable the championship teams to pick up a bit of prize money for the cold winter."[2] However, the series almost failed to come off. Pittsburgh owner Barney Dreyfuss offered to let his players divide all of his team's gate receipts, but Boston management was not as generous. They wanted to give Collins and his men only half of the box office take, which angered the players so much that many did not want to play the series at all.

Collins, anxious to prove the mettle of the new league against the old one, did his best to convince his teammates to play regardless of the financial considerations involved. They "yelled murder," said Collins later, "and it was useless to argue with them." The Americans finally relented when the Boston owners offered a 60–40 split of the proceeds, and, though some of the players still grumbled about their shares, the first modern World Series became a reality.

The first three contests were played in Boston, including a raucous third game in which fans surged through the rope barriers and stood on the field during the game. The umpires could not clear the field, so they ruled that any ball hit into the mass of people in the outfield was an automatic double. Jimmy Collins drove in two runs, but the Pirates won the game 4–2 and returned to Pittsburgh with a 2–1 lead in games. Pittsburgh won the fourth game as well, defeating Game 2 winner Bill Dinneen, but the Americans rebounded with an 11–2 win by Cy Young in the fifth contest and a 6–2 victory behind Dinneen in Game 6 to even the series at three games apiece. Another well-pitched game by Young in the seventh contest gave Boston a 4–3 lead in games in the best-of-nine struggle. Through it all, "Nuf Ced," "Honey Fitz," and the Royal Rooters cheered their heroes, paraded on the field before the games, and sang "Tessie," a popular song of the day. "They must have figured it was a good luck charm," remarked Pittsburgh outfielder Tommy Leach to Lawrence Ritter in *The Glory of Their Times*, "because from then on you could hardly play ball[,] they were singing 'Tessie' so damn loud."[3]

Young performed well for the Americans, winning the fifth and seventh games, but Dinneen emerged as the pitching star of the Series. By the eighth contest, he had thrown three complete games, two of which were victories, in his three starts against the Pirates. He was ready to see the Series end. "I want to get back to Syracuse," said Dinneen. "I got a lot of things I want to do. This thing has gone far enough." In Game 8, he pitched a masterful shutout, his second of the Series, and struck out Honus Wagner for the last out of the game to clinch Boston's first World Series title.

Determined to defend their world championship, the Americans were hobbled in June of 1904 when league president Ban Johnson prevailed upon Boston management to trade its best hitter, left fielder Patsy Dougherty, to the New York Highlanders for utility infielder Bob Unglaub. Dougherty's addition strengthened the New Yorkers and helped them mount a serious pennant charge, resulting in the first exciting American League pennant race between the Americans and the Highlanders. Boston and New York swapped the league lead several times during the last two months of the season, culminating in a season-ending doubleheader between the two teams on October 10. Boston could clinch the pennant by winning either of the two games, and when New York's Jack Chesbro, a 41-game winner that year, heaved a ninth-inning wild pitch that allowed the winning run to score, Collins and the Americans won their second consecutive flag.

John McGraw, still smarting from the American League's victory in the baseball war of 1901–1902, refused to let his pennant-winning New York Giants challenge the Boston Americans that fall, so no World Series was played in 1904. As it was, the conclusion of the 1904 pennant race was the last high point of Jimmy Collins' managerial career in Boston. The team had been purchased from its original owners by Charles Taylor, a Civil War veteran and publisher of the *Boston Globe*, and turned over to Taylor's son John to operate. Charles Taylor, a general in the state militia, was one of the wealthiest and most respected men in Boston, but his baseball-mad son was a young man with little ambition. He preferred to spend his time watching the Americans with his friends rather than enter the business world. The general, perhaps figuring that John was at the ballpark every day anyway, made his son president of the team.

John I. Taylor was a disaster as a baseball executive, and it did not take long for him to alienate Jimmy Collins, the players, and many of the fans. He started off on the wrong foot when he traded Patsy Dougherty to New York at Ban Johnson's behest, a deal which nearly cost Boston the pennant. The new team president was known to barge into the clubhouse and make insulting remarks to his charges after losses, and he and Collins were soon at odds. Taylor rarely bothered to consult his manager before making player transactions, and in early 1905, he took it upon himself to deal George Stone, a promising young outfielder, to St. Louis for the aging Jesse Burkett. Burkett batted only .257 in 1905 and then retired, while Stone led the league in hits that year and won the batting title for the Browns in 1906. The Boston newspapers so thoroughly criticized Taylor for those two disastrous trades that he subsequently refused to make any deals at all, leaving Collins with a stagnant roster and no way to improve it.

Injuries, Collins' own decline as a player, and meddlesome ownership dropped the Americans to fourth position in 1905. The following campaign was even worse, as a wave of injuries and retirements, coupled with Taylor's stubborn refusal to help the team in the trade market, doomed the Americans before the season began. A 20-game losing streak in May put the Americans in last place to stay, and by June Collins began to manage in street clothes, not even bothering to take the field anymore. Taylor, who was paying Collins to play third base, was ready to fire his manager, but Collins retained the loyalties of the Royal Rooters and the Irish fans of Boston. The demoralized team played disinterested ball, and attendance, tops in the league two years earlier, fell to last in 1906.

Taylor and Collins had long ceased to communicate, but an incident in August forced the owner to finally deal with his manager. Collins, nursing a knee injury that kept him out of the everyday lineup, stayed away from the park for days at a time with no explanation or warning. He had become an absentee leader, expressing his frustration with the team in the most direct way possible and virtually daring Taylor to remove him from the manager's chair. In late August Taylor did exactly that, suspending Collins and appointing right fielder Chick Stahl to replace him. The Boston Americans, once the powerhouse of the American League, finished the 1906 campaign in last place, and at season's end Collins was dismissed as manager, though retained as a player. Stahl, Collins' longtime friend and old Beaneater teammate, was given command of the team for the following season.

The Americans (renamed the Red Sox by John I. Taylor after the 1907 campaign) hired and fired several managers, some Irish and some not, during the next few years. Stahl, apparently depressed over issues in his personal life, stunned the entire league in March of 1907 by committing suicide during spring training. Pitcher Cy Young took over briefly as manager, only to be replaced by George Huff, a college coach with no major league experience, and later by infielder Bob Unglaub. Finally, in early June, Taylor made a break with the past by trading Jimmy Collins to the Philadelphia Athletics for infielder John Knight. This transaction was the first player trade Taylor had completed in nearly two and a half years. He then bought Jim (Deacon) McGuire, a veteran catcher, from the New York Highlanders to manage his club.

McGuire, whose Irish immigrant father worked in the steel mills of Youngstown, Ohio, was one of the most respected men in the game at the turn of the 20th century. He had begun his playing career in 1884 as a teenager with Toledo, playing on the same team as popular Irish-American stars Tony Mullane and Curt Welch. McGuire, a durable catcher and solid hitter, was Washington's best player during the 1890s, and managed the Senators for four seasons. Since then, he had bounced around both leagues, appearing for Brooklyn, Detroit, and the Highlanders before landing in Boston in 1907. Dignified and soft-spoken, McGuire had reportedly never been ejected from a game by an umpire. His knowledge of the game was top-notch, and his 26 seasons of major league playing experience leaves him behind only Cap Anson and Nolan Ryan (both with 27 seasons) in baseball history.

McGuire had little to work with, though outstanding young players such as outfielder Tris Speaker and pitcher Joe Wood were beginning to make a mark with the team now known as the Red Sox. In mid–1908 the impatient John I. Taylor dismissed McGuire and replaced him with another old catcher, the Canadian-born Fred Lake. Lake brought the Red Sox home in third place in 1909 and restored the club to the top of the circuit in attendance, but asked for a raise at season's end and was bitterly disappointed when Taylor refused his request. Taylor, offended by his manager's attitude, fired Lake and gave the job to another Irishman, Patsy Donovan, a native of County Cork who had managed the Pittsburgh Pirates (succeeding Connie Mack) in 1897 and had earned a reputation as a fine judge of baseball talent. Donovan also failed to lift the team out of the doldrums and was dismissed after two seasons, though he remained with the Red Sox as a scout. By the end of the 1911 campaign, it appeared that the club was hopelessly mired in mediocrity.

John I. Taylor built a lasting legacy, Fenway Park, which opened in April of 1912, but he was ready to step down from the day-to-day operations of the club. Though he was willing to keep a partial ownership stake in the Red Sox, he made it known that he and his father were looking to sell their controlling interest. Several groups of politicians, businessmen, and other investors quickly formed, and some of the suitors were Irish political leaders with ties to the Royal Rooters. However, the league was determined to find a suitable ownership consortium, and Ban Johnson took control of the search. He wanted a group of his choosing to take control, so he directed the negotiations between the Taylors and the prospective buyers of the ballclub.

The team had nearly gained an Irish-American owner several years earlier. John (Honey Fitz) Fitzgerald, a future mayor of the city, put together a syndicate and made overtures to buy the club in 1904, when the original

PHILADELPHIA, MARCH 13, 1897.

PATRICK J. DONOVAN,
The Manager, Captain and Outfielder of the Pittsburg Club.

Born in County Cork, Ireland, Patsy Donovan managed the Red Sox in 1910 and 1911. He had replaced Connie Mack as field leader of the Pirates in 1897 (author's collection).

ownership group sold out. Johnson, however, may have feared that Fitzgerald, a son of Irish immigrants who was already a powerful political force in Boston, would be too independent for the league to control. Fitzgerald's leadership role in the boisterous Royal Rooters may also have worked against him, so Johnson instead engineered the sale of the team to Charles Taylor. However, the time was now right for the Irish, well represented in the playing and managing ranks of the team since its inception, to play a role in owning the Red Sox. Johnson gave his approval to the veteran player and manager Jimmy McAleer, the former Cleveland Spiders outfielder, who assembled a group of investors that included Robert McRoy, Johnson's personal secretary, and bought the Red Sox in September of 1911.

McAleer, the center fielder on Patsy Tebeau's "Hibernian Spiders" during the 1890s, had not been idle since playing his last game for Cleveland in 1898. He was one of the first established National Leaguers to cast his lot with Johnson's circuit, managing the American League's franchise in Cleveland in 1900 and 1901. Moving to St. Louis in 1902, he filled the roster of the new Browns by raiding the crosstown Cardinals of seven of its biggest stars, including Hall of Famers Jesse Burkett and Bobby Wallace. In 1909 he moved on to Washington, where he persuaded President William Howard Taft to throw out the first ball at the Senators' home opener in 1910, establishing a tradition that continues to this day. Though the Senators did not win many games, McAleer earned much of the credit for developing pitcher Walter Johnson into a star.

A born entrepreneur, McAleer popularized the concept of the all-star game three decades before the major leagues arranged to play one each summer. In 1910 and 1911, after the Philadelphia Athletics clinched the league title in each season, McAleer assembled the stars of the other seven American League teams to play the Athletics in tune-up matches to keep Connie Mack's players in shape before the World Series. It must have helped, because the Athletics won both post-season classics, against the Cubs and Giants respectively. Another of McAleer's all-star aggregations, which featured Ty Cobb, Tris Speaker, Eddie Collins, and many other top players, defeated Cleveland in a benefit game for the widow of pitcher Addie Joss in July of 1911. That team, with eight future Hall of Famers on it, drew a sellout crowd at Cleveland's League Park and represented one of the most powerful collections of talent in the history of the game.

McAleer became president of the Red Sox, but under the conditions of the sale, did not have a free hand in choosing a manager. Garland (Jake) Stahl, no relation to the late Chick Stahl, was a former Boston infielder who retired from the playing ranks after the 1910 season and took a job at a Chicago bank, working for his wife's wealthy father. As fate would have it, Stahl's father-in-law was one of the leading investors in the syndicate headed by McAleer and McRoy. Stahl expressed interest in leaving his bank job and trying his hand at managing the Red Sox, so McAleer acquiesced, releasing Patsy Donovan and hiring Stahl as playing manager.

The 1912 season, the first in which an Irish-American held the presidency of the Boston Red Sox, was a resounding success. The team's new stadium, Fenway Park, opened on April 20 and gave the team a home and an identity that has lasted for nearly a century. Pitcher Joe Wood burst into stardom, winning 34 games and losing only five, while center fielder Tris Speaker established himself as perhaps the second-best player in the league after Detroit's Ty Cobb. The Red Sox took advantage of a down year for the defending champion Philadelphia Athletics and swept to the pennant, Boston's third in the American League. In one of the most exciting World Series ever played, the Red Sox defeated the New York Giants in eight games to win their second World Series title.

Despite winning an unexpected world championship in his first season as club president,

McAleer was not happy with the field leadership of Stahl, who was not his choice to manage the Red Sox. McAleer was an experienced manager himself, but his unsolicited advice was not appreciated by Stahl and strained their relationship. Tensions boiled over before the sixth game of the World Series, when McAleer ordered his manager to start right-hander Buck O'Brien instead of the team's ace, Joe Wood, with the Red Sox on the verge of clinching the Series over the Giants. Stahl protested, but McAleer had his way, and O'Brien gave up five runs in the first inning, losing the game by a 5–2 score. Wood started the seventh game the next day and failed to retire a batter, as the Giants won the game 11–4 and knotted the Series at three games apiece (with one tie). Fortunately, right-hander Hugh Bedient kept the Red Sox close in Game 8, and Wood came on in the late innings to keep the score tied after nine. In the tenth, a series of Giant misplays, a run-scoring single by Tris Speaker, and a sacrifice fly by Larry Gardner gave the Red Sox the title. Still, the acrimony between Stahl and McAleer remained and would become more pronounced during the following season.

McAleer's popularity among the Irish fans of Boston took a severe beating during the World Series. The Royal Rooters had traditionally been allocated a block of about 300 seats in the left-field stands for Red Sox games, and when a seventh game of the Series became necessary, the Rooters naturally assumed that they would occupy those chairs as usual. In what was later called a "clerical error," Boston management put those tickets up for sale to the general public, and when the Rooters finished marching around the field before the game, they found their seats already occupied. A near-riot ensued that held up the start of the game for nearly an hour, as police on horseback labored to keep the irate Rooters from reclaiming the seats by force. Eventually, the Royal Rooters were allowed to stand in the left-field area behind a fence that had been damaged in the disturbance, but an outraged "Nuf Ced" McGreevey called for a fan boycott of the eighth contest the next day. So influential was "Nuf Ced" in Boston that Fenway Park was only half-filled for Game 8. Only about 17,000 people watched the Red Sox clinch the championship in one of the most thrilling games in baseball history.

The 1913 Red Sox were expected to defend their title, but the team started slowly, and the bickering between McAleer and Stahl increased. Exacerbating the problem was the fact that the club was divided into factions, with the Irish Catholics on the team, most of whom were from the northern and eastern states, opposed by the Southerners and Protestants. Tris Speaker and Joe Wood, the two biggest stars, were leaders of the "Masons," the Protestant faction, while catcher Bill Carrigan, outfielder Duffy Lewis, and other Irishmen were in the "Knights of Columbus" (Catholic) group. Manager Jake Stahl, who retired as a player and led the team from the bench in 1913, was in the Mason corner, as he was a friend and off-season hunting companion of Speaker and Wood. Local reporters divided the Red Sox into "Carrigan men" and "Stahl men," and since team president Jimmy McAleer was an Irish Catholic, it appears that he, too, was a "Carrigan man."

The friction between Catholic and Protestant Red Sox was no secret to the rest of the American League. Left fielder George (Duffy) Lewis, center fielder Speaker, and right fielder Harry Hooper were considered the greatest outfield in the game during that era, but Speaker and Lewis wanted little to do with each other. Lewis, a San Franciscan who survived the catastrophic earthquake of 1906 that struck the city on his 18th birthday, was the son of immigrants from Ireland and used his mother's maiden name as his nickname. A cocky sort, Lewis had rebelled against the rookie hazing meted out by the Red Sox veterans when he arrived in Boston in 1910, earning the enmity of Speaker and others. As Hooper's biographer, Paul J. Zingg, stated, "[Lewis'] attitude particularly put Lewis on a collision course with Speaker, and initiated ill feeling between them that lasted throughout their careers."[4] Hooper, a Catholic whose parents were immigrants from Canada, was friendly with Speaker and the other Protestants, but Lewis rarely, if ever, communicated with his center fielder outside the playing field.

Though Duffy Lewis was an outgoing individual, he was sensitive about his appearance, especially when it came to his quickly receding hairline. Lewis' vanity was well known to his teammates, and Speaker, an enthusiastic practical joker, decided to take advantage during the 1913 season. In front of a large crowd at Fenway Park one day, Speaker repeatedly swatted Lewis' cap off, revealing the left fielder's bald head. "Do that again and I'll kill you," Lewis warned. Speaker did it again, and Lewis finally lost his temper, grabbed a bat, and threw it at his outfield mate, smacking him in the shins with it. Speaker had to be helped off the field, and the relationship between the two outfielders deteriorated further.[5]

Violence between the Protestants and Catholics on the club had erupted during the previous World Series. After McAleer ordered manager Stahl to start the Irish Catholic Buck O'Brien instead of the Protestant Joe Wood in Game 6, Wood was so outraged by the subsequent loss that he attacked O'Brien with a bat before the start of the seventh game. Teammates broke up the ugly fight, but Wood pitched so poorly afterward that many believe to this day that he lost the game on purpose. He faced only nine batters in Game 7, allowing six runs and seven hits before giving way to a reliever. He appeared to be merely lobbing the ball across the plate, perhaps to show his disgust with McAleer, or possibly because he was exhausted from the pregame fight with O'Brien and the hour-long delay caused by the Royal Rooters. In any case, questions about the integrity of the seventh game of the 1912 World Series have lingered ever since.

The Red Sox, with Wood suffering from a sore arm that eventually derailed his promising career, struggled to stay in the pennant race during the early part of the 1913 season. The Philadelphia Athletics built a sizeable lead, and by mid–July the dissention-ridden Red Sox were mired in fifth position, 18 games behind the Athletics and two games under the .500 mark. The tension between the Catholics and Protestants had to be resolved, one way or another, and on July 15 McAleer came down firmly on the side of the Irish Catholics. He fired Jake Stahl as manager and replaced him with Bill Carrigan.

The new manager, a no-nonsense veteran who was called "Rough" Carrigan by the sportswriters, was widely to be considered the toughest player in the American League at the time. Born in 1883 in Lewiston, Maine, his parents had escaped poverty in Ireland and sailed to America in the late 1850s. John Carrigan

George (Duffy) Lewis, Boston Red Sox left fielder. The incline that existed in front of the left field wall in Fenway Park was called "Duffy's Cliff" (author's collection).

worked as a deputy sheriff in Lewiston, while his youngest child, Bill, worked as a farmhand while attending school. After starring in both football and baseball at Lewiston High, Bill entered the College of the Holy Cross in Worcester, Massachusetts, a school with a strong baseball program that had sent many other Irish Catholic boys to success in the major leagues. The Holy Cross coach was Tommy McCarthy, an icon of Boston baseball during the 1890s who had devised many innovations in strategy while leading the Beaneaters to pennants in 1892 and 1893. Carrigan arrived at Holy Cross as an infielder, but McCarthy convinced him to take up catching, which proved to be the youngster's best position. In 1906, Boston team owner Charles Taylor signed Carrigan, and by 1908 he had claimed a permanent spot on the Boston club. He did not hit much, but was an excellent handler of pitchers and gave no ground to incoming baserunners. When sliding into the plate against Carrigan, "You might as well try to move a stone wall," said Chicago's Jimmy Callahan.[6]

Carrigan, who displaced veteran Lou Criger as Boston's main catcher, projected an air of authority. He insisted upon calling all the pitches in a game, even as a rookie catching the likes of Cy Young. Carrigan was an intelligent and well-spoken man off the field, but one of baseball's best fighters on it. A brawl between Carrigan and another Irishman, Detroit's George Moriarty, in 1909 was the stuff of legend, with players from both teams gathering at home plate to watch the action. Moriarty won that fight, but Carrigan's later battle with another Tiger, Sam Crawford, ended in a victory. Though some of the Protestant Red Sox (including Speaker, who never warmed to Carrigan's personality) apparently resented this Irish Catholic's aggressive attitude, Carrigan was a winner who demanded much from his teammates. "The first great requisite for success in baseball is nerve," Carrigan once said. "I have

Bill Carrigan (left) and Jake Stahl in 1912. One year later, Carrigan succeeded Stahl as manager of the Red Sox (author's collection).

seen players with speed, hitting, strength, and grace, but they did not make good. They lack the prime essential, stoutness of heart."[7]

Carrigan's appointment as manager steadied the Red Sox, who played better ball during the last half of the 1913 season and finished in fourth place. However, McAleer's dismissal of Jake Stahl spelled the end of his tenure as president of the team. The moneymen behind the club, especially the fired manager's father-in-law, were angry at McAleer for dumping Stahl only nine months after winning the world championship. Fans were upset by the team's poor performance, and the Royal Rooters were still seething over the World Series ticket fiasco of the previous fall. League president Ban Johnson was distressed by the turmoil in Boston and secretly began looking for a new team president and part-owner to replace McAleer. A few months later, he found one in the person of a Canadian-born businessman, Joseph Lannin, who bought half of the stock in the club. Lannin, with Johnson's help, bought out McAleer, former manager Jake Stahl, and several of the previous investors. The Red Sox now had a new majority owner, and a tersely-worded telegram from Johnson, sent to McAleer in early 1914, brusquely ended McAleer's association with the Red Sox and, as it turned out, baseball as well.

Joe Lannin, a native of Canada, became an Irish-American success story. Born in 1866 in Quebec to immigrant parents from Ireland, Joe was the ninth of ten children. Orphaned at age 14, Lannin traveled to Boston (some say he walked all the way there) and found work as a hotel bellboy. Intelligent and ambitious, Joe earned a promotion to doorman, and soon worked his way into management. All the while, he made it a point to engage in conversation with the hotel's wealthy patrons, gathering stock tips and financial advice. Lannin saved his money, invested in the commodities market, and by age 30 was a wealthy man with interests in hotels, apartment buildings, and other forms of real estate. He was not only rich enough to buy control of the team, but also to fight off the Federal League, a new circuit which was already making large offers to Tris Speaker and other Boston stars. He was also an Irishman, which no doubt pleased the Royal Rooters and the Irish fans of the Hub.

Jimmy McAleer was bitter and depressed over his rude dismissal. He and Ban Johnson had worked together closely since the formation of the American League, and its eventual success was due in no small part to McAleer's skill and leadership. Unfortunately for McAleer, his services were no longer needed by Johnson, who had a history of ending relationships when they no longer benefited him personally (as he had done several years before in driving "Rowdy Jack" O'Connor, McAleer's former Cleveland teammate and fellow Irishman, out of the league). McAleer, once one of Johnson's closest friends, never spoke to the American League president again. The old outfielder spent his remaining years in his hometown of Youngstown, Ohio, where he dabbled in real estate and followed the fortunes of the Cleveland Indians until he died in 1931 at the age of 66.

The Federal League threat to the established circuits was real enough that Joe Lannin was required to double Tris Speaker's salary, signing him to a contract for a sum of $18,000 per season, to keep him away from the new league. Bad feeling between the Protestants and Catholics on the Red Sox remained, but Bill Carrigan managed to keep the Boston players from fighting each other and concentrate on the job at hand. Under Carrigan's leadership, the Red Sox jumped back into contention in 1914, claiming second place and, after the post-season breakup of the champion Philadelphia Athletics, expecting to win the pennant in 1915. Their success was suddenly a matter of importance because the Red Sox faced real competition for the loyalties of the Boston fans. Across town, the Boston Braves had won the National League title and defeated the Athletics in the 1914 World Series, challenging the Red Sox for baseball supremacy in Boston for the first time in more than a decade.

Lannin, a skilled businessman, had no intention of losing the Boston baseball war to the upstart Braves, and was savvy enough to turn the Federal League threat to his advantage. Many minor league clubs suffered in competition with the new league, and the Baltimore Orioles, owned and managed by former pitcher Jack Dunn, were especially hard hit. The Feds had placed a team in Baltimore called the Terrapins, under the direction of the long-retired Ned Hanlon, and the Orioles of the International League saw their attendance shrink. Dunn could no longer afford to keep many of his star players, and in June of 1914 he sold two of his promising young pitching prospects, right-hander Ernie Shore and a 19-year-old left-hander named George (Babe) Ruth, to Lannin and the Red Sox for a reported price of $8,000. Ruth played only briefly for Boston that season, but in 1915 both Ruth and Shore were ready to join the starting rotation. Shore won 19 games and Ruth 18 as the Red Sox battled the Detroit Tigers for the pennant, eventually winning the flag by two and a half games.

A five-game victory over the Philadelphia Phillies that October gave Boston its third World Series title in three post-season appearances, and the team entered 1916 as favorites to repeat as champions. However, the bickering between the Catholics and the Protestants had never been resolved, and some of the Red Sox chafed under the leadership of the Irishman Carrigan. They respected him, and perhaps feared him, but some resented his style. Babe Ruth, a Catholic (though not an Irishman), later called Carrigan the best manager he played for during his 22-year major league career, but some of his teammates would have disagreed with that assessment, despite the convincing win over the Phillies in the World Series.

In addition, Tris Speaker, the leader of the Protestant faction, was deeply unhappy with his contract situation as the 1916 season dawned. The failure of the Federal League after two years ended the competition between the established leagues and the new circuit, and the club owners no longer needed to pay huge salaries to keep their stars. Accordingly, Joe Lannin took a cleaver to Speaker's salary, slashing it to $9,000 per year, the same level at which it had been before the Federal League appeared on the scene. This move infuriated the star center fielder, who became angrier still when manager Carrigan failed to support him. "That [$9,000] was considered a big salary then," said Carrigan to the sportswriters, undercutting Speaker's position in the public relations battle.[8] Speaker offered to sign a five-year deal for $12,000 a season, but Lannin turned him down, leaving Speaker with no alternative but to threaten a holdout. Speaker showed up at spring training camp in Hot Springs, Arkansas, that March, but refused to sign a contract for less than what he thought he was worth.

Joe Lannin, however, was as stubborn as Speaker. Lannin believed that Speaker, at age 28, was on the downside, as his batting and slugging averages had declined during each of the previous three seasons. Also, he had played well, but not spectacularly so, during the World Series against the Phillies. The team owner had already sent feelers around the league to gauge the level of trade interest in his biggest star, and when contract talks with Speaker hit an impasse, Lannin decided to act. On April 12, the opening day of the 1916 season, he traded Speaker to the Cleveland Indians for two players and $55,000 in cash. "I never dreamed I could get so much money for [Speaker's] release. I do not believe that any ball player is worth the money I received for Speaker," said Lannin happily after the deal was consummated.[9]

Carrigan, in an interview with reporter Ward Mason from *Baseball Magazine*, was sanguine about the deal. "The trade was a business deal, pure and simple," he said. "Mr. Lannin felt that in disposing of Speaker he was getting back part of the money he had spent in building up a great club and still had a great club in the bargain. We shall miss Speaker, there is no use to deny that. But we are no longer top-heavy favorites and if we win, as we shall make every effort to do, we shall win entirely on our merits."[10]

The loss of Speaker made Bill Carrigan's task of defending Boston's world championship more difficult, but the trade also removed one of the leading sources of conflict on the ball-club. Joe Wood, too, left the Red Sox that spring, as his sore arm failed to respond to treatment and obligated the pitcher to remain inactive for the entire season. Speaker and Wood, for all their undeniable talent, were the leaders of the anti–Irish Catholic faction on the Red Sox, and their absence promised a more pleasant clubhouse in 1916. *The Sporting News* agreed with this assessment, stating in an editorial, "It is comforting to hear that the transfer of Speaker and the absence of Joe Wood have made for harmony on the Red Sox ball team."[11]

Called upon to prove his skill as a field leader in 1916, Carrigan did so in spectacular fashion. The pennant race was one of the most jumbled in history, with six teams ending the season above the .500 mark and one other, the Washington Senators, one game below it. Mired in fourth place in mid-season, Carrigan whipped his charges into shape and climbed the standings, aided immeasurably by Joe Lannin's pitching acquisitions. Ernie Shore won 18 games that season, while Babe Ruth achieved stardom, posting 23 wins and leading the league in earned run average. In mid–September the Red Sox pulled away, winning the flag by two games over the White Sox and four over the Tigers. The Red Sox then needed only five games to defeat the Brooklyn Dodgers in the World Series, bringing the world championship to Boston for the third season in a row (counting the Braves' unexpected title in 1914).

Bill Carrigan had managed the Red Sox to two world titles, but did not view baseball as a lifelong career. He had tried to retire after the 1915 season to take a position at a bank in his native Maine, but Lannin had convinced him to stay for one more year. His performance in 1916, winning the championship despite the loss of Tris Speaker, cemented his reputation as a field leader but made him more determined to leave. His wife was pregnant, and Carrigan decided to trade his baseball success for a career in the business world. He resigned as manager after the 1916 World Series and was succeeded by another Irish playing manager, veteran shortstop Jack Barry.

To the surprise of almost everyone in Boston, team owner Joe Lannin also decided to quit at the pinnacle of success. Though Lannin was only 50 years old, he found that the day-to-day strain of operating a world championship team was too much for him. He missed the days when he would buy a ticket and sit in the stands, rooting anonymously for his favorite team. "I am too much of a fan to run a baseball club and found that it was interfering with my health," he said, as quoted in *The New York Times*." I have turned over to the new owners the best team in the world. It is now up to them to keep the champions at the top."[12] On November 1, 1916, Lannin completed the sale of his Red Sox and returned, happily, to the ranks of the fans.

The new majority owner was Harry Frazee, a theatrical producer whose tenure started in a promising way. His Red Sox, under Jack Barry's field leadership, finished in second place behind the White Sox in 1917 and then, with Ed Barrow as manager, won the pennant in 1918 and defeated the Chicago Cubs in the World Series. However, Frazee was a New Yorker who knew little of the ways of Boston, and his businesslike approach to the sport offended many of the city's most loyal fans. "Baseball is essentially a show business," said the new owner to F. C. Lane of *Baseball Magazine*. "Surely it is a sport, but it's an exhibit just the same. If you have any kind of a production, be it a music show or a wrestling bout, or a baseball game that people want to see enough to pay good money for the privilege, then you are in a show business and don't let anyone ever tell you different."[13]

He cut back on free and discounted passes for the Royal Rooters, alienating powerful political leaders such as "Honey Fitz" Fitzgerald and Joseph P. Kennedy, Fitzgerald's son-in-law who had tried, and failed, to buy the team from Lannin. Frazee also harassed the local sportswriters, barring them from Fenway Park if their reporting met with his disapproval. Such tactics were accepted in the theatrical realm, but not in the baseball world, and the writers attacked Frazee at every opportunity. For the first time in several years, the ballclub was not owned by an Irishman, and only the team's success on the field in 1917 and 1918 kept the Irish fans of Boston content.

Frazee's success in the theater world soon turned sour, with a Broadway production called *My Lady Friends* losing money hand over fist in 1919, and the Boston owner found himself in serious financial difficulty. The solution to his financial woes, in Frazee's mind, was simple. He intended to trade or sell his star players to the highest bidder. The 1919 Red Sox had finished in sixth place, and Frazee saw no reason to pay high salaries to members of a team that had finished five games under the .500 mark. Several key Boston players, including shortstop Everett Scott, pitchers Herb Pennock, Joe Bush, and Waite Hoyt, and catcher Wally Schang, were transferred to the New York Yankees during the next few seasons. The Yankees, flush with cash from millionaire owners Jacob Ruppert and T. L. Huston, were more than willing to build a championship team in New York by purchasing the stars of the Red Sox.

The most famous (or infamous) transaction consummated between Frazee and the Yankees, the sale of pitcher-turned-outfielder Babe Ruth for $100,000 in cash in January of 1920, was the most damaging to the Red Sox. However, the departure of Boston manager Ed Barrow after the 1920 season was nearly as significant. Barrow joined the Yankees as general manager and oversaw the construction of the Yankee champions of the 1920s, while the effect of Frazee's fire sale was felt in Boston for decades. The Royal Rooters, demoralized by the decimation of their beloved team, disbanded, and the Red Sox finished last in the circuit in attendance each year from 1921 to 1925. The team dropped to the bottom of the standings, and though Frazee (who sold the club at a profit in 1923) and his successors hired a string of Irish-American managers such as Hugh Duffy, Marty McManus, and Shano Collins, the love affair between the team and the Irish fans of the Hub was over.

Bill Carrigan, the most successful manager in Red Sox history, was lured out of retirement to lead the team again in 1927, but three last-place finishes proved that not even Carrigan could lift the talent-poor Red Sox out of the depths. Not until millionaire Tom Yawkey bought the club in 1933 would the Red Sox begin to turn their fortunes around. Yawkey refurbished Fenway Park, which had fallen into a state of disrepair under the previous owners, and in 1935 hired another Irishman, shortstop Joe Cronin, to lead the club. A second-generation Irish-American, Cronin was a San Francisco native whose family lost everything in the 1906 earthquake. He went on to manage the club for 13 seasons and led the Red Sox to the 1946 pennant, its first in 28 years. In 2004, a World Series victory over the St. Louis Cardinals put the Red Sox on top of the baseball world for the first time since 1918, shortly before Harry Frazee's financial problems consigned the team to baseball purgatory for decades.

Making the circle complete, a new incarnation of the Royal Rooters has made its presence felt on the Internet. More than 6,000 people have registered on the Royal Rooter website, called redsoxnation.net, and groups of 21st century Rooters follow their heroes in bars, clubs, and in the stands at Fenway Park. No longer a predominantly Irish fan group, the new Royal Rooters keep the spirit of "Red Sox Nation" alive. A Boston-area band called the Dropkick Murphys even recorded a rock version of the traditional Rooter anthem, "Tessie," which was played repeatedly during the club's successful 2004 World Series run. A second world championship in 2007 solidified the popularity of the Red Sox, once a largely Irish team with a mostly Irish fan base, among all ethnic groups in New England and around the nation.

Epilogue

Jennings and McGann, Doyle and Callahan.
Hanlon, Scanlon, Kirk and Donlin,
Devlin, Keeler, Walsh and Conlin.
Joe McGinnity, Shea and Finnerty,
Farrell, Carroll, Darrell and McAmes.
Connie Mack and John McGraw
All together shout hurrah!
They're all good Irish names.
      —1911 baseball song, "They're All Good American
      Names" by Jean Schwartz and William Jerome.[1]

The lasting nature of the Irish contributions to baseball's legacy is generally acknowledged. Indeed, a 1906 article in *The Sporting News* gave the Irish the lion's share of credit for the status of baseball (then spelled as two words) as the national pastime:

> The foundation stone, superstructure and even the base ball roof is as Irish as Paddy's pig. Some of the wainscoting and trimmings are German, French, and mayhap Swede and English, but underlying and encompassing all the great Irish brawn and sinew permeates and sustains the whole mass, giving it characteristic form and coloring. The finest athletes in the world are Irish and it is due to the predominance of the Irish in base ball that the American nation's chosen pastime is the most skillful in the world.
>
> Take the great names in base ball — Kelly, Sweeney, Welch, O'Neill, Glasscock, Denny, Fogarty, McAleer, O'Connor — and a host of others, and up to the present decade it was nearly all Irish. Of course, we had the mighty Swede, "Pop" Anson, and the great second baseman, "Dutch" Fred Pfeffer, but to find a very great ball player who was not an Irishman was an exception.[2]

However, by the time this article appeared, the percentage of Irish-American players on major league rosters had been stagnant for more than a decade. Hall of Fame historian Lee Allen determined that, of players who debuted in the National League from 1891 to 1899, 22 percent could be identified as having Irish ancestry, down from 36 percent during the last half of the 1880s. The number rose slightly, to 23 percent, for the period from 1901 to 1909, but fell after 1910 as German-American players rose to nearly a third of the total. Allen's statistics for 1910 to 1919 indicate that the Irish presence fell to 18 percent of the total during the decade.

During the years immediately preceding World War One, half or more of the major league managers were Irishmen. However, some ballclubs had few or no Irish players in their ranks. In 1914, Washington Senators manager Clark Griffith remarked to a local newspaper, the *Post*, that his roster contained Germans, Englishmen, Scotsmen, and a Cuban (outfielder Merito Acosta), but no Irishmen. John McGraw's New York Giants club was perhaps the most Irish in the game, but even "The Little Napoleon" recognized that the ethnic composition of the sport was changing. As the *Post* reported, "Several years ago [during spring training] the Germans on the Giants wanted to play the Irish a game on St. Patrick's Day, but McGraw would not permit it, as he said he did not care to see any Irish slaughtered by the Dutch on the 17th of March."[3]

While the numbers of second- and third-generation Irishmen in baseball decreased, Irish-born players virtually disappeared. Of the 40 players in major league history who were natives of the Emerald Isle, only one (Joe Cleary, who pitched in one game for Washington in 1945) was born in the 20th century, and the last active Irish player before Cleary, the Dublin-born catcher Jimmy Archer, suited up for the final time in 1918. Since then, major league performers have hailed from nations as diverse as the Netherlands, Poland, Aruba, and Curacao, as well as South America and the Pacific Rim, but none have come from Ireland.

Irishmen retained a presence in the managerial ranks, at least for a while. Joe Cronin, born in San Francisco shortly before the 1906 earthquake, led pennant-winning teams in Washington and Boston before becoming president of the American League in 1956. Joe McCarthy, who grew up near Philadelphia and idolized his fellow Irishman, Connie Mack, was the first field leader to win four World Series in a row from 1936 to 1939, and accrued seven world championships in all. Mack remained as manager of the Philadelphia Athletics until 1950, though his final two decades were notable for their lack of success. Casey Stengel, who broke McCarthy's record with his fifth consecutive world championship title in 1953, was half Irish, as was Charlie Dressen, the Brooklyn Dodgers manager who opposed Stengel's Yankees in two Series appearances. However, other ethnic groups also earned success in the dugouts, and Irish domination of the managerial end of the game had disappeared by the middle of the 20th century.

The Irish arbiter remained a part of the game even after World War Two, with second-generation Irishmen Bill McGowan and Jocko Conlan carrying on the tradition begun by "Honest John" Gaffney and "Honest John" Kelly during the 1880s. Inevitably, representatives of other ethnic groups entered the umpiring profession, which lost its former Irish character as the decades passed. By 1966, when Emmett Ashford became the first African-American umpire at the major league level, the Irish presence had disappeared from the field.

American society had changed significantly in the decades after the Great Famine sent more than a million Irish refugees across the ocean. Intermarriage, social mobility, and other factors had diversified the country's population, and in the 20th century, most Americans claimed ancestry from two or more countries. The Irish Diaspora of the 1840s and 1850s had created heavily Irish communities of Brooklyn, Boston, St. Louis, and other large metropolitan areas, but these were rapidly becoming less homogeneous. Baseball, perhaps more than other professional sports, has always been a microcosm of society, and as the brogue-speaking, second-generation Americans of purely Irish parentage disappeared from American life, so did they from the rosters of major league baseball teams. Still, Irish-Americans left their mark on baseball as well as American society at large, and their influence on both is nearly immeasurable.

It seems fitting that baseball has slowly, but steadily, taken root in Ireland, the ancestral home of many of the sport's early stars. Softball had been played there, mostly in the Dublin area, but in the early 1990s a group of young Irishmen, looking for a greater challenge, decided to take up baseball. They played the game on soccer pitches and rugby fields, and by 1995, several adult-level baseball teams had formed. An organization called Baseball Ireland, the sport's governing body for both the Republic of Ireland and Northern Ireland, was created shortly thereafter. Interest in baseball grew and was given a boost by Los Angeles Dodgers owner and president Peter O'Malley, who donated $140,000 to Baseball Ireland for facilities and equipment. The Irish Baseball League began play in 1997 and includes teams representing Belfast, Greystones, and Dublin. These clubs play most of their games at the home of Irish baseball, O'Malley Fields at Corkagh Park in Clondalkin, West Dublin. Baseball Ireland also sponsors an Irish national team which won a bronze medal at the European championships in 2004, and took the silver at the next continental tournament in 2006.

The Irish Baseball League is ever mindful of the debt that the sport owes to the long-ago Irish-born stars of American baseball. Each year, its outstanding player is presented with the Andy Leonard Most Valuable Player Award, named for the native of County Cavan who starred for the Red Stockings of Cincinnati and Boston. The league's top hurler receives the Tommy Bond Best Pitcher Award, in remembrance of the Irish-born right-hander of the Boston champions of the late 1870s. The "Dirty Jack" Doyle Silver Slugger Award and the Patsy Donovan Batting Champion Award recall two other natives of the island who succeeded in American baseball.[4]

There are no Irish-born players in the Baseball Hall of Fame, though Tony Mullane, Andy Leonard, and Tommy Bond are early stars who may be worthy of induction. The American-born sons of famine refugees, however, are well represented, with plaques honoring Mike (King) Kelly, Ed Delahanty, Tim Keefe, Mickey Welch, and more than two dozen other stars of Irish parentage. These men clearly illustrate the importance of the Irish to the national pastime, and though these sons of immigrants passed from the scene many decades ago, their exploits and achievements will be recalled and revered as long as the game is played.

Notes

Prologue

1. There are many outstanding sources of information about the famine and resulting exodus. This summary came from Kevin Kenny, *The American Irish: A History* (New York: Longman, 2000), page 98.

2. H. G. Wells, *The Outline of History: Being a Plain History of Life and Mankind, revised edition* (Garden City, New York: Doubleday, 1971), page 855.

3. Ibid.

4. Ron Kaplan, "The Sporting Life," *Irish America*, February/March 2003. This article can be seen online at http://www.aoh61.com/history/sporting_life.html.

Chapter 1: Beginnings—The Irish in Boston

1. "The American Experience" web site at http://www.pbs.org/wgbh/amex/murder/peopleevents/p_immigrants.html.

2. Stephen D. Guschov, *The Red Stockings of Cincinnati: Base Ball's First All-Professional Team* (Jefferson, North Carolina: McFarland and Company, 1998), page 34. Also referenced in the *New York Clipper*, 1874 Pre-Season Guide.

3. The other Irish-born players in 1871 were Ed Duffy, who played in 25 games for Chicago, and Jimmy Hallinan, who played in five games for Fort Wayne.

4. *The Sporting News*, February 10, 1968. Some regard this story as apocryphal, though it may have come from Tim Murnane, a teammate of O'Rourke's who later wrote sports for the *Boston Globe*.

5. Peter Levine, *A. G. Spalding and the Rise of Baseball: The Promise of American Sport* (New York: Oxford University Press, 1985), page 18.

6. From the 19th Century Base Ball web site at http://www.19cbaseball.com/tours-1874-world-baseball-tour-4.html.

7. Tim Murnane's 1874 diary, offered for sale in 2007 by Robert Ward Auctions. A sample of the text can be seen at http://www.robertedwardauctions.com/auction/2007/792.html.

8. Albert G. Spalding, *Base Ball: America's National Game, new edition* (San Francisco, California: Halo Books, 1991), page 207.

9. Harold Kaese, *The Boston Braves* (New York: G. P. Putnam's Sons, 1948), page 21.

10. Kaese, page 40.

11. Curt Smith, *Storied Stadiums* (New York: Carroll and Graf, 2003), page 30.

12. Frederick Ivor-Campbell and Robert L. Tiemann (editors), *Baseball's First Stars* (Cleveland, Ohio: Society for American Baseball Research, 1996), page 153.

13. Mike Roer, *Orator O'Rourke: The Life of a Baseball Radical* (Jefferson, North Carolina: McFarland and Company, 2006), page 78.

14. Kaese, page 33.

Chapter 2: The Irish White Stockings of Chicago

1. "Irish Immigrants in America during the 19th Century" website at http://www.kinsella.org/history/histira.htm.

2. Albert G. Spalding, *Base Ball: America's National Game, new edition* (San Francisco, California: Halo Books, 1991), page 195–196.

3. Howard Rosenberg, *Cap Anson 1: When Captaining a Team Meant Something* (Arlington, Virginia: Tile Books, 2003), page 192.

4. New York Clipper, September 13, 1879.

5. Benjamin G. Rader, *Baseball: A History of America's Game* (Champaign, Illinois: University of Illinois Press, 2002), page 54.

6. Adrian C. Anson, *A Ballplayer's Career* (Chicago, Illinois: Era Publishing, 1900), page 116.

7. Spalding, page 516.

8. Spalding, page 525.

9. Mike Kelly, *Play Ball: Stories of the Ball Field* (Boston: Press of Emery & Hughes, 1888).

10. Anson, page 115.

11. Rosenberg, page 194.

12. Spalding, page 525.

13. Spalding, page 525.

14. *Washington Post*, October 7, 1885.

15. Robert F. Burk, *Never Just a Game: Players, Owners, and American Baseball to 1920* (Chapel Hill, North Carolina: University of North Carolina Press, 1994), page 131. Burk's data came from a study by Baseball Hall of Fame historian Lee Allen, and summarized in Allen's "Notebooks Containing Statistical Data on Baseball Players" in the National Baseball Library, Cooperstown, New York.

16. David Nemec, *The Great Encyclopedia of 19th-Century Major League Baseball* (New York: Donald I. Fine Books, 1997), page 291.

17. Anson, page 137.

18. *The New York Times*, January 3, 1887.

19. *The New York Times*, February 21, 1887.

Chapter 3: Shamrocks, Trojans, and Giants

1. The city makes this claim, anyway. See the parade web site at http://newsite.holyokestpatricksparade.com for details.

2. Robert L. Tiemann and Mark Rucker (editors), *Nineteenth Century Stars* (Kansas City, Missouri: Society for American Baseball Research, 1989), page 171.

3. Frederick Ivor-Campbell and Robert L. Tiemann (editors), *Baseball's First Stars* (Cleveland, Ohio: Society for American Baseball Research, 1996), page 38.

4. "A Different Kind of Performance Enhancer," Internet column by Robert Smith on http://www.npr.org, March 31, 2006.

5. Ivor-Campbell and Tiemann, page 125.

6. *The Sporting News*, February 10, 1968.

7. Ivor-Campbell and Tiemann, page 125.

8. Ivor-Campbell and Tiemann, page 138.

9. John Montgomery Ward, "Is the Base-Ball Player a Chattel?" *Lippincott's Magazine*, August 1887.

10. James S. Mitchel, "The Celt as a Baseball Player," *The Gael*, May 1902.

11. *New York Clipper*, July 13, 1889.

12. *Sporting Life*, February 26, 1890. The proposed salary must have been for a multi-year contract, as no established player made anything close to $15,000 per year during that era.

13. *The New York Times*, January 14, 1890.

14. *Sporting Life*, February 5, 1890.

15. *New York Clipper*, November 30 1889.

16. *The Sporting News*, November 22, 1890.

Chapter 4: Charlie Comiskey and the St. Louis Browns

1. G. W. Axelson, *Commy: The Life Story of Charles A. Comiskey* (Chicago: Reilly and Lee, 1919), page 80.

2. Axelson, pages 40–41.

3. Axelson, page 59.

4. Axelson, page 103.

5. Robert L. Tiemann and Mark Rucker (editors), *Nineteenth Century Stars* (Kansas City, Missouri: Society for American Baseball Research, 1989), page 52.

6. Axelson, page 74.

7. Internet site at http://www.TheBaseballPage.com/players.

8. *The New York Times*, September 12, 1887.

9. David Nemec, *The Beer and Whiskey League* (New York: Lyons Press, 1994), page 146.

10. Daniel Ginsburg, *The Fix Is In: A History of Baseball Gambling and Game Fixing Scandals* (Jefferson, North Carolina: McFarland and Company, 2004), page 67.

11. *The Sporting News*, May 24, 1890.

12. Marty Appel and Burt Goldblatt, *Baseball's Best: The Hall of Fame Gallery* (New York: McGraw-Hill, 1980), page 288.

13. The other three are Bert Blyleven (287), Jim Kaat (283), and Tommy John (258).

Chapter 5: White Stockings, Colts, and Cubs

1. *Sporting Life*, December 14, 1887.

2. *The Sporting News*, October 27, 1954.

3. Harold Kaese, *The Boston Braves* (New York: G. P. Putnam's Sons, 1948), page 70.

4. *The Sporting News*, January 15, 1942.

5. *The Sporting News*, January 18, 1890; this report made reference to a statement that appeared in the *Chicago Tribune* on January 3, 1890.

6. *The Sporting News*, March 1, 1961.

7. Adrian C. Anson, *A Ballplayer's Career* (Chicago, Illinois: Era Publishing, 1900), page 132.

8. Howard Rosenberg, *Cap Anson 1: When Captaining a Team Meant Something* (Arlington, Virginia: Tile Books, 2003), page 187.

9. *St. Louis Globe-Democrat*, April 12, 1890; referenced in Howard Rosenberg, *Cap Anson 4: Bigger Than Babe Ruth: Captain Anson of Chicago* (Arlington, Virginia: Tile Books, 2006), page 211.

10. Rosenberg, *Cap Anson 4,* page 211.

11. Ibid.

12. *The Sporting News*, July 12, 1890.

13. *Chicago Tribune*, January 3, 1890.

14. Jerome Holtzman and George Vass, *Chicago Cubs Encyclopedia* (Philadelphia: Temple University Press, 1997), page 15.

15. Anson, page 302.

16. Peter Golenbock, *Wrigleyville: A Magical History Tour of the Chicago Cubs* (New York: St. Martin's Press, 1997), page 87.

17. *Chicago Tribune*, December 20, 1913.

Chapter 6: Patsy Tebeau and the Hibernian Spiders

1. John Phillips, *The 1898 Cleveland Spiders* (Cabin John, Maryland: Capital Publishing Company, 1997), page 17.

2. *Worcester Telegram*, January 11, 1953.

3. *The Sporting News*, May 7, 1931.

4. Fred Stein, *And the Skipper Bats Cleanup: A History of the Baseball Player-Manager* (Jefferson, North Carolina: McFarland and Company, 2002), page 55.

5. Frederick Ivor-Campbell and Robert L. Tiemann

(editors), *Baseball's First Stars* (Cleveland, Ohio: Society for American Baseball Research, 1996), page 53.

6. John Phillips, *Cleveland Spiders Who Was Who* (Cabin John, Maryland: Capital Publishing Company, 1993).

7. Ibid.

8. *The Sporting News*, May 23, 1918.

9. *The Sporting News*, January 12, 1949.

10. *The Sporting News*, May 23, 1918.

11. Frank Ceresi, "The Battle of 1895: The Temple Cup Games," on the FC Associates Internet site at http://www.fcassociates.com/nttemplecup.htm.

12. *The New York Times*, August 5, 1897.

13. John Phillips, *The '99 Spiders* (Cabin John, Maryland: Capital Publishing Company, 1988), July 12 entry.

14. Phillips, *The '99 Spiders*, September 27 entry.

15. Charles Alexander, *John McGraw* (New York: Viking Penguin, 1988), page 71.

16. Undated article by Sid Keener in the Patsy Tebeau file at the National Baseball Library, Cooperstown, New York.

17. *The Sporting News*, February 23, 1933, page 3.

Chapter 7: The Old Orioles

1. *Baltimore Sun*, September 30, 1892.

2. Wilbert Robinson biography at SABR's Baseball Biography Project, http://bioproj.sabr.org.

3. *Washington Post*, September 26, 1897.

4. Charles Alexander, *John McGraw* (New York: Viking Penguin, 1988), page 41.

5. Joseph Durso, *The Days of Mr. McGraw* (Englewood Cliffs, New Jersey: Prentice-Hall, 1969), page 25.

6. Alexander, page 41.

7. Alexander, page 44.

8. *Philadelphia Inquirer*, March 16, 1890.

9. J. C. Kofoed, "A Twenty-Five Year Record," *Baseball Magazine*, April 1916, page 81.

10. Frederick Ivor-Campbell and Robert L. Tiemann (editors), *Baseball's First Stars* (Cleveland, Ohio: Society for American Baseball Research, 1996), page 68.

11. *Sporting Life*, September 19, 1896; Michael Glazier (editor), *The Encyclopedia of the Irish in America* (South Bend, Indiana: University of Notre Dame Press, 1999), page 46.

12. Alexander, page 54.

13. Burt Solomon, *Where They Ain't: The Fabled Life and Untimely Death of the Original Baltimore Orioles* (New York: Simon and Schuster, 2000), page 119.

14. Alexander, page 63.

15. Tom Simon (editor), *Deadball Stars of the National League* (Washington, D. C.: Brassey's Inc., 2004), page 43.

16. The Ned Hanlon page on the National Baseball Hall of Fame web site, http://www.baseballhalloffame.org.

Chapter 8: The Heavenly Twins and the Boston Irish

1. Harold Kaese, *The Boston Braves* (New York: G. P. Putnam's Sons, 1948), page 44.

2. George V. Tuohey, *A History of the Boston Base Ball Club* (Boston: M. J. Quinn and Company, 1897), page 93.

3. Tuohey, page 94.

4. Kaese, page 40.

5. Howard Rosenberg, *Cap Anson 2: The Theatrical and Kingly Mike Kelly* (Arlington, Virginia: Tile Books, 2004), page 161.

6. Marty Appel, *Slide, Kelly, Slide: The Wild Life and Times of Mike "King" Kelly, Baseball's First Superstar* (Lanham, Maryland: Scarecrow Press, 1996), page 138.

7. Kaese, pages 52–53.

8. Howard Rosenberg, "Tommy Tucker Appreciation Day," posted at *http://plunkbiggio.blogspot.com* on July 13, 2005.

9. Ibid.

10. Ibid.

11. Kaese, page 63.

12. *The New York Times*, July 18, 1893.

13. *The New York Times*, October 20, 1954.

14. David Nemec and Dave Zeman, *The Baseball Rookies Encyclopedia: The Most Authoritative Guide to Baseball's First-Year Players* (Washington, D.C.: Brassey's Inc., 2004), page 54.

15. *The Sporting News*, March 11, 1943, page 5.

16. Ibid.

17. Ibid.

18. *Boston Globe*, November 10, 1895.

19. John Phillips, *The 1895 Cleveland Spiders* (Cabin John, Maryland: Capital Publishing Company, 1990), June 12 entry.

20. *The Sporting News*, October 2, 1897.

21. Kaese, page 100.

22. Ibid.

Chapter 9: Comiskey and the White Sox

1. Lawrence S. Ritter, *The Glory of Their Times* (New York: William Morrow and Company, 1984), page 56.

2. Billy Sullivan biography at SABR's Baseball Biography Project, http://bioproj.sabr.org.

3. During the 81 seasons that the White Sox played in Comiskey Park, only one Chicago player managed to win the American League batting title (Luke Appling, who did it in 1936 and 1943). The Sox also did not have a league home run leader until Bill Melton turned the trick in 1971.

4. *The Sporting News*, August 26, 1915.

5. The White Sox sent pitcher Ed Klepfer and outfielders Bobby (Braggo) Roth and Larry Chappell to the Indians. Chappell played only three games in a Cleveland uniform, while Roth and Klepfer were both gone from the Indians by the end of the 1919 season.

6. Warren Brown, *The Chicago White Sox* (New York: G. P. Putnam's Sons, 1952), page 83.

7. John J. Ward, "The New Leader of the White Sox," *Baseball Magazine*, March 1919.

8. Clipping, dated 1938, from the Kid Gleason file at the National Baseball Library, Cooperstown, New York.

9. Ibid.

10. Brown, pages 83–84.

Chapter 10: The Umpires

1. *The Sporting News*, April 25, 1891.

2. *The Sporting News*, April 8, 1943.

3. *Brooklyn Eagle*, June 17, 1888.

4. *The Sporting News*, July 5, 1886.

5. Providence Grays Vintage Base Ball Club Internet site at http://providencegrays.org.

6. *The New York Times*, July 9, 1896.

7. *Brooklyn Eagle*, July 19, 1896.

8. John Phillips, *Buck Ewing and the 1893 Spiders* (Cabin John, Maryland: Capital Publishing Company, 1992), June 29 entry.

9. Charles Alexander, *John McGraw* (New York: Viking Penguin, 1988), page 55.

10. Christopher Mathewson, *Pitching in a Pinch, reprint edition* (New York: Stein and Day, 1977), page 177.

11. Internet article by Harvey Frommer from http://www.around-the-horn.com.

12. *Washington Post*, February 12, 1896.

13. Harvey Frommer, *Primitive Baseball: The First Quarter Century of the National Pastime* (New York: Athenum, 1988), page 121.

14. Joe Dittmar, "Tim Hurst," *The National Pastime #17* (1997), page 99.

15. Norman Macht, *Connie Mack and the Early Years of Baseball* (Lincoln, Nebraska: University of Nebraska Press, 2007), page 450.

16. Hank O'Day biography at SABR's Baseball Biography Project, http://bioproj.sabr.org..

17. Mathewson, pages 174–175.

18. Silk O'Loughlin biography at SABR's Baseball Biography Project, http://bioproj.sabr.org.

19. Bill James, *The New Bill James Historical Baseball Abstract* (New York: Free Press, 2001), page 623.

20. Eugene C. Murdock, *Ban Johnson: Czar of Baseball* (Westport, Connecticut: Greenwood Press, 1982), page 99.

21. *The New York Times*, April 17, 1989.

22. "Books of the Times," *The New York Times*, May 10, 1960. The story has been featured in several books by Joe Garagiola.

23. John (Jocko) Conlan and Robert W. Creamer, *Jocko* (Lincoln, Nebraska: University of Nebraska Press, 1997), page 179.

Chapter 11: McGraw and the Giants

1. Cappy Gagnon, "The Debut of Roger Bresnahan," *Baseball Research Journal #8 (1979),* page 41.

2. Tom Simon (editor), *Deadball Stars of the National League* (Washington, D. C.: Brassey's Inc., 2004), page 55.

3. Eugene C. Murdock, *Ban Johnson: Czar of Baseball* (Westport, Connecticut: Greenwood Press, 1982), page 39.

4. John McGraw, *My Thirty Years in Baseball* (New York: Boni and Liveright, 1923), page 175.

5. Charles Alexander, *John McGraw* (New York: Viking Penguin, 1988), page 89.

6. *Albany Evening Journal*, February 19, 1907.

7. Simon, page 58.

8. Alexander, page 131.

9. Simon, page 56.

10. Alexander, page 143.

11. Alexander, page 171.

12. McGraw, page 68.

13. Frank Deford, "Giants Among Men," *Sports Illustrated*, August 25, 2003.

14. Ibid.

15. Lawrence Ritter, *The Glory of Their Times, enlarged edition* (New York: William Morrow, 1984), page 213.

16. Ritter, page 179.

17. David Cataneo, *Casey Stengel: Baseball's Old Professor* (Nashville, Tennessee: Cumberland House Publishing, 2003), page 22.

18. *The New York Times*, July 7, 1933.

19. *New York World-Telegram*, August 9, 1934.

Chapter 12: Wild Bill, Whiskey Face, and the Tall Tactician

1. Frederick G. Lieb, *The Detroit Tigers* (New York: G. P. Putnam's Sons, 1946), page 54.

2. Robert W. Creamer, *Stengel: His Life and Times* (New York: Simon and Schuster, 1984), page 134.

3. Undated clipping in Eppa Rixey file, National Baseball Library, Cooperstown, New York.

4. Pat Moran biography at SABR's Baseball Biography Project, http://bioproj.sabr.org.

5. *New York Sun*, January 9, 1946.

6. Frank Graham, "Setting the Pace" column, *New York Sun*, February 15, 1939.

7. *The New York Times*, October 1, 1920.

8. Norman Macht, *Connie Mack and the Early Years of Baseball* (Lincoln, Nebraska: University of Nebraska Press, 2007), page 24.

9. Macht, page 89.

10. Macht, page 49.

11. Danny Murphy biography at SABR's Baseball Biography Project, http://bioproj.sabr.org.

12. Jack Barry biography at SABR's Baseball Biography Project, http://bioproj.sabr.org.

13. Danny Murphy biography at SABR's Baseball Biography Project, http://bioproj.sabr.org.

14. Ibid.

15. Ibid.

16. Daniel Okrent and Harris Lewine, editors. *The Ultimate Baseball Book* (Boston: Houghton Mifflin Company, 1981), page 120.

Chapter 13: Red Sox and Royal Rooters

1. *Boston Globe*, March 10, 1901.

2. *Sporting Life*, October 17, 1903.

3. Lawrence Ritter, *The Glory of Their Times* (New York: William Morrow and Company, 1984), page 27.

4. Paul J. Zingg, *Harry Hooper: An American Base-*

ball Life (Champaign, Illinois: University of Illinois Press, 1993), page 79.

5. Zingg, page 114.

6. Bill Carrigan biography at SABR's Baseball Biography Project, http://bioproj.sabr.org.

7. Randy Voorhees and Mike Gola, *As Koufax Said...: The 400 Best Things Ever Said About How to Play Baseball* (New York: McGraw-Hill Professional, 2003), page 115.

8. Charles C. Alexander, *Spoke: A Biography of Tris Speaker* (Dallas, Texas: Southern Methodist University Press, 2007), page 100.

9. *Sporting Life*, April 22, 1916.

10. *Baseball Magazine*, December 1916, page 34.

11. *The Sporting News*, April 20, 1916.

12. *The New York Times*, November 2, 1916.

13. *Baseball Magazine*, March 1919, page 268.

Epilogue

1. Ron Kaplan, "The Sporting Life," *Irish America*, February/March 2003.

2. *The Sporting News*, September 1, 1906, page 2.

3. *Washington Post*, June 7, 1914.

4. To learn more about the sport in Ireland, go to the Baseball Ireland web site at http://www.baseball ireland.com.

Bibliography

Books

Alexander, Charles. *John McGraw* (New York: Viking Penguin, 1988).

_____. *Spoke: A Biography of Tris Speaker* (Dallas, Texas: Southern Methodist University Press, 2007).

Anson, Adrian C. *A Ball Player's Career* (Chicago, Illinois: Era Publishing, 1900).

Appel, Marty. *Slide, Kelly, Slide: The Wild Life and Times of Mike "King" Kelly, Baseball's First Superstar* (Lanham, Maryland: Scarecrow Press, 1996).

_____, and Goldblatt, Burt. *Baseball's Best: The Hall of Fame Gallery* (New York: McGraw-Hill, 1980).

Axelson, Gustav W. *Commy: The Life Story of Charles A. Comiskey* (Chicago: Reilly and Lee, 1919).

Brown, Warren. *The Chicago White Sox* (New York: G. P. Putnam's Sons, 1952).

Burk, Robert F. *Never Just a Game: Players, Owners, and American Baseball to 1920* (Chapel Hill: University of North Carolina Press, 1994).

Cataneo, David. *Casey Stengel: Baseball's Old Professor* (Nashville, Tennessee: Cumberland House, 2003).

Creamer, Robert. *Stengel: His Life and Times* (New York: Simon and Schuster, 1984).

Durso, Joseph. *The Times of Mr. McGraw* (Englewood Cliffs, New Jersey: Prentice-Hall, 1969).

Ginsburg, Daniel. *The Fix Is In: A History of Baseball Gambling and Game Fixing Scandals* (Jefferson, North Carolina: McFarland, 2004).

Glazier, Michael, editor. *The Encyclopedia of the Irish in America* (South Bend, Indiana: University of Notre Dame Press, 1999).

Golenbock, Peter. *Wrigleyville: A Magical History Tour of the Chicago Cubs* (New York: St. Martin's Press, 1997).

Guschov, Stephen D. *The Red Stockings of Cincinnati: Base Ball's First All-Professional Team and Its Historic 1869 and 1870 Seasons* (Jefferson, North Carolina: McFarland and Company, 1998).

Holtzman, Jerome, and George Vass. *The Chicago Cubs Encyclopedia* (Philadelphia: Temple University Press, 1997).

Ivor-Campbell, Frederick, and Robert L. Tiemann, editors. *Baseball's First Stars* (Cleveland, Ohio: Society for American Baseball Research, 1996).

James, Bill. *The Bill James Historical Baseball Abstract* (New York: Villard Books, 1986).

_____. *The New Bill James Historical Baseball Abstract* (New York: Free Press, 2001).

_____. *The Politics of Glory* (New York: Macmillan, 1994).

Jones, David, editor. *Deadball Stars of the American League* (Dulles, Virginia: Potomac Books, 2006).

Kaese, Harold. *The Boston Braves* (New York: G. P. Putnam's Sons, 1948).

Kelly, Mike. *Play Ball: Stories of the Ball Field* (Boston: Press of Emery & Hughes, 1888).

Levine, Peter. *A. G. Spalding and the Rise of Baseball: The Promise of American Sport* (New York: Oxford University Press, 1985).

Lieb, Fred. *The Boston Red Sox* (New York: G. P. Putnam's Sons, 1947).

_____. *The Detroit Tigers* (New York: G. P. Putnam's Sons, 1946).

Macht, Norman. *Connie Mack and the Early Years of Baseball* (Lincoln: University of Nebraska Press, 2007).

Mathewson, Christopher. *Pitching in a Pinch,* (New York: Stein and Day, 1977).

McGraw, John. *My Thirty Years in Baseball* (New York: Boni and Liveright, 1923).

Murdock, Eugene C. *Ban Johnson: Czar of Baseball* (Westport, Connecticut: Greenwood Press, 1982).

Nemec, David. *The Beer and Whiskey League* (New York: Lyons Press, 1994).

_____. *The Great Encyclopedia of 19th-Century Major League Baseball* (New York: Donald I. Fine Books, 1997).

Okrent, Daniel, and Harris Lewine, editors. *The Ul-*

timate Baseball Book (Boston: Houghton Mifflin, 1981).

Phillips, John. *Buck Ewing and the 1893 Spiders* (Cabin John, Maryland: Capital Publishing Company, 1992).

_____. *Chief Sockalexis and the 1897 Cleveland Indians* (Cabin John, Maryland: Capital, 1991).

_____. *Cleveland Spiders Who Was Who* (Cabin John, Maryland: Capital Publishing, 1991).

_____. *The 1895 Cleveland Spiders* (Cabin John, Maryland: Capital Publishing, 1990).

_____. *The 1898 Cleveland Spiders* (Cabin John, Maryland: Capital Publishing Company, 1997).

_____. *The '99 Spiders* (Cabin John, Maryland: Capital Publishing, 1988).

Ritter, Lawrence. *The Glory of Their Times* (New York: William Morrow, 1984).

Rosenberg, Howard. *Cap Anson 1: When Captaining a Team Meant Something* (Arlington, Virginia: Tile Books, 2003).

_____. *Cap Anson 2: The Theatrical and Kingly Mike Kelly* (Arlington, Virginia: Tile Books, 2004).

_____. *Cap Anson 4: Bigger Than Babe Ruth: Captain Anson of Chicago* (Arlington, Virginia: Tile Books, 2006).

Simon, Tom, editor. *Deadball Stars of the National League* (Washington, D.C.: Brassey's, 2004).

Spalding, Albert G. *Base Ball: America's National Game* (San Francisco, California: Halo Books, 1991).

Tiemann, Robert L., and Mark Rucker, editors. *Nineteenth Century Stars* (Kansas City, Missouri: Society for American Baseball Research, 1989).

Tuohey, George V. *A History of the Boston Base Ball Club* (Boston: M. J. Quinn, 1897).

Voorhees, Randy, and Mike Gola. *As Koufax Said...: The 400 Best Things Ever Said About How to Play Baseball* (New York: McGraw-Hill Professional, 2003).

Ward, Geoffrey C., and Ken Burns. *Baseball: An Illustrated History* (New York: Knopf, 1994).

Wells, H. G. *The Outline of History: Being a Plain History of Life and Mankind* (Garden City, New York: Garden City Books, 1961)

Zeman, Dave, and David Nemec. *The Baseball Rookies Encyclopedia: The Most Authoritative Guide to Baseball's First-Year Players* (Washington, D.C.: Brassey's, 2004).

Zingg, Paul. *Harry Hooper: An American Baseball Life* (Champaign: University of Illinois Press, 1993).

Newspapers

Albany Evening Journal
Baltimore Sun
Boston Globe
Chicago Tribune
New York Clipper
New York Sun
The New York Times
New York World-Telegram
St. Louis Globe-Democrat
Washington Post
Worcester (MA) Telegram

Magazines

Baseball Magazine
Baseball Research Journal
Lippincott's Magazine
The National Pastime
Sporting Life
The Sporting News
Sports Illustrated

Internet Sites

Baseball Almanac (http://www.baseball-almanac.com)

Baseball Library (http://www.baseballlibrary.com)

The Baseball Page (http://www.thebaseballpage.com/players)

Baseball Reference (http://www.baseball-reference.com)

The Dead Ball Era (http://www.thedeadballera.com)

Library of Congress — American Memory (http://memory.loc.gov)

National Baseball Hall of Fame and Museum (http://www.baseballhalloffame.org)

Paper of Record (http://www.paperofrecord.com)

SABR (Society for American Baseball Research) Biography Project (http://bioproj.sabr.org)

The Sporting News (http://www.sportingnews.com)

Index